The Wishing Years

❖❖❖

ISBN: 0-923568-32-0

Cover design by BDW Designs, Inc.

Wildwood Press
P.O. Box 970152
Ypsilanti, Michigan 48197-0803

Manufactured in the United States of America

To Lenda ~
Enjoy the trip
down memory Lane!
A celebration of
wishes and
dreams ~

The Wishing Years

❖ ❖ ❖

Coralie Cederna Johnson

Coralie Cederna
Johnson

Notes from the Author

I dedicate this book to Mom and Dad and thank them for their love, generosity, and wisdom . . . to Corinne, who left me her pink vanity with the secret drawer . . . to John, who finally gave in and took me—blindfolded—to his and his pals' secret hideaway down in the old gravel pit . . . to Connie, who still goes to the movies with me, but whom I no longer have to pay to walk home . . . to Jim, even though he had a hand in Mom beating me in the Great Canasta Tournament . . . to Jerry who, never, ever, misses the opening day of bird season . . . and to all the other characters in this book who made my wish for adventure come true.

I also wish to thank Erin Sims-Bardsley, my editor, and Clayton Klein, Wilderness Adventure Books, who "discovered" me and made possible this book.

Table of Contents

Wishing in the Wilds

Everyone has their wishing years—years filled with the wonders of growing up, the trials and tribulations of being a kid in a grown-up's world, and the unquestionable certainty that coming of age is only a distant dream that will probably never ever really come true.

Mine were spent in Michigan's wild, rugged, and somewhat isolated Upper Peninsula, in a small iron mining community called Dober Location just down the hill from the rusty shafts of the Hiawatha Mine where Dad worked.

Our area's claim to fame—besides iron ore production—was the hundreds of clear blue lakes and streams teaming with trout, bass, and bluegills; the pine forests thick with deer, bear, and partridge; and the remains of abandoned Ojibway villages and burial grounds where it was rumored Indian spirits still stomped around in the woods. But, believe me, while this wonderful world of wildlife was a Paul Bunyan paradise for the male portion of the population, a girl could easily feel lost in the maze of woods, water, and world history.

Spread-eagled in a patch of sweet purple clover surrounding our potato field near a steep gravel pit, I would stare, for hours, upward into space. Wishing. The sky was the limit. I could go anywhere, do anything, be anyone I wanted. I wished I were a gorgeous, silver screen, movie queen like Lana Turner. I wished I could assume a new identity and call myself by my dreamy, made-up name, Lynette Swan. I wished I knew how to drive. I wished I were old enough to get a job scooping ice cream at Lenny's Soda Bar or taking tickets at the Perfect Theater in Stambaugh. I wished I were a bird and could fly away.

Rolling over with the stealth of a spy, I would flatten myself like a snake, slither silently to the sunburned grass on the edge of the pit and watch bug-eyed grasshoppers flex their lanky green legs, then jump and spit. I wished I could live with such abandon. I wished I could take off and go rabbit hunting like Dad and my brother John whenever I felt the urge and not have to be faced with a future of fussy female things like ironing ruffled blouses, shaving legs, and plucking eyebrows into perfectly shaped arches.

Yet, prowling the aisles of Newberry's Five and Dime in Iron River with Mom, I hunted not for rabbits but for any hint of glamour that would take me away from the pines, the birchbark, and the fungi of the northwoods. Standing in fascination over the midnight blue, imitation velvet display of fake sapphires and diamonds, I became a woman of the world, a Bohemian artist, a concert pianist on world tour, not just a wide-eyed, curly-haired, broomstick-skirted girl born to the Great Lakes' wilderness.

Wherever I was, I longed for adventure. I wished Mom and Dad would loosen up the apron strings. Sometimes, I wished I lived in Chicago with my grown up sister Corinne. Other times, I wished I could just be one of the guys and hang out with my brother John and his pals in their secret clubhouse hidden somewhere down by the iron ore piles, near Old Nick's, the hermit's, shack.

I didn't exactly want my Guardian Angel to take a hike, but I wanted to experience danger, mystery, chance. I wished that, by some miracle, life in Dober Location, in Iron County, in the Upper Peninsula of Michigan—practically the middle of nowhere—could somehow be exciting, daring, memorable. And, as it turned out, it was. Sometimes we laughed. Sometimes we cried . . .

Bleeding Hearts

Following The Great Depression, when the Oliver Mining Company sold the Dober Mining Location houses, Mom and Dad bought ours, House #13, for $450.

My cousin Joanne lived just three doors down the block and even though she was a grown up seven and I was only four, we were the best of friends.

When she went off to school in the fall of 1943, I thought I'd die without her. I gave up trying to count the long hours of each weekday, convinced that the weekend would never arrive. But somehow the days ticked slowly away until we could once again be together, make up for lost time, and play our favorite games in my back yard.

But then something terrible happened.

We'd been warned not to play piggyback. Caught in the act, we'd been told it was too dangerous. But the older kids in the neighborhood all did it. As soon as our parents were out of sight, Joanne would boost me up on her shoulders and away we'd go, wobbling, pitching, and stumbling until we'd tumble to the ground, giggling so hard we could barely pick ourselves up again.

One Saturday afternoon, as Joanne strutted about the yard with me on her back, our laughter sent us sailing with such speed around the front of the house that we nearly fell headlong into Mom's Snowball bushes. Joanne tried to stop the fall by taking a quick step backward, but her feet got tangled and she ran straight into the sharp corner of our front porch, jabbing her side and hurling us into a sorry heap.

I thought, at first, she was still laughing but, when I tried to roll her over, I could see she wasn't. She was crying. I begged her not to go home, but she didn't seem to hear me. I watched her limp along down the block, holding her side and sobbing.

I hoped she would come back after supper. I waited and waited, but she didn't come.

I waited for her the next day, again, but she still didn't come.

At our house, a strange thing was going on. Mom and Dad seemed to have a secret. They would often whisper to each other, then stop when I came into the room.

Finally on Monday evening, Mom told me Joanne was sick. She had a ruptured appendix. Auntie Sep had been told by their doctor that there was a new drug called penicillin that might cure her, but it was not yet available in our small town. Auntie Sep was beside herself with frustration and fear.

"Is Joanne better yet?" I kept asking my mother on Tuesday, but each time the answer was no.

On Tuesday night, I heard the phone ring, then Mom's voice sounding sad.

When she hung up the phone, she looked at me and said, "Coralie, come into the living room. Let's sit down. I want to talk to you."

She took my hand and led me to the sofa in the living room.

"That was Auntie Sep on the phone," Mom continued, looking at me in an odd way.

"Is Joanne better?" I asked.

"Coralie," she hesitated, "Joanne isn't going to get better." She put her arm around me as we sat of the sofa. "She's gone to heaven. She's one of God's special little angels now . . . She was very sick, you know, and now she won't be in pain anymore."

"She's going to be an angel? Then I won't see her anymore?" I tried hard to imagine what that meant.

In my restless dreams that night, I could see Joanne's face. Her short, soft curls spilled out from underneath the brim of her favorite hand-knit Scandinavian cap, forming a soft golden halo around her sky-blue eyes. But when I reached out and tried to touch her, I couldn't, because she was an angel, floating in heaven with all God's other special angels. Her face was happy, but I woke up crying and sad. I would never see my friend again.

"Can I go to the funeral?" I asked Mom.

"No, dear, you are too little. Only the grown-ups will be there," Mom answered, her eyes red-rimmed.

Standing in our back yard on the day of Joanne's funeral, I could see the mourners in black walk slowly in the cold drizzling rain from their cars to Auntie Sep's back door, then disappear inside. I stood silently watching until there were no more people, only empty cars. I felt small, chilled, and terribly alone.

I would never see Joanne again. I didn't have anyone to play with. Even when Mom read me my bedtime stories, I felt sad and lonely. All winter long, I thought about her, dreamed about her, and sometimes even pretended that she was with me, just invisible.

There were hushed conversations I sometimes overheard during those winter months. "I don't know how she's ever gonna' get through it," Dad told Mom, referring to his sister, Auntie Sep. "She hardly eats enough to keep a bird alive and she cries all the time."

I worried about her. I missed Joanne, but I missed my favorite aunt, too. It was a long winter.

When spring came, I stood at our northerly dining room window, looking off across the street to the field where topsy-turvy patches of burnt brown Indian tobacco, wild wheat, and weeping white milkweed waved invitingly in the sun. I wished Joanne was there so we could go exploring for buttercups, birds, and berries.

"I think the strawberries are ripe," Mom said brightly, interrupting my daydreams. "How would you like to go and see?"

"By myself?" I'd never been across the street alone before.

Mom hesitated, then went to the kitchen sink, rinsed out her little tin measuring cup, dried it on a blue and white striped kitchen towel and handed it to me. "By yourself. It's time you learned to cross alone. I'll walk you to the edge of the street, but when you come back, remember to look both ways for cars, just like we've talked about." She pressed the tin cup into my hand, smiled, and walked me to the street.

Excited about my adventure, I looked back only once to see if Mom was still watching me, but she'd gone back inside. So, I made my way through the waist-high waving grass, stooping now and again to press grass and leaves aside to look for berries.

Suddenly, I came upon a huge boulder hidden in the grass. Bigger than me and polished by years of sun, snow, and rain, it had a smell all its own, like the shoreline of a lake. I ran my hands over the pocked surface, found a notch halfway up just big enough for the toe of my white sandal and scrambled up.

Stretching out on its cool surface like a tricky toad, I moved not at all, blending into my surroundings so convincingly that the orange and black Monarch butterflies fluttering by could not tell me from the rock. The breath of their wings tickled my knees as they landed, then took off again.

To the musical trill of a meadowlark nesting nearby, I gazed up toward the serene sapphire sky, letting my thoughts float along with the puffy white clouds overhead as they scudded slowly along, taking the shapes of dancing dogs, circus elephants, and . . . angels, like Joanne.

Spring came and went. Then, one day in early summer, the phone rang.

"Coralie, that was Auntie Sep. She wants you to come for a visit. How would you like that?" Mom asked, obviously pleased.

"You mean I can go alone?" I'd been across the street, but never on a visit by myself.

"Yes, I think you're big enough now," Mom said in her sun-shiny way.

I was thrilled. Not only was I going on a visit by myself, but I would finally get to see Auntie Sep again, too.

Mom slipped my white embroidered pinafore over my head, then hooked each of my long curls around her forefinger and brushed it into a perfect bobbing spiral. She polished my white sandals, gave me a pair of white anklets to pull on and, finally, gave my face a few swipes with a warm wet washcloth that smelled sweetly of Fels Naphtha.

Heady with happiness, I hopped along down the sidewalk to Auntie Sep's house, counting the sections of cement and carefully skipping over each crack.

I slowed when I reached the pruned entrance to the yard and walked like a lady to the back door. There, behind the screen door, stood Auntie Sep waiting, but she had a strange look on her face. Was something wrong? I didn't know what to do. We just stood there looking at each other for what seemed like a long time, until I began to wonder if I should go back home.

But then she opened the door, stepped out, and looked off over my head.

"The wrens have come back," she said wistfully, pointing to the tiny birdhouse hung in the maple tree just outside her kitchen window. "They are such hard workers. Never stop from dawn 'til dusk." Her thoughts seemed far away as she watched the little brown birds flitting back and forth from her garden to their house.

"They're so tiny!" I exclaimed.

"Yes, they are, tiny but hearty," she answered, turning and walking toward her back yard garden.

"Look at all those sad little faces," she said more to herself than to me as we examined clusters of bright lavender, purple, and yellow pansies peering up at us.

I followed her from flower to flower enjoying the colors of her garden. Grouped in perfect little patches were pink carnations, white Shasta daisies, and blue bachelor buttons, bordered by orange nasturtiums, yellow four-o'clocks, and red moss roses. At each new plant, she stopped and pulled away dead leaves and stems.

"Your flowers are so pretty. I love the colors," I said, hoping to cheer her up, hoping she would look at me. She didn't seem to remember I was there.

"Yes, the garden is comforting," she replied. Her voice was somber, her thoughts far away, her eyes clouded over. She seemed lost from me.

But after several seconds, she finally spoke again. "Come," she said looking off across the garden, "I have something to show you."

I followed her to the far corner of the garden. "These are new this year," she said pointing to a clump of pink and white flowers.

I walked over to get a closer look. Here grew the most amazing flowering plant I had ever seen, abundant green branches weighted down with small pink heart-shaped flowers, each split down the middle by a white pendulum.

"They're called Bleeding Hearts," Auntie Sep said, studying the flowers.

"They look like broken hearts," I said. Just like mine, I thought.

She didn't respond at once. I began to wonder if she'd ever look at me.

"Yes, dear." I heard grief in her voice. "They are one of God's little miracles. He knows when our hearts are sad and has given us a symbol of His understanding to remind us that He understands our pain."

"Can we pick them?" I thought how pretty they'd look in a vase.

She fell silent . . . thinking. I looked up at her and tried to see her eyes but they were still turned from me. However, she seemed to be making an important decision. I wondered what it was.

"I have a better idea," she finally answered. "We'll let them be for now. Then we can come back each day and see how they've grown."

With this, she summoned up her courage and turned to look me squarely in the eyes. She forced herself to smile through her tears. "Would you like to come and visit me again," she asked, "tomorrow?"

"And we can walk in the garden again?" I asked.

"We certainly can, Coralie. We can walk in the garden . . . together," Auntie Sep answered.

Then, as she reached, out taking my tiny hand in hers, and I felt the wonderful warmth of her touch ease the pain of my broken heart, I knew everything was going to be all right. I had thought Joanne was lost forever, but there in the garden I felt her presence, her memory blessed by the Bleeding Hearts.

Our visits to the garden became the most important events in our lives during the summer of 1944. As hand in hand we shared the beauty, peace, and joy of God's wonders, we also held Joanne silently within our grieving hearts. And through this gentle companionship of love and hope and grace our hearts, at last, began to heal.

My cousin Joanne in her mother's garden.

The Luck of the Irish

Not long after St. Valentine's Day in 1945, some pretty peculiar things started to happen at our house. For no special reason—it wasn't even Mom's birthday—some of her lady friends threw a big party in her honor.

They popped up the extra leaf in the dining room table and set up two card tables in the living room on which they placed pretty crocheted cloths, Mom's good dishes, and a fancy luncheon of grated carrots and raisins in green jello, cream cheese and olive finger sandwiches with the crust cut off, and white frosted pineapple bars. When they finished nibbling their lunches and picking at the mints and peanuts from pink accordion pleated nut cups, the tables were cleared and a load of gift-wrapped packages set in front of Mom's place.

Mom happily opened each package from the odd assortment of gifts and thanked her friends for their thoughtfulness. But I wondered how she could keep a straight face, because there wasn't a single thing that wasn't just plain silly. There were teeny-tiny sweaters, pink floral rattles, small striped flannel blankets and a lot of other stuff we couldn't possibly have had any use for. I was way too big for the sweaters, too old to play with rattles, and we didn't even have a dog that could have used the blankets.

And if that wasn't strange enough, Mom's pals, Marguerite DeRocher and Irene May gave her a large greeting card and matching book with this really weird looking bird on them. It wore a blue porter's cap, a short matching jacket, and carried a baby trussed up in a diaper in its long skinny sharp yellow beak.

"What kind of a bird is that?" I asked after the women had left.

"It's a stork, honey." Mom smiled at the goofy bird and set the card on a table so it stood up like a picture.

"How come he's flying around with a baby?"

"Because that's what he does, delivers babies to their new homes," Mom answered.

"Have you ever seen him?" I asked.

"Well, he's been to our house a few times. To bring your sister Corinne and your brother John," Mom explained, "and you."

"Me?" I was trying to get the picture, but it wasn't making much sense.

"Yes, you." Mom answered.

"He's not coming *again*, is he?" I was pretty sure Mom was teasing me, but if she wasn't, I wanted to make sure she knew we didn't need any old bird bringing a baby to our house.

"Well, he's not coming to the house anymore. He'll be going to the hospital from now on," Mom explained.

"Why does he have to go to the hospital?"

"Because I decided that's where he should go," Mom answered.

"So, did you write him a letter, or what?"

"Honey," Mom laughed, "times are changing and he just knows." I didn't know why Mom was telling me these silly stories, but there was definitely something funny going on.

A couple of days after the big party, things went from weird to worse. I found Mom in her bedroom, packing her suitcase. I'll admit the party was pretty bizarre, but I didn't think it was bad enough to make her want to leave home.

"Where are you going?" I asked in astonishment.

"Don't worry, honey," she said, "I've just got to go meet the stork and then I'll be coming right back home in a few days."

"I want to go with you!" I pouted.

"Dad will be here with you and so will your brother John. You'll see, it won't take long at all. I'll be back in no time."

I thought the whole thing was pretty chintzy, but what did I know, I was just a kid. I sure wished I would hurry and grow up so I could understand some of the crazy things my mom did.

Anyway, on March 17, Mom got all dressed up in her best clothes, put John in charge of baby-sitting me, and instructed Dad to drive her to the hospital. I told her I hoped she'd have a good time and she promised to tell me all about it when she got home.

And she did. She said the stork met her there and asked what kind of a baby she wanted. She told him a little girl would be nice and he looked over what he had on hand and forked one over. Then, the nurses at the hospital, who announced that all the babies born on St. Patrick's Day were Irish, held a party for Mom, the other mothers, and their babies. They had a cake trimmed with green frosting, little paper plates with Leprechauns on them, and dainty napkins plastered with shamrocks. After the celebration, the stork flew away, the other mothers and their babies went home, and Mom called Dad on the telephone to come and pick her up.

I had a hard time swallowing some of this story, but I know the part about the napkins was true because Mom brought one home for me to save. The part about the baby was true too, because she brought one of those home to keep. I don't think the part about the baby being Irish was true, since Mom's family was Finnish and Dad's, Italian, but the part about it being a girl was. And that turned out to be pretty terrific, after all, because I got to have a little sister all my own. I named her Connie Lynn.

My mother, Carrie Cederna, and my little sister Connie at
Chicaugon Lake.

The Web of War

Thousands of miles from Dober Mining Location, the Allied troops united to defend our rights, our freedom, our lives. World War II raged. Mom, her women friends, and other community volunteers, under the guidance of the Red Cross, gathered to roll bandages for the boys overseas. From billboards and recruiting posters, flag-waving sailors and marines singled out passersby, signaling them to join the armed forces. Rationing stamps were hoarded, and tokens carefully counted, before and after each trip to the grocery store.

With our nation's sons noticeably missing from cities, villages, and communities, a sense of mourning hovered overhead like a sinister shroud. Fear knew no boundaries. It lurked in blackened bedrooms by night and sunny kitchens by day. Parents, siblings, and friends lived in constant dread. Denial did nothing to banish visions of uniformed officers arriving in an official black sedan, telegram in hand. Grief. Hopes and dreams dashed forever.

Neighborhoods such as ours, normally separated by ethnic variance, bonded together in times of loss. Gifts of money for grieving families were collected, then delivered in stoic silence. This sharing created a unity that overrode the confines of "old country" privacy, strict religious beliefs, and diverse cultural backgrounds. Loss was universal, no interpretation necessary.

Every man, woman, and child attempted to escape the fear and depression which surrounded the war and pervaded the world, our nation and each small community. Music, that alluring antidote, took on new rhythms. "Big Band" sounds and ballrooms sprung up around the country and sheet music became a popular item. I listened to my teen-age sister Corinne play the piano and sing *Paper Doll* and *Besume' Mucho*, bright melodies underscored with longing.

At the Perfect Theatre in Stambaugh and the Delft Theatre in Iron River, newsreels brought home the reality of war-torn countries—pain, suffering, devastation. We witnessed vicious front line battles; emaciated refugees trudging along pulverized paths, forced to leave their families, homes, and possessions; air raids followed by bombs blasting from fighter planes, dropping to targets far below, and bursting into horrific explosions. Struggling soldiers with savage machine guns, bayonets, and tanks skirmished in bloody battles, sweeping the screen with sordid details of death, dying, and despair. Harry Truman, dapper in his white suit and straw hat, flashed his friendly smile and tried to convince us we were winning, that one day soon the war would come to an end.

The war's end was a unified goal shared by all ages. It loomed over our heads. Intangible. Elusive. We did our best to cope, to understand, to go on with our everyday activities.

Even five-year-olds were aware of a world larger, stranger, and more threatening than the one they could see, smell, and touch. We could only be protected so much. The reminders of war were everywhere . . .

"Form a circle, children," Miss Young, my kindergarten teacher, instructed. "Let's see who can be first to be seated and ready to start the day. Don't forget. Fold your hands."

There was a frenzied scraping of small wooden chairs against the highly varnished wooden strip floor as twenty-two girls and boys raced, squealing and giggling, to place their chairs in a circle, be seated, and win the approval of the teacher.

"Silence is golden," Miss Young said in a low quiet voice. "Take out your imaginary keys. Good. Now lock your lips and throw away your keys."

It was the same every day. I loved Miss Young, but I always put my key in my pocket so I could find it when I needed it. Silence may have been golden, but for me it was painful. I knew I couldn't last in a silenced state for long.

"Now, what do we recite each morning as we start our day?" Miss Young asked. No one answered. I figured they had all flung their keys too far away. "Can anybody tell me?"

I furtively withdrew my key from my pocket, sneaked it up to my lips, and turned the lock. Then I raised my hand.

"Coralie?" Miss Young called on me.

"We're supposed to say, 'Politeness is to do and say the kindest thing in the kindest way,'" I answered proudly.

"That's right, Coralie." She smiled at me in the kindest way and I just knew I'd get a gold star on my day chart. How I loved gold stars, charts, and school. "Girls and boys, let's repeat our *Politeness Poem* in unison. Stand up please."

We all stood and delivered the *Politeness Poem* together.

"Remember now, everybody, you must be kind to each other. The world will be a better place if we remember every day, in every way, to be polite and kind to others," Miss Young told us.

I wondered about the war . . . people were getting killed. I guessed they had stopped being kind and polite.

"Who would like to hold the flag?" Only the boys volunteered for this honor. It was too heavy for the girls to handle. Larry Smitham raised his hand, walked over to the heavy wooden handled flag, and lifted it as high as he could. His little arms quivered, but he fought to keep them under control. Standing at attention, his face reflected the somberness of the subdued kindergartners.

"Put your hands on your hearts, children, and face the flag," Miss Young said with reverence. As if in church, we recited, "I pledge allegiance to the flag of the United States of America and to the republic for which it stands, one nation, indivisible with liberty and justice for all."

A sober silence followed, until the flag was replaced in its holder next to the backboard. Then, the usual chaos broke out.

"Be seated," Miss Young ordered. "Now, how many of you have brought your money for War Bonds today? Line up with your pennies and I will record your contributions."

Most of us remembered our pennies. It was difficult not to remember when cautioned each day in the classroom by a thoroughly threatening Uncle Sam pointing down from an immense colored poster on the bulletin board. "Uncle Sam Wants *You!*" it read. I knew I wasn't going to let him get *me*—that's for sure—so I always remembered my pennies. His ferocious eyes focused on me as I stood in line, waiting to pay, and I wondered if he had ever heard of the *Politeness Poem.*

Each War Bond contribution, no matter how small, guaranteed a tiny paper stripe of red, white, and blue would be glued to the shoulder of the giver's poster child. Each kindergartner, depending on their gender, had a mimeographed girl or boy poster pinned in a row across the top of the blackboard, individualized with their names printed in bold block letters and creatively personalized by the owner's coloring crayons.

When Miss Young was through collecting War Bond money, she went directly to the piano, sat down, and struck a chord. "Are you ready, children?" she asked.

We were always ready to sing. *My Country 'Tis of Thee* was one of our favorites. We sang at the top of our lungs, "Sweet land of libery, of thee I sing . . . land where our fathers died, land of the pilgrims' pride, from e-e-vry-y mountain-side, le-et freedom ring . . ." No one could have been more enamored with the music, the words, the business of being patriotic. We knew in our little hearts that somehow our voices raised in song would lead the world out of battle and put an end to war . . .

At St. Agnes Catholic Church in Iron River, Dad, Corinne, John, and I sat in the balcony and listened to Fr. Dingfelder preach about the wickedness of war. After the homily, he asked for our special support and prayers.

"Let us all kneel and pray for the end of the war," he beseeched. "Let your hearts and souls be generous and give your love and prayers to the leaders of this great country, our boys who have left their families to serve us, and their families who have so willingly given them up to the Lord's wisdom and care. Pray for peace and may God's blessing be with you."

Day-to-day discussions of death and dying were all too commonplace. Kids at school talked about relatives who had been wounded or killed in action. Everyone knew someone who had lost their life in the war.

"Coralie, will you help me with this box," Mom asked as we worked in the basement, sorting out old coats, suits, and shoes. "Just hold the end of it open, while I pack these suits inside."

"Sure," I said, grabbing the sturdy cardboard flap, "but why are we packing them if we're going to throw them out?" The clothes were old, out of style, drab black, brown, and gray woolens. I'd heard Mom say they weren't much good any more.

"We're not going to throw them out," Mom explained. "These clothes are still sturdy and warm. We're sending them to Aunt Hannah and her family in Helsinki, Finland."

"But Mom, why would they want our old clothes?" I wondered if Mom realized they might think it was impolite to send them our old things. "Won't they feel bad if we send them this old stuff?"

"Honey, not everyone is as lucky as we are to live in the United States. Our cousins in Finland can't buy warm clothes like these. There are none for sale. And they can't buy things they need like soap, socks, and shoes. Aunt Hannah wrote and begged me to send any kind of warm clothes that we could spare," Mom answered.

"Gosh," I gulped. I'd never given a thought to not being able to have soap, socks, or shoes. Those things were just taken for granted.

"We're very lucky." Mom stuck bars of soap and several pairs of socks down in along the sides of the clothing. Then she stacked all of our old shoes on top of the suits and coats and taped the box shut. "They may not even get these things."

"Why not?" That didn't make sense.

"All of these boxes will be opened and checked by the authorities. If the government feels others need these things more than Aunt Hannah, they'll just keep them. That's the way it is in many other countries," Mom said. "Just be glad you live in America."

"Is there a war in Finland, too?" I asked.

"Almost the whole world is at war," Mom answered bleakly. "When Aunt Hannah and her family go to bed at night, they lay on top of their beds, completely dressed, in case they have to flee from invading troops. Their bags are always packed."

"I hope the war is over soon," I told Mom.

"Yes dear, that's what we're all hoping and praying for." Mom took a ball of twine, looped it many times over and around the box, and carefully knotted the loops with short strong lengths of string.

The war continued until, at last at summer's end, on August 15, 1945, surrender to the Allies was announced.

Harry Truman signing the final documents was immortalized on the front page of our newspaper. In a frenzy of celebration, locals jumped into their automobiles and drove through the neighborhood streets blasting their horns in thanksgiving.

"We won the war. We won the war!" the other neighborhood kids and I shrieked as we ran up and down the sidewalk alongside the street where a parade of people tooted, hollered, and banged their relief.

We had grown older, stronger, and wiser. We had experienced loss beyond our years but survived with a greater sense of God, our neighbors, and selves. We called it Victory.

Teen-age sister Corinne played the piano and sang *Paper Doll* and *Besume' Mucho*—popular WWII songs.

The Letter

Though World War II had come to a victorious end in 1947, its aftermath created complications, confusion, and heartache for people in cities large and small. In 1947, many were still struggling to find and put the pieces of their lives back together.

Going on with life was difficult enough, but resolving the issues surrounding loss was sometimes nearly impossible. Families mourning a member killed in action were usually able to feel a measure of relief once the body was returned home to the States and given a final resting place in hallowed ground. But, while these families put their loved ones and grief to rest, others agonized over relatives missing in action. For them there would be no rest, nor would the war really be over, until the last pieces of their devastating puzzles were uncovered and set into place.

Even if a family was notified their loved one's name had been taken off the Missing In Action list, a government snafu of identification, regulations, and shipping orders could create further disturbing complications. "Damned red tape," Dad called it, and Mom agreed.

An underlying tension of unresolved worry and waiting was evident at our house. I had no idea what Mom and Dad were dealing with, but I was soon to learn.

The April winds of the Upper Peninsula of Michigan, traveling swiftly down from Canada and across the Great Lakes, brought with them yet another stormy week of blowing cold and snow flurries. Daffodils and crocuses, bravely poking their tiny yellow and purple heads up from the earth, were covered over in a veil of white. The winter, longer than anyone could remember, seemed to go on forever. All the neighbors agreed it was the worst in years. They threw up their mittened hands, wondering if spring would ever come.

As my little sister Connie, who had reached the toddling age, and I sat in the breakfast nook nibbling peanut butter and banana sandwiches, Mom burst into the kitchen, pinning on her wide-brimmed grey felt hat and shrugging on her grey muskrat coat.

"Bundle up, Coralie. Let's take a run up to the Post Office and see if there's any mail." Mom handed me my outdoor clothes and whisked Connie out of the nook, wiped her face and hands with a damp dish towel, and started tugging on her baby blue snowsuit, white boots, and white knitted cap.

"The Post Office!" I loved going to the Post Office. Even though I couldn't reach the dial on our mailbox, I knew the combination and also knew it wouldn't be long before I'd be able to open Box 642 myself. I crammed the last bite of banana and bread into my mouth, slipped out of the nook, and quickly washed the signs of peanut butter from my face and hands. "I'll be ready in a second." I pulled on my brown rubber boots, my fashionable navy blue wool military style coat, and fixed the matching soldier's cap over my long brown curls, setting it jauntily to one side. Then, I hurried along after Mom as she walked briskly out to the garage, carrying my little sister.

"I don't know how long this car is going to hold up," Mom murmured to herself, looking at the old green Chevy sitting on the concrete floor, dripping oil. "It's never been quite right." Holding Connie on her hip, she opened the garage door, then the passenger door on the car so I could hop into the front seat, and finally her own door. She stood Connie between us and slid behind the steering wheel. "I just hope it lasts a while longer," she added, starting the sputtering car, backing it slowly out of the garage, and onto the street alongside our house.

We drove west on Nineteenth Street past Mottes' neighborhood store, around the corner at Judish's Gas Station, and headed north up to Stambaugh. We passed the coal bins, overflowing with black sooty nuggets, outside the Caspian Lumber Company building where Mrs. Judish worked, the entrance to Thirteenth Street where Auntie Andy and Uncle Ray Hereau lived, and the Stambaugh School playground at the top of the hill. We sailed by the manicured campus of the school, zipped past the Carnegie Library, and coasted around the corner near the Stambaugh General Hospital before coming to a stop in front of Lenny's Soda Bar.

"Want to wait in the car?" Mom asked, as she opened her car door and started to step out.

"No! I'm coming in, too." I wasn't about to miss going into the Post Office. It was the highlight of any day.

Connie reached out her arms and, while Mom hitched her up under one arm and waited for me, I managed to thrust the heavy creaking green car door open by myself. Pleased, I jumped out on the sidewalk, stepped to the other side of the door, and slammed it shut with all my might, causing the car to sway and tremble.

We hustled across the snow-spotted street, opened the heavy glass Post Office door, and hurried inside where we were greeted by the teeming smells of sweet raspberry jelly bismarcks and glazed doughnuts from Roberg's Bakery next door, brewing coffee blending with a shot of tobacco, and a heavy odor of fresh newsprint. The busy little two room office was bustling with energy, chatter, and good spirits.

"You're getting mighty tough," Jack Corbett, who'd been watching us through the plate glass window, called out from behind the wall of mailboxes where he was sorting letters and small packages, feeding them into the hungry boxes. I could just make him out through the tiny glass windows of the partially filled mailboxes. "We're going to have to get you out for football, get you to play on the team with your brother John and Mel Holmes. What do you think, Harold?" He nodded to Harold Anderson who was taking in the joke while weighing a stack of letters behind the main window. "Think Willard could use a good fullback?" he continued, referring to Willard Anderson, my brother's high school football coach. Harold just chuckled.

I started to giggle, as usual, and put my hand over my mouth to smother the sound. Jack always said something silly to make me giddy, but no matter how hard he made me laugh, he always held a poker straight expression on his own face, and that made me giggle even harder.

I pivoted on the toes of my brown rubber boots, still giggling, and walked over to the package delivery door where the wall was plastered with handbills decked out with black and white photos. Wanted posters! I silently sounded out the words, "Re-ward $100 lead-ing to con-vic-tion and ar-rest. Armed and dan-ger-ous." Dangerous! I stared at the vicious criminals' eyes, some beady and mean, some vacant and haunted, and wondered if they would ever come to our town. A hundred dollars was a lot of money, I figured. I could buy that horse I was always dreaming about. Still, how could a kid my age hope to catch one of them. Dad, maybe could, but probably not me. I shivered, turned away, and caught Harold watching me, a big grin on his face. "Looking to make some money?" he asked. I shrugged my shoulders, wrinkled up my nose, and caught another giggle in the palm of my hand. Now how did he know what I was thinking?

"Letter from Minnesota, Carrie," Jack said to Mom who had set Connie down and was still dialing the numbers to the combination on Box 642. "Hope it's good news." She pulled out a white square-shaped envelope, peered into the four by six inch opening of the box to see if there was any other mail and, when she saw there wasn't, slapped the door shut, simultaneously giving the round combination dial a twist to lock it.

"I hope so." Mom's voice sounded sort of concerned, her expression troubled, as she turned the envelope over, inspecting it.

"Wonder how much snow they've got up there," Jack said. "They always seem to get it worse than we do. You've got to be pretty hardy to live in Minnesota."

"Or crazy, hey?" Harold laughed.

"That's what I keep telling my Dad," Mom answered, picking Connie up, "but he loves it up there in Keewatin."

"See you Monday," Harold called after us as we approached the door to leave.

"I don't know . . ." Mom said absentmindedly, staring at the unopened letter clutched in her hands and leaving both Jack and Harold behind with puzzled looks on their faces.

Even after we got back in the old Chevy, Mom remained quiet. She set Connie on the seat between us and didn't say a word. I kept waiting for her to open her letter, but she didn't. This was odd because Mom always opened her mail as soon as she got her hands on it. Something strange was going on.

"Aren't you going to open your letter?" I asked curiously.

"I will. Later." Mom adjusted her mirror, turned the key in the ignition, and pumped the gas pedal to get the Chevy started. It caught, chugged, and sputtered. "Oh no, not again." She tried again and the car started.

"Look, Mom," I said to cheer her up, "the sun's coming out. Maybe it'll melt all this snow away."

"That would be nice, wouldn't it," Mom said, trying to sound cheerful. "We certainly could use some sunshine." She backed the car out of the diagonal parking space, drove down the street to Tri-City Drugs and, checking carefully in all directions to make sure the Stambaugh Police Car was nowhere in sight, flipped a U-turn. Then we drove back home in silence.

"It's time for your nap," Mom said to Connie, removing her snowsuit. "But, Coralie, you can go and play." I could tell Mom wanted to be alone, but that was okay with me since I wanted to start working on my new Uncle Wiggly puzzle.

While Mom put Connie into her crib in the downstairs bedroom, I got busy at the dining room table, scrambling up the pieces of the jigsaw puzzle, then building and rebuilding it. It wasn't long before Mom came back into the living room and sat on the old mauve sofa, picked up the envelope from Minnesota, and finally pushed her finger under the glued flap to open it. She eased the letter out, read it, and reread it, then sat silently looking out the window, the letter momentarily abandoned in her lap. Her eyes looked damp.

"What's wrong?" I asked.

"I think you're too little to remember Johnny Sippola," she said, finally picking up the letter, folding it, and placing it back in its envelope. "He was with us when we vacationed at Swan Lake in Minnesota just before he shipped out for overseas duty."

"I remember Johnny," I said. He was the tall handsome young man with sandy blonde hair and smiling eyes—the one who teased and laughed and swam like a fish. I could still see him slipping under the water like a shimmering eel, popping up in the most unlikely places to surprise us little kids, and splashing us with water. With broad breaststrokes, he'd spin away towards shore, grab his towel, and run as fast as he could so we couldn't catch him. "He was fun!"

"Yes, he was," Mom said sadly.

"What's wrong?" What was going on? Mom never acted sad like this. How come one little letter was causing all this trouble?

"Johnny's not coming back from the war." Mom said softly.

"But the war's over!" It had been more than two years since we'd celebrated the horn-blowing victory. I looked at Mom, more curious now than ever, just as I heard Dad coming in the back door. "Dad's home from the mine!" I jumped off my chair at the dining room table, ran to the kitchen door, and peered around the corner. Dad was ready for me. He'd set his dinner pail on the kitchen counter and was coming toward the doorway, leaning over like a gorilla, and trying to catch me with his dangling arms. I squealed in mock terror, darted under his arms, and escaped into the kitchen to safety.

Mom followed me into the kitchen, carrying the letter like it was glass. "You'd better get back to your puzzle," she said, nodding to Dad to stop his gorilla antics. "I want to talk to Dad, alone."

"Okay." Disappointed, I shuffled back to the colored and curved pieces of Uncle Wiggly I'd left scattered over the dining room. As I crawled back up on my chair, I hardly had to strain at all to hear what they were saying.

"A letter came from "Sanna," today." Sanna was the Finnish name Mom used when referring to her stepmother Susan, Grandpa Wierimaa's wife. "It looks like Johnny is finally coming home," Mom said quietly to Dad. I perked up my ears, surprised. Hadn't Mom just told me Johnny was not coming home?

"You mean they're finally gonna' ship him home?" Dad sounded angry. "First they said they didn't know what happened, then they said they couldn't find him, then they wouldn't give him up. Makes you wonder just what all has been going on over there. These guys give up their lives for their country and the government can't even get them sent back home for a decent burial."

"I guess we're lucky they were able to locate him at all," Mom pointed out, "under the circumstances."

"I suppose," Dad mumbled.

"With so many bodies never even found after the ship went down, I guess we need to be thankful. Think of those families who still don't know what happened to their sons," Mom answered. There was a long silence before Mom spoke again and when she did, she sounded like she was crying. "I just can't believe this happened to Johnny."

"Yah, those Liberty Ships were supposed to be protected," Dad agreed.

"Here he was on a rescue mission, carrying all those women and children from England to freedom in Norway. It's so unfair."

"War's about as unfair as it gets," Dad grumbled. He sounded even more angry about all the war business. Again there was a long silence, then Dad spoke up again. "What I can't figure out is why he didn't just swim away—like a lot of the other guys did—the ones who made it away alive. You know what a heck of a swimmer he was. It just doesn't make any sense."

"Well, we'll never know the answer to that," Mom said in a hushed voice, "but I wish we would. It would be a big help to Sanna. I just don't know how she'll ever heal from all this."

"It's rough, that's for sure."

Mom and Dad's voices stopped. Time seemed to stretch out in a long endless space. In the stillness, I slipped off my chair, tiptoed to the kitchen doorway, and peeked around the corner. As if fastened to their places, Mom and Dad sat motionless in the breakfast nook, staring down at the top of the table where the letter lay open between them.

I turned soundlessly on my toes, went back to my puzzle, and started looking for the piece with the blue tip of Uncle Wiggly's stovepipe hat. A lump welling up in my throat, I now understood what had happened to Johnny. He had died. I tried to call up the memory of his laughing eyes reflecting the blue-green waters on the shore of Swan Lake, but they were shadowed by the sun at his back. Perplexed, I listened to the silence, punctuated only by the constant drip-dripping of the kitchen faucet against the porcelain sink.

The Trip

Our household became a whirlwind of activity that evening as Mom and Dad started getting ready to pack us all up and travel to Grandpa's and Sanna's home in Keewatin, Minnesota.

We'd barely finished dinner when Mom started organizing. She was back to her old self again. There was no more time for silence or tears. "We're going to Minnesota," she announced, "for Johnny Sippola's funeral. We've got a lot of work ahead of us. I want you all to pitch in and help get ready to go."

"I'll be out under the hood. There's got to be a few hundred miles more left in that heap of junk," Dad said, throwing on his leather jacket and grabbing his hat as he escaped to the garage.

"John," Mom said to my brother, "I want you to go down to the basement, find the suitcases, and throw a scoop of coal in the furnace while you're down there." I half hoped John would come out with one of his usual teasing comments to lighten the tension, but he didn't. The tone, while hectic, was as solemn as Sunday on church. It wasn't the time, nor place, for fooling around and we all knew it without being told.

"Coralie, I want you to keep an eye on your little sister while I go down and wash clothes." It wasn't even Monday—in fact, it wasn't even daytime—and Mom was headed for the ringer washing machine in the basement.

By the time Dad got back in the house from working on the old Chevy, Mom had washed and hung all the clothes on lines in the basement next to the coal furnace so they'd dry overnight, prepared the suitcases to be packed with the dry clothes once morning dawned, and made sure we all had our baths before we climbed into our beds.

Much as I loved riding around the county roads, I hated taking long distance trips. For one thing, I always got carsick—it was a fact of life. And sitting in the car all day, just driving—rather than adventuring—was an entirely different matter. Restless, I didn't think I'd ever fall asleep. I wondered what it would be like to finally go to a real funeral. I thought about Johnny and all the fun we'd had on our vacation a few years earlier. I imagined I was in the row boat with Mom, Corinne, and John paddling slowly along the shore of Swan Lake and, at last, lulled to sleep by the lap-lap of the waves against the wooden boat, I drifted off into an uneasy stupor. The night was filled with sketchy dreams of wild scenes. Even though I dreaded being in the car all day, it was a relief to hear Dad calling us kids to get up at four o'clock the next morning.

Then, the whirlwind resumed. While Dad packed the overnight bags and suitcases, bursting with clean clothes, into the car, Mom tried not to rush us kids through a hot breakfast of cream of wheat, but we could feel her urgency to be on the road, so gulped our food as fast as we could.

Meanwhile Mom rushed around the kitchen preparing baloney, salami, and peanut butter sandwiches; packages of store-bought windmill cookies, Fig Newtons, and pink frosted ginger snaps; and apples, bananas, and pears and packed them into shoe boxes for the trip. By five o'clock, all signs of breakfast had been cleared from the kitchen and we were on US 2, in the coughing old green Chevy, on our way to Grandpa's place in Keewatin, Minnesota.

"We should be able to make it to Ironwood by seven," Dad said, pulling his stainless steel pocket watch out for the fourth time in five minutes. "We can look up a church there. That'll put us in Ashland, Wisconsin right about nine, nine-thirty."

Sunday Mass. No matter what, Dad never missed church on Sunday. There was no excuse good enough in the whole entire world for not going to church on Sunday. It was a day of thanks and praise and we—Dad reminded us often enough— had plenty to be thankful for.

"What if we can't find a church?" I seemed to have a knack for posing questions that were best left unasked.

"We'll find one!" Dad growled, but now that I'd brought it up he was worrying about that as well as how the rumbling old car would make it to Minnesota.

Mom turned around in her seat, put her fingers to her lips, and shook her head, cautioning me to be quiet. "Why don't you read for a while," she suggested.

I pulled out my new Bobbsey Twins book, *The Bobbsey Twins in Echo Valley*, opened to the chapter I'd marked with a pink hair ribbon, and started to read. From other books in the series, I'd come to know The Bobbsey family quite intimately. They traveled to all sorts of exotic areas of the country, having astonishing adventures wherever they went. I thought they were kind of like us, but they had a maid and she traveled with them, too. Now where would we put a maid in our car? There was just barely room in the back seat now for John, little Connie, and me. But, I did envy the girls, Flossie and Nan, as they never seemed to get carsick.

I couldn't seem to take my mind off my nervous stomach. I was sure to get carsick. Just thinking about it, my stomach started making little lurching leaps. I tried to think of something else, but it was no use.

"I think I'm going to throw up," I gagged, tossing my book on the seat beside me.

"Stop the car!" Mom yelled at Dad.

"What the heck's going on?" Dad hollered, jamming on the brakes, downshifting, and swerving to a stop just off the shoulder of the road.

"Get out!" Mom opened her door and jumped out, pulled back her seat, and grabbed hold of my coat shoulder, engineering me out of the back seat to the side of the road. I gagged a couple of times, but nothing would come up. "Stick you finger down your throat!" Mom said, closing the car door to shut the rest of the family out of this private moment.

"I can't, when you're looking at me!" I griped, still gagging.

"Oh, for heavens sake." Mom gave a heavy sigh as she opened the car door, climbed back in, and pulled it almost closed. Then she called through the little crack of an opening, "And don't get any on your coat."

I walked to the back of the car where the smell of gasoline caught in my eyes, nose, and throat. All it took then was one gigantic gag and I didn't have to stick my finger down my throat after all. It was all over in seconds and I'd kept my coat clean—of course, I was an old hand at this car-sickness business.

I stepped away from the gas tank, took a few deep breaths of cold April air, then stood catching my breath and looking into the forest filled with long needled pines bathed in green black morning light. The sight of the long slender boughs weighted down with molded mounds of melting snow was wondrous as was the ground below still covered with smooth white winter snow. It was fascinating to watch the melting banks trickle in little trails down the slopes of hills, form lazy rivulets, and course out toward the road. It was too bad I had to get back in that old car again.

"If you're done, get back in here," Mom ordered from the car—she was an old hand at my car-sickness business, too. Reluctantly, I left the enchanted snow scene and crawled back into the car.

"Now we're gonna' be late," Dad complained, pulling his watch out to get another glimpse of the time as he pulled the snorting car back onto the road. Everyone knew we weren't really on a time schedule, but we also knew Dad would worry about being late no matter where we were going, or when we got there.

"I'm sure we'll find a Mass starting when we get to Ironwood," Mom said, trying to reassure him. Now we were all anxious about the time.

It seemed to take forever, but we finally reached the outskirts of the city. Mom grabbed hold of Dad's sleeve and pointed to a shiny white gas station on the right side of the road above which galloped an amazing sign in the shape of a bright red horse with wings. "Let's pull in there and ask directions," Mom urged.

"I'm not gonna' pull in there without buying gas," Dad answered, "I'm sure that guy's got better things to do than stand around giving out directions all day long."

"Well, pull in and *get some gas*, then," Mom said.

Dad made a jerky turn into the station, pulled up alongside the gas pump, and rolled down his window. A wiry grey haired man dressed in oily coveralls came bounding out of the station door, wiping his black greasy fingers on a black greasy rag. "Fill 'er up, hey," Dad said with a big grin.

"Ask him about the church," Mom whispered.

"I will, I will," Dad mumbled. "Just hold on, will you."

When the gas had been pumped, the oil checked, and the windows meticulously washed, the greasy fingered man danced back to the window. Dad took out a five dollar bill, grinned again, and held it out to the man. Only then did he ask the burning question—where was the church?

"See that big old black lamppost down the way? Take a left there. You'll see a water tower on your right—turn left—then make a quick jog right. Go another hundred yards or so and it'll be right in front of your nose. You folks ain't from around here, are you," he said, which I figured was a really brilliant deduction on his part.

"We're from Stambaugh," Dad said proudly.

"Stambaugh?" He'd never heard of it.

"It's right up the hill from Iron River," Dad answered.

"Oh, Iron River." Now he had a handle on where we were from—he'd heard of Iron River. "I got a cousin lives there, maybe you know him. Name's Maki, Wilbur Maki. Married to my first cousin, Sophie. Moved over to Iron River a couple of years back, but lived here most of their lives." Dad had been wrong. This man obviously had nothing better to do than stand around all day giving directions and visiting.

"Uh, there's a lot of Maki's over our way." Dad shifted in his seat, impatient to leave but not wanting to be impolite.

"In town for a visit?" This man was not about to let his only customer get away that fast.

"Nope. Heading up to Minnesota," Dad said, starting the car—a cool hint that we wanted to get out of there.

"Business or pleasure?" The man still had one greasy hand glued to the window frame, trying to keep us from leaving.

"Business," Dad said gruffly, losing his smile. This guy was getting too familiar to suit him.

"Oh," the man said suspiciously, leaning down to stare into the car at Mom and the three of us kids, "I see." Of course, he didn't see at all, but he obviously wanted to know more about what our business might be. Three kids and a wife on a business trip? On Sunday? Sounded pretty fishy to him. He finally let go of the window frame, stood back, and pulled off his cap. Scratching his head, he added, "Well, good luck."

"Yah, we gotta' go," Dad said, edging the car away from the pump, rolling his window up, and shaking his head as he watched the place disappear in his rear-view mirror. "Nosy old codger," he grumbled.

"He was just trying to be friendly. You could have been nicer to him," Mom remarked.

"If I'd have been any nicer, he'd have hog-tied us and made us stay for dinner." The back of Dad's neck was getting red. All this stopping and talking was getting us late for church. "You remember those directions he just gave us?"

"I wasn't really paying attention. I thought you were listening." Mom looked from one side of the street to the other. We were already a block and a half away from the gas station.

"I was trying to listen but he kept chewin' the fat, throwing in all that stuff about his cousin Sophie married to some Maki. I've never heard of any Wilbur Maki in Iron River—"

"He said something about a big old black lamppost," John piped up from the back seat, trying to help.

"Lamppost, you say?" Dad asked, looking nervously up the street ahead which was lined with one big old black lamppost after another.

"Turn here," Mom said suddenly.

"Are you sure?" Dad gave the steering wheel a sharp twist and almost didn't see the on-coming old blue pick-up truck. At the last second, he slammed on the brakes, just barely missing the truck and avoiding a head-on collision. The three of us kids in the back seat came flying forward, squealing, into the back of the front seat.

"Watch out!" Mom shrieked, but we were already at a dead stop in the middle of the street. The smell of sizzling rubber seeped up from the tires.

"I can't turn on a dime you know," Dad yelled, trying to cover up his own fright at what he'd almost done, pinning the blame on Mom. "I gotta' have some warning. That's all we need is to pile up this old wreck of a car and end up stranded back at Wilbur Maki's cousin's place."

"Are you kids okay?" Mom's voice was rising frantically. She jumped up on her knees in the front seat and pulled little Connie up from the floor. John and I had already picked ourselves up, dusted ourselves off, and were excitedly looking out the rear window, watching the beat-up blue pick-up pull over to the side of the road and stop.

"We're okay," John and I said together, still watching the pick-up intently. A man with long straight black hair stepped out of the car. His high cheekbones, hawk-like nose and angular chin made it look like his face had been chiseled from stone. His expression was as sober as a cemetery as he walked slowly toward our car.

Dad turned the key in the ignition, put his foot on the gas pedal, and pumped but the old Chevy's motor wouldn't turn over. "Oh, for crying out loud," Dad groaned as he pumped more furiously.

"What's wrong?" Mom was getting more nervous by the second.

"It's flooded," Dad said with a snort.

"You mean we're stuck out here in the middle of the street?" Mom asked.

"Indian," John gasped.

"What's that you're saying?" Dad demanded.

"That guy in the pick-up—he's coming over to the car," John said, "and he looks mad."

We all turned to look at the stone-faced man approaching the car—all but Dad. Dad urgently turned the key in the old Chevy, pressed the accelerator to the floor, and held it there until the he heard the miraculous sound of the engine coming to life. Then he thrust the shift into first gear, carefully looked both ways, and cautiously completed the left turn he had attempted a few short anxious minutes earlier. When we were safely across the street, Dad rolled down his window and called, "Hey, we're just trying to get to church."

The stone-faced man stopped in his tracks, but didn't say a word. He just stared at Dad. Dad didn't know what else to say, so he just stared back—waiting and readying himself for whatever would happen next. Then the stone-faced man, putting an end to the stand-off, nodded solemnly, pointed in the direction we were headed, and turned, leaving us to continue our search.

Dad drove slowly away, still a little stunned by the encounter.

"Well, he certainly was nice," Mom said, recovering from the ordeal.

"Nice?" Dad said.

"Yes, he was showing us the way to the church, wasn't he?"

"I guess," Dad answered, trying to figure out where to turn next.

"Lucky he didn't come right over and scalp us," John giggled.

"Oh stop it," Mom said. "We don't need any of that kind of talk around here. He was a very nice man and he could have been really angry with us for almost wrecking his truck."

"Wrecking his truck? Did you see that thing? It was strung together with chicken wire," John laughed, ignoring Mom's scolding.

"He's probably from one of the reservations—probably very poor, which is nothing to laugh at," Mom pointed out.

"Am I supposed to turn right, or left, now?" Dad interrupted. "Does anyone know where we're going?"

"There's the water tower," I yelled from the back seat. "I think you're supposed to go left."

"You sure he didn't say right? I thought he said right." Dad stretched his neck out to the right and then to the left, craning to see which way looked the most promising.

"Left, then right." Mom set us all straight and as Dad followed these final instructions, the tall steepled white wood church came into view. We all gave a sigh of relief until we realized the street was lined with cars—all empty. Everyone was already in church. From Dad's rolled down window, we could hear the strains of *Ave Maria*, pouring from the organ and choir within.

"They're halfway through the service," Dad grumbled. "We can't go in there now." He pulled into an alley alongside the church, backed out, and stopped the car alongside the curb, trying to figure out what to do. Suddenly, his back went taut with tension.

"Oh no," Dad said, glancing nervously in his rear-view mirror, "I think we've got trouble." We all looked out the back window to see what he was talking about and nearly jumped out of out skins when we say the old beat-up blue pick-up lumbering slowly up from behind.

"It's that Indian again." John wasn't giggling this time.

"We'd better get out of here," Mom said, quickly forgetting about what a nice man she had previously thought he was.

Dad stalled for just a second. Then, he decided to take matters into his own hands. "I'd better find out what the heck he wants. Lock the car doors until I get back." Leaving the motor to idle, he opened his car door, stepped out, and waited for the pick-up to stop. We watched apprehensively from the safety of the car while Dad strode around to the driver's side of the pick-up.

Although we couldn't hear what was being said, we could see the stone-faced man was no longer silent and was apparently giving Dad a piece of his mind. His deep-set eyes were squarely on Dad's. Then we saw Dad nodding and talking back to the man. It seemed an eternity before Dad returned to the locked car. As Mom unlocked his door, the pick-up drove off.

"What did he say?" Mom asked. "Was he trying to make trouble? He's not going to bother us anymore, is he?" Her eyes, worried and fearful, became wide with astonishment as Dad began to grin.

"He says there's an eight o'clock Mass at the Bad River Indian Reservation in Odanah, Wisconsin," Dad said. "It's only about twenty-five minutes away from here. We can get there just in time."

"You mean he came all the way around here just to tell us that?" Mom asked.

"Yah," Dad answered, "that's exactly what he did."

"I told you he was a nice man," Mom said as Dad drove away from the Ironwood church. "He must be from the reservation."

"That's right," Dad answered. "That's where he's from. Well, looks like we're gonna' be able to get a few more miles under our belts before we have to stop again."

"A blessing in disguise," Mom sighed. "We'll be there in no time."

"I have to go to the bathroom," I announced.

"Why didn't you think of that before we left the gas station?" Dad snorted.

"I didn't have to go when we were at the gas station," I argued.

"Maybe we'd better go back there," Mom said quickly.

"We're not going back," Dad said adamantly. "I've heard all I ever want to about Sophie Maki and her pal Wilbur. You can hold off for another twenty minutes, can't you?"

"I guess" I grumbled. I wanted to be out of Ironwood as much as he did.

Dad drove around the block, got back on the main road, and followed it out of town. In less than a half hour, we started seeing signs of Odanah and the Bad River Indian reservation.

"Odanah," Dad announced. While the rest of us gawked at the run-down paint-peeling shacks, Dad checked his pocket watch. "And we should be right *on time* for Mass," he added happily.

"Look at the Indians," John said, nodding his head at the people sitting out on the front porches of their dilapidated homes. "And look at those shacks. Can you believe people really live like that?"

"I thought Indians lived in wigwams," I said.

"Not these Indians," John answered.

"Look Mom," I said pointing, "real Indians."

"Geez, don't point." John grabbed my hand and pulled it down from the window. "You want them to come after us with tomahawks." He gave a tug on my long curls, sending chills up my spine.

"You two, stop that this instant," Mom exclaimed. "Where's your sense of decency?" But she couldn't take her eyes off the people and their living conditions, either.

"I guess this is the main drag," Dad said, slowing the car and ignoring us kids. He was intent on getting to church. Nothing else mattered at the moment. "And there's the church." He parked the car right in front of the big red brick church, pulled out his pocket watch, and heaved a sigh of relief. We'd made it—and on time. "Let's go," he said, picking up Connie and rushing the rest of us out of the car and into the vestibule.

"We'll be right back," Mom said, taking me by the hand and hurrying me into the restroom near the entrance door. Dad stood guard outside the restroom, and as soon as we opened the door, ushered us into the last pew in the back of the church.

"They're *all* Indians," I whispered to my brother.

"Yah, all except us," he whispered back.

"Look, there's more of them coming in," I whispered, watching in wonder as more Indians arrived, filling the church except for the front two rows of pews. Finally a group of Indian children, led by a stone-faced nun in black robes, filed down the main aisle and into the empty pews. Both boys and girls were dressed in navy blue and white uniforms—the girls in skirts and the boys in dark dress pants. They knelt, prayed silently, and stood in unison as the resounding church bell began to peel and the priest and altar boys walked out onto the altar.

"The priest is an Indian, *too*," I whispered to John.

"Sh—" Mom gave us a warning look.

Church had never before been so interesting. I couldn't take my eyes off the congregation, the children and, most of all, the priest. I'd never seen anything like it. I couldn't wait to get back home and tell the kids at school I'd been to church with real Indians at a real reservation.

"Well, that was truly inspiring," Mom said as we drove away from the church. "I've always wondered what it would be like to go to a Mission Church."

"Well, now you know," Dad said pleasantly, "and we were only in there an hour. We should make good time now, getting to Superior, Wisconsin and over the bridge to Duluth, Minnesota. You kids are getting quite an education today. Do you realize you'll be traveling in three states in just a matter of a couple of hours?" He was a happy man. He'd been to church, actually gotten there on time, and now we were on the road again. Nothing could dampen his pleasant disposition, except maybe the weather.

"It looks like it's going to rain," Mom said, just as the drizzle on the windshield turned into a downpour.

"I can barely see in this stuff," Dad complained. Even with the wipers on full blast, it was clear we were going to have to slow down to a snail's pace.

"Well, maybe it'll wash away all the snow," Mom said cheerily.

"If it keeps up like this, we'll have a flood on our hands," Dad said, leaning his head toward the windshield to get a better view of the road.

"Well, there's nothing we can do but take our time," Mom said. "Why don't we have a bite to eat? Anybody hungry?"

"I'm starving," I said, suddenly realizing I'd worked up an awful appetite.

"Me, too," Dad agreed, "I'm hungry as a horse."

John opened one of the shoe boxes on the floor next to him, pulled out the waxed papered sandwiches, and handed them around—baloney for him and me, peanut butter and banana for Mom and Connie, and salami for Dad. We devoured our sandwiches, opened the shoe box filled with desserts, and polished off our lunches with fruit and cookies. I couldn't remember when I'd had anything that had tasted as good. I was stuffed and sleepy . . .

"Look at the size of that ore boat!" Dad exclaimed, startling me back to my senses after a long sleep. "Boy, oh boy, I just can't believe the size of those things. You kids better get a good look. Those freighters travel all around the Great Lakes, carrying iron ore."

"Where are we?" I asked sleepily.

"We're just outside of Superior, Wisconsin," Mom said, her excitement matching Dad's. I saw we were high on a bridge over the water and the rain had stopped. "We'll be in Duluth, Minnesota in minutes."

"Can we drive down to the docks and get a closer look?" John asked. "There's a boat right there in port."

"Maybe on the way home," Mom replied, sure Dad wouldn't want to make another stop.

"It might not be there when we go home," John pointed out.

"Well, I suppose it's not that far out of our way." Dad was as excited as a kid about the ore boats. Once over the bridge, we wound our way through a maze of small roads that led eventually to the ore docks. There sat a beauty of a boat, practically right alongside the road. We all got out of the car, walked over to the edge of the water, and stared silently at the gigantic ship covered in a rusty cloud of ore dust—awed by it size, its intricate machinery, and the massive expanse of its intriguing deck.

"Imagine what it must be like to live on a boat like this," Dad said with reverence. "You wouldn't see shore sometimes for days."

"But there would be plenty of sights to see along Lake Superior," John said. "Boy, I wonder what it's like when they get caught in a storm."

"It would take some mighty bad weather to sink a boat like this, but there have been some serious shipwrecks in these parts over the years. Still, I've always wanted to take a ride on one of those things." Dad, absorbed in his musings, stared in wonder at the great vessel, almost forgetting about his pocket watch. When he remembered, he looked like a kid who'd been caught playing hooky from school. He grabbed his watch, checked it sternly, and waved us all back into the car. "We'd better hit the trail right now, if we're gonna' make it to Keewatin today."

The old Chevy chugged up the steep hills of Duluth, purred along the skyline drive, then rattled along the highway toward Hibbing. Lost in thought, hardly anyone said a word. The time had come to face the inevitable, the real reason for our trip . . . Johnny's funeral.

The Saloon

Some of my friends' grandfathers were miners, some farmers, some teachers, but none of them owned and operated a saloon. As always, the sight of the Keewatin Saloon, the only tavern any of us kids had ever been inside, was foreign and deliciously exciting.

We saw him as soon as we walked in the door, standing behind the bar polishing his crystal clear beer mugs with a clean white cloth. His grey pin-striped shirt was tacked at the neck with a black bow tie, his sleeves caught up and held by black elastic bands. Handsome and debonair with flowing white hair and wire-rimmed spectacles, Grandpa Olli Wierimaa looked like he might have just stepped off a Hollywood movie set.

"Oh, Kaari." He set the mug and towel aside to give Mom a tender hug. "Kaari, it's good to see you. Come and sit down at the bar," he said to John and me. "Let's have a look at that baby girl. Oh my, not even a baby anymore. Walking? Oh Kaari, the time goes by too fast. How long has it been? Johnny, you're looking good." Grandpa pumped Dad's hand happily. He was overwhelmed with our entrance. Living here in Minnesota, so far from Stambaugh, we didn't get to see each other nearly often enough. "Sanna's upstairs waiting for you, Kaari. Let John and Coralie stay here and visit with me, while you go up. Johnny, you want something to drink?"

There was no one else in the saloon. Dad pulled a stool up to the bar and indicated that John and I should do the same. "Nothing for me, Olli, maybe the kids would like a pop."

"John, you're getting so grown up, pretty soon, we're not going to know you anymore. How's the football team?" Grandpa pulled up the top of a big red cooler behind the bar. "What flavor pop would you like? Orange, cherry, strawberry? Grape? I've got a new grape flavor here in the cooler."

"I'll have an orange," I butted in, my eyes darting from the colorful beer advertisements, serving trays, and signs decorating the walls to my own reflection in the mirrored wall above the bar, just behind the rows of glistening beer mugs.

"I'll take the grape," John said. "I'm on the second string this year."

"Well, sure, but you'll make first string as soon as you're old enough," Grandpa said reassuringly. "And what have you been up to?" he asked, pouring my orange pop into a glass and setting it on the bar in front of me.

"Just school," I answered, trying to think of something I'd done lately that he'd find interesting. "Oh, and I'm taking piano lessons."

"Piano lessons. I'll bet you're good at it, too." Grandpa beamed. "Your uncles play the piano, you know. Had orchestras of their own during the war."

"I played in a program last month," I offered, sipping the sweet soda pop slowly to make it last.

"How about a stick of gum?" Grandpa opened a brand new pack of Juicy Fruit gum and handed John and me each a piece. I unwrapped mine, popped the gum into my mouth, and was about to crumple up the paper when Grandpa stopped me. "See this here?" he asked, handing me a lightweight silver ball about the size of a softball. "You know what that is?" I shook my head. "Here, I'll show you." He took my gum wrapper, carefully removed the silver layer from the white paper, and pressed the silver onto the metallic ball, adding yet another layer. "I've been saving these ever since the war started. Isn't this *something*?"

"It's swell," I exclaimed. It *was* swell. I didn't know what he'd ever do with it, but it was swell and he obviously was thrilled with it. "Really *swell!*" I tossed it back and forth from one hand to another and then gave it to my brother to examine.

"It's really dandy. It must have taken a lot of patience to save up all this silver," John said. He gave the ball back to Grandpa, who held it briefly in his hands as if it were a precious jewel, then placed it once again in its special spot, against the mirror behind the bar, amidst glasses of red swizzle sticks, bottles of maraschino cherries, and stacks of small white napkins.

"Well, Johnny." Grandpa turned his attention to Dad. "How are things with the M.A. Hanna Mining Company?"

The two men talked about mining, the economy, and the war. They talked about the inevitable strikes soon to come both in Stambaugh and in nearby Hibbing. Many families would have to tighten their belts, but the miners felt it was the only way they could bargain for more money. Dad, being a company man, believed the strikes did more harm than good, but had to admit he was glad he'd never been out of work. Once they got to the topic of war, Grandpa lowered his voice so my brother and I couldn't hear what he was saying. But we knew he was talking about Johnny.

I slipped off my bar stool, unnoticed, and slowly walked the length of the long rectangular room, investigating. High-backed dark wood booths lined one length of the room. Each was decorated with an amber glass shaded lamp which, affixed to the red and gold striped wallpapered wall just beneath a fancy curlicue gold framed mirror, shed streams of red-gold light. The glow looked like shimmering twilight on a misty rose-hued evening as it fell softly over black marble tabletops and flickered through pairs of tapered glass salt and pepper shakers, silver topped glass sugar shakers, and round red ashtrays.

Sets of Bentwood chairs and round oak ice cream tables, all intricately supported by vine-like black wrought iron bases, were sprinkled here and there throughout the rest of the room. I guessed it was a busy bustling place when the booths and tables were filled with customers.

I ambled back to where Dad and Grandpa were talking, picked up my orange pop, and slipped into an ice cream chair at a table just behind Dad so I could listen in on their conversation.

"Too cold to bury him in the ground," Grandpa was saying. "They'll have to keep him in the Mausoleum until they can break ground. By the looks of the cold weather that may not be until June."

"Well at least he'll be back home," Dad said.

"Miracle they ever found him," Grandpa went on. "There were many lost at sea that day."

"That's what Carrie said." Dad shifted uncomfortably on his stool. He stood up suddenly. "I think I'll take a walk down the main drag—get some fresh air." He'd had enough of riding in the car, sitting around the saloon, and talking about the funeral.

"I'll go with you." Leaving my brother to keep Grandpa company, I downed the rest of my orange pop, and slipped out the door with Dad. In the cold damp air of winter's end, we silently strolled down the wet snowy sidewalk that passed in front of a five and dime store, a hardware store, a bank, a drug store, a gas station, and two small cash and carry grocery stores. It took us less than five minutes to cover the entire main street of Keewatin and return to the saloon door.

"You'd better let Mom know where you are," Dad said, without even giving me a glance. "I'm gonna' walk a little further." I knew he wanted to be alone for a while, so I walked around to the back of the saloon, found the door to the upstairs apartment, and climbed the wavy wooden steps. I stopped in front of the closed door at the top of the stairway, wondering if I should knock, or just walk in. I could hear voices inside. I decided I'd better let them know I was coming. I made a fist and rapped on the heavy oak door.

"Come on in," Sanna called from the kitchen. She, her daughter Mary from Spokane, Washington, and Mom were gathered in the steamy kitchen, visiting and cooking dinner.

Since there was no high chair for little Connie, she had been set on a high backed carved oak kitchen chair—a dishtowel tied around her waist to keep her from falling. Content, she patted the table with one fist, thrust a piece of buttered toast into her mouth with the other, and gave me a big smile.

I hadn't realized how hungry I was until I smelled the juicy meatloaf hamburgers simmering in onion gravy, fresh whole kernel corn, and large new potatoes waiting in water to be mashed. Sanna carefully tended the bubbling pans filled with dinner, stirring, spearing, and turning as she expertly lifted and replaced boiling hot lids. While Mary washed and carved red radishes, carrot sticks, and celery stalks for a relish tray, Mom frosted a spongy yellow cake with creamy brown sugar butter frosting.

My stomach growled as I took sat down next to Connie on one of the ornate chairs arranged around the oval oak claw-footed dining table. Plain white dishes, ancient silverware, and sea green cloth napkins folded in fourths, sat in waiting on a white tablecloth printed with splashes of lavender lilacs, blue roses, and trailing pink ribbons.

"Are you hungry?" asked Sanna, wiping her hands on her long white cobbler apron. "It won't be long before we eat." Her eyes were red from crying.

It seemed to take forever for the women to finally finish cooking dinner, put the food in serving dishes, and call down for the men to come up and eat. But once we all gathered around the table, dinner took no time at all. Grandpa, who had locked the saloon doors in order to join us for dinner, crammed his food down at top speed, said he'd be back to visit later, and rushed back downstairs to work until closing time.

Mom, Mary, and Saana talked the entire time we sat at the table, but the rest of us just packed away the food like it was going out of style. When we were through, Dad and John went back down to the saloon to keep Grandpa company and, while the women cleaned up the dishes and prepared more food for the following day, Connie and I were sent into the living room to entertain ourselves with toys and books brought from home.

I took out my Richmond Educational Spelling Board, an oval board with moveable wooden letters that could be pushed into slots to form words. F-U-N-E-R-A-L, I spelled. It was a disturbing thought. I laid the game aside, wondering what I could do instead.

There didn't seem to be anything for a kid to do in this place. It was a home for grown-ups, not kids. Sanna's spotlessly polished red-brown mahogany tables, topped with filmy lace crocheted cloths upon which sat her assorted collections of pink crystal glass slippers, fluted edged vases, and cut glass candy dishes—all empty—were untouchable. And Grandpa's Black Forest coo-coo clocks hanging on two walls, the pendulums precisely set to match those of his three tall grandfather clocks which commanded attention from the corners of the room set the perfect picture of paradise for grown-ups. But for a kid in need of something to do, it took every stretch of the imagination to come up with something interesting.

Amber light, flowing from frosted glass chandeliers, traveled down the leaf green painted walls, through the glass slippers, and inside the vases and empty candy dishes, creating pastel rainbows on the rose patterned wool rug. Dancing on the rug, the walls, and on my fingertips if I held my hands just under the light, the flickering rainbow rays—along with the constant movement of the gold pendulums, the chirping of the coo-coos, and the low mellow chimes of Grandpa's clocks—gave the room a life of its own. I leaned my head back on the sofa, watched the ever changing light, and listened to the room.

"I think everything's ready for tomorrow," I heard Sanna tell Mary and Mom in the kitchen. "The military guard will arrive just before the funeral, along with the minister from the Lutheran Church."

"What about an organist? And flowers?" Mom asked.

"No music," Sanna answered, "and no flowers. It somehow just didn't seem fitting. The casket will be draped and there'll be taps. It seems anything else would be, well, too much."

"Yes, you're right," Mom said thoughtfully. "What time should we get to the chapel?"

"The funeral will be at eleven," Mary answered, "so we should get there at least an hour before."

"I'd better get the girls to bed then," Mom said, coming into the living room. "It's been a long day for you two. Let's get your pajamas on and get you to bed." She led us to a room that looked more like a living room than a bedroom. "You two will sleep in Sanna's sitting room." There were two small rollaway beds turned out in fresh white bedding in the middle of the floor. Mom sat on the edge of Connie's bed and sang a gentle lullaby and by the time she reached the last line, Connie was fast asleep. Mom tucked the blankets under her chin, gave us each a peck on the cheek, and hurried back to the living room, leaving the door cracked open only wide enough for a single stingy slice of light to sneak inside.

It may have been a long day, but I was far from ready for sleep. Unaccustomed to the strange bed and bedroom so far from home, I felt at odds with the world. I tried closing my eyes, counting sheep, and daydreaming myself into sleep, but nothing worked. While Connie lay peacefully wrapped in slumber, I lay wriggling in wakefulness.

Though I could hear the grown-ups talking in the living room, I couldn't hear what they were saying, but I knew what they were talking about—the war, the funeral, and Johnny lying in the cold mausoleum. Their voices went on late into the night, but I was still awake when they finally quit talking, turned off the lights in the living room, and made their way to their beds. The only sounds left in the night were the clocks, tick-ticking the time slowly away, the silly coo-coo's bursting out of their little locked doorways, plunging noisily into the darkness, and the low bonging of the grandfather clocks. The living room never slept. I was certain I'd never fall asleep either.

"Breakfast is ready." Mom walked into the little sitting room, briskly pulled the sheets and coverlets into place over the bed on which my little sister had slept, and began folding her nightclothes into a suitcase. Connie was nowhere in sight. "Everyone is already up and at the breakfast table. You must have had a good rest."

If only she knew. I'd probably slept less than three hours all night and even then I could still hear the sassy coo-coo's calling out in my dreams. Yet, I was hungry and anxious for the day to begin. I was going to my first funeral—a military funeral, at that—and even though it was a tragic affair, I couldn't help feeling a strangely exciting sort of anticipation.

The kitchen, heavy with the smell of bacon, eggs, and toast, was also weighted down with an air of solemn sadness.

The family was now faced with the awful reality of Johnny's body lying in the lonely mausoleum chapel.

"I'm going outside to get some fresh air." Dad, all spruced up in his brown three-piece Sunday suit, got up from the table, lit a cigarette, and started toward the door. His face was drawn and tense, his voice strained and taut.

"We've got to leave soon." Mom was cleaning up the crumbs and crusts from Connie's toast. Though I could only see her back, I could feel her tension—a mirror image of Dad's.

"Hold on. I'll go down with you." My brother's cheeks were pale as he shot out the door, following Dad.

I sat down at the table and attacked the plate of steaming fried eggs, bacon, and toast. Nervous, or not, I was famished, but as soon as I began to eat, I found the inside of my mouth tasted like cardboard. Sanna and Mary, their faces white and drawn, cleaned the kitchen in silence. The family's bleak mood was contagious. My breakfast only half eaten, I pushed away from the table, got up, and went into the living room to wait until it was time to leave for the chapel.

Strands of light crept in through the lace curtained windows, shot through the glass slippers, and projected prisms of moving light on the green walls. The clocks, relentless, tick-tocked their dreary tune, which today sounded not only monotonous, but mournful as well. I thought of Dorothy stuck in the Emerald City of Oz, far from Kansas, wishing to be back in her happy home. I knew just how she felt.

The Funeral

In a lonely two-car procession, we slowly wound our way on the gravel roadway through the cemetery to the chapel.

The faceless names, etched in stone, loomed from the flat fronts of old round topped tombstones. An imposing cement cherub peered eerily down into the window of our car from its perch amidst several smaller stones, announcing the plot of a long gone area family. A tiny stone, off by itself, carved with the words, "Beloved Baby," spoke of anguish and loss. Another larger, rectangular stone was embellished with crusty chipped roses, and read, "At Peace, In the House of the Lord."

I felt my skin sort of prickling as I read one epitaph after another and wondered who all those people were, what their lives had been like, and how they had died. The wind blowing through the waving pines overhead seemed to whisper, "Remember me . . . remember me . . ." I shivered, but not from the chilling cold forcing its way into the heated car.

"There's the chapel," Mom whispered to Dad.

"Yah, I see it. Not many cars."

"We didn't expect there would be many people—just a few of Dad's and Sanna's close friends."

"What about Johnny's friends?" I asked. "Won't they be here?"

"Grandpa and Sanna didn't move here until after Johnny was grown up, so this isn't really his hometown. I doubt if there'll be any young people. No one who lives here really knew him." Mom sat upright in her seat, closer to the dashboard, and anxiously peered out at the small assemblage of cars.

The chapel's heavy arched wooden doors, like two massive angel wings, stood open to the damp dismal air, beckoning us inside. Grandpa parked his car close to the doors, Dad pulled in behind, and we all got out and started toward the doors. We were met at the archway by three young uniformed men in full Navy dress. Two of them led Grandpa and Sanna, Mary, and Mom to their places in the front row of the small dimly lit chapel. The third man stayed posted at the outer doors of the chapel.

Once inside, I had hoped we'd find refuge from the cold clammy air, but it was just as chilling indoors as out. Dad and the three of us kids hurried behind the procession led by the uniformed men and silently slipped into the second row of pews. When the young men had delivered their charges, they marched side by side to the middle of the chapel, separated, and turned, each taking a position at either end of the long flag covered casket. Staring at some unknown objects in space, they looked like pictures I'd seen of the guards at Buckingham Palace. Fascinated, I watched their eyes, waiting for them for blink, but they didn't. They made not the slightest movement, nor sound.

A handful of people took up the pews behind us—mostly people Grandpa's age who frequently blew their noses, wiped their eyes, and coughed. Grandpa and Sanna stared straight ahead, almost like the Navy men, but Mary wept openly while Mom dabbed at her eyes with her handkerchief. Dad sat with his arms tightly folded across his chest as if to keep inside any hint of sadness he may have been feeling. My brother's eyes, especially solemn, were fastened to the brilliant red, white, and blue of the stars and stripes covering the casket. I wondered what he was thinking.

My little sister stood next to Dad, clung to the back of the pew, and looked out over the sparse congregation. I contained my desire to turn around and look, too, entertaining myself instead with thoughts of death. I wondered about Johnny's last hours at sea, imagining angels descending from the blue skies above, attempting to gather him up and take him with them to heaven. But, as usual, my daydreams got out of hand when the angels started getting wildly splashed by towering ocean waves. I abandoned the vision and forced my attention back to the stars and stripes.

Finally, the preacher stepped out from a side door in the front of the chapel, walked over to a quaintly carved wooden lectern to the left of the casket, laid his black bible down, and looked sadly over the congregated group. "We are gathered together today to pay our last respects to one of our country's finest young men, John Sippola. John, who in the course of duty was bringing others to freedom, was called away in the youth of his years. He served our country with honor, giving his life so that we might all have a better future . . . We may not ever know why our Lord chose to call Johnny home on that dark day at sea, but we should rest easier knowing he is in the House of the Lord." The preacher closed his bible, bowed his head, and asked us all to do the same.

After a moment of silent prayer, he raised his head, nodded at the uniformed young men, and stood back as they took up the corners of the flag, folded it end over end until it became a small triangular shape, and placed it into Sanna's trembling hands.

Just outside the arched doors, in the cold April air, the third naval guard who'd been stationed at the back of the chapel, stepped out, lifted his trumpet to his lips, and played the simple soldiers' tune. Taps. The music, mournful and mellow, brought back memories of the joyful afternoons, not so very long ago, when we had all been together, laughing, teasing, gliding over the peaceful waters of Swan Lake. I felt tears well up and spill.

The Final Piece of the Puzzle

I felt like a blubbering idiot when Dad handed me the big white freshly ironed handkerchief Mom had tucked into his pocket just before we'd left for the funeral. I'd tried hard to act grown up and not cry, but I just couldn't seem to stop myself. I'd have been all right, too, if that Navy guy hadn't started playing his trumpet. Taps. I thought it must be the most lonesome song in the world. I dried my eyes and nose with quick furtive dabs, folded the damp hanky end over end until it was a tiny triangle, and stuck it away in my coat pocket.

The grey smooth casket, now cold and dull without its patriotic drape, sat forlornly on the silver castered dolly in the front of the church as we quietly filed out of our pews and down the aisle toward the open doors. I couldn't resist the urge to turn back and take one last look, but then I only felt worse. Why had this awful thing happened to Johnny? Why didn't he swim away and save himself? What had happened? I knew the rest of the family was thinking the same thing, but there was nothing any of us could do to find the answers.

We got back into our cars, drove in silence past the chipped rose encrusted monuments, the peering cement cherubs, and the rows of gravestones until, with relief, we passed out of the cemetery and onto the road back to Grandpa's place.

We had barely climbed the steps to the apartment, when Sanna set the flag she'd been cradling in her arms down on the hall table, untied the eye-covering navy netting of her hat, and removed her coat and wide-brimmed hat, exchanging them for a long light blue bib apron. She immediately began making coffee, preparing food platters, and laying out dishes and silverware on the dining room table. Her eyes were a tell-tale pink, but she resolutely went about her business. It seemed she was determined to put the funeral behind her. Being together with the family now was the best medicine. That and food.

Mary and Mom stashed their coats and hats in the hall closet, dashed into the kitchen to help Sanna, and eagerly loaded bowls, plates, and platters with food. I'd never seen so much food for one meal. I figured the women must have been cooking while I was "sleeping in." There was fresh home baked bread, mounds of hot and cold sliced ham, relishes, and home canned stewed tomatoes, pickles, and bright red beets. There were platters of cheese, fresh fruit, and buttermilk biscuits along with immense bowls of potato and macaroni salads, a gigantic roaster of baked beans, and baked sweet potatoes topped with marshmallows. I wondered if we'd find room to sit at the table, but we managed. It seemed everyone had worked up an appetite. I piled my plate high with a helping of everything that passed my way, careful to leave room for dessert—scrumptious frosted coffee cakes, apple cinnamon and lemon meringue pies, and banana, raspberry, and orange nut breads.

"It was a beautiful ceremony," Mom finally remarked. "Johnny would have liked it."

"Yes, I believe he would have. It was a hero's send-off and Johnny deserved that." Mary's eyes misted over and I thought she was going to start crying all over again, but she cleared her throat, pushed her shoulders back, and changed the subject. "This ham is just delicious. Can I pass anyone, anything?" The topic of food, its sweet, tart, and salty scents filling the apartment, put everyone at ease. It was time to break away from the dreariness of the weather and the funeral and find satisfaction in the simple pleasures of sharing good food, talk, and family history.

Grandpa started reminiscing about the good old days, telling his favorite story about coming to America from Finland, seeing the country for the first time from the ship, and then making his way to the Upper Peninsula of Michigan to seek his fortune by working in the iron mines in Victoria until he had saved enough money to open his own business. The talk quickly traveled to iron mining and both Grandpa and Dad entertained us, exchanging tales of underground conditions and disasters.

Dad told about the daring rescue mission his father, Grandpa Cederna, had taken on with his partner Tony Shubat. When a pipe broke, poisonous fumes had overcome the miners on the sixth level of the mine. Those who had made it up to the surface looked back, shook their heads, and told the others there was no chance of anyone else making it up and out. But that didn't stop Grandpa and Tony from going back down into the mine to try to save the men, facing possible death themselves. Two of the remaining men were found alive by Grandpa and Tony, carried up to the surface, and lived to tell their daring tale.

We lingered long at the dining table, following the big feed. The conversation was lively, the tales exciting, and it was fun listening to the men talk about old times, but my thoughts kept creeping back to Johnny. I guessed maybe everyone was going through the same thing, but it was easier just to talk about other things.

Eventually, the men moved into the living room to continue their talk while the women cleared the table of dishes, silverware, and what was left of the food. Everything back in order, the long evening stretched out before us. We'd all be leaving for home in the morning and I knew Dad, who was looking at his pocket watch every five minutes, was getting itchy to go. We'd been away from home too long already. Mom, picking up on Dad's tension, kept looking at the hands on the big Grandfather clocks as if this would help move them along a little faster. I was ready to leave, too. It was time to go home.

One of the crazy coo-coo birds jumped out of its clock cage and cackled just as the slender-necked black telephone on the hallway table rang out. Puzzled, everyone looked first at the clock and then toward the telephone, wondering if they had really heard a phone ring, or not. But when it rang out again, Grandpa rushed to answer it.

"Yah," he murmured into the receiver, "that's me. You got the right number." There was a long pause and Grandpa's eyes got big as saucers. "You did? You are? Oh, sure, sure, come right over. Please! Do you know how to get here? It's the only saloon in town. Around the back and upstairs. Okay, we'll be waiting for you."

When Grandpa placed the receiver back in its cradle, he could barely speak, he was in such a state of disbelief. Then, he got hold of himself and called out to Sanna in the kitchen, "Sanna, we've got company coming right over. Oh my Lord, I can't believe it. Two young guys traveled all the way over here from Minneapolis for the funeral, but they had some car trouble and got held up."

"Two young guys?" Sanna looked at Grandpa with bewilderment.

"Yah, two young guys who were on the same ship as Johnny!" Grandpa shook his head as if to clear his mind.

"The same ship—?" Sanna's face was pale, but her eyes were bright, fresh with new hope.

"The same. They're right around the corner from us and will be here any minute." Grandpa went over to the sheer ivory lace panels covering the set of double windows and looked through them down to the side street.

Within minutes, there was a quick rap at the door, and even though we knew the men were coming, we all jerked to attention. As if in shock, no one moved. Then, everybody moved at once, getting up, going in a little group toward the door to welcome the travelers from Minneapolis.

"Come on in. Sit right in here." Grandpa and Sanna ushered them into the living room, gave up their own over-stuffed chairs, and pulled in two extra chairs from the dining room for themselves, creating a circle of seating around the room. Everyone looked to the young men, anxious to hear what they had to say.

"I'm Andy Voitanen and this here's Rusty, uh Ray, Torvensen. We're—uh, that is—we were, shipmates of Johnny's." Andy, a big blond guy with ham-like hands held his hat politely on his lap. The quieter man, Rusty, didn't say a word, but nodded at Sanna and Grandpa. "Sorry to barge in on you like this, but we had a flat on the way over here and had to hitchhike thirty miles to a station to get it fixed. That's why we missed the funeral."

"Well, you couldn't help that," Grandpa said.

"We were just gonna' turn around and head back home, but Rusty and me, well, we talked it over and we just had to see if we could track you down—tell you what a great guy Johnny was."

"You knew him well?" Sanna's anxious eyes were fixed on Andy's.

"He was a buddy," Andy continued. "Wasn't nothing he wouldn't have done for us. That's just the way he was, always watching out for everybody."

"How about you two have some coffee and a bite to eat?" Grandpa asked.

"No thanks. We already ate. It does smell good though," Andy replied. "Maybe just coffee." Rusty nodded in agreement.

Sanna started toward the kitchen, but Mom motioned her to sit down. "I'll get it. You stay and visit." She was off like a flash, rattled a few dishes around in the kitchen, and back in seconds with two brimming cups of coffee and a plate of coffee cake wedges fanned out in a fancy circle.

"Yah, we sure had some good times," Andy said, gratefully accepting the coffee and sipping thoughtfully as he reminisced.

"And would still be, if it hadn't been for that damn torpedo." Andy looked at his partner, surprised to hear him speak up.

"He's right. Rammed us right in the side—and us a protected ship. Oh, the war department claimed they made a big mistake, but I got my doubts about that, too. Here we were, not far off the coast of Norway, in neutral waters, when we got hit. It was awful. All those kids and their mothers . . ." Andy looked at Sanna, hung his head, then finally looked back at her. "You don't need to hear all this. Geez, I'm sorry."

"No, no. Go on." Sanna couldn't help reaching out and touching the young man's sleeve. "We want to know everything. No matter how bad it is."

"Your son was a hero, Ma'am," Andy went on. "While the rest of us were saving our skins, he was helping the women and kids into lifeboats. While everyone was running around half crazy, he was issuing orders. Me and Rusty, here, we jumped ship and swam, then hung onto some floating planks until a hospital ship came and picked us all up. It's not that we were "chicken," or anything like that, we just knew that ship was doomed to sink and if we wanted to make it, we'd have to leave."

"What about Johnny? What happened to my brother?" Mary asked.

"Why didn't he get off the ship and swim, too?" Grandpa asked.

"You'd have to have seen Johnny on duty to understand, I guess. For him, it was the most natural thing in the world—what he did, when the rest of us were swimming away."

"What?" Sanna asked.

"He went down with the ship." Rusty spoke up a second time.

"Last I saw of him, he was standing on the bow of the ship, along with our Captain. They were sinking fast," Andy said.

"But why?" Mary had new tears in her eyes.

"Why?" Andy's voice was gentle and kind. "Because Johnny would never let a man go to his death alone. No, not Johnny."

Sanna reached over and patted Andy's hand. "Thank you for coming to us today. Thank you. Johnny would be so pleased and proud." Her eyes were moist, but in them shone the pride, acceptance, and relief she felt in learning of her son's final decision. The final piece of the puzzle was now in place. The war, for Johnny, had ended in glory—the glory of giving the most precious gift of all.

John Sippola leaving for overseas duty.

There's No Place Like Home

"Everything's packed and in the car." Dad was standing in the doorway at the top of the stairs, checking his watch as usual, shifting from one foot to another, and impatiently waiting for Mom to finish her farewells. "I'll be out in the car waiting for you." He couldn't stand it any longer. He just had to get on the road and get home.

While Mom, Mary, and Sanna hugged, making promises to write soon, I was caught trying to make my getaway by Grandpa who gave me his famous good-by handshake, palming a silver dollar from his hand into mine, telling me to be a good girl. With a quick thank you and the shiny silver piece clutched tightly, I was off down the stairway from the apartment to the car with visions of how I'd spend my newfound fortune. Like Dad, I couldn't wait to get on the road, even if it was still raining.

Out the back window of the old green Chevy, I watched Grandpa's saloon get smaller and smaller and finally disappear as we pulled off the main street of Keewatin and out onto the highway. It had been a memorable visit. I mulled it all over as we sped silently along toward home—my first funeral, Taps, and the surprising visit and explanation of Johnny's death by his pals, Andy and Rusty.

I watched the windshield wipers sweep back and forth against the rain. The whoosh-whoosh sound was hypnotizing. "There's no place like home . . . no place like home . . ." I thought again of Dorothy trying to get out of Oz and get back home . . . if only I had a pair of red glittery shoes.

"We're never gonna' make it home by suppertime with all this rain." For several hours, Dad had been grasping the steering wheel tightly with both hands, leaning intently forward, and struggling to see the road.

"Maybe we should pull off the road for a while and let it pass," Mom suggested.

"No, we're not gonna' pull over," Dad snapped. Nothing was going to stop him from getting home.

"It was just a suggestion." Our nerves had been rubbed raw from lack of sleep, the tension of the funeral, and the long trip to Minnesota and now home. "I thought it might be good for you to take a break from driving."

"I don't need a break from driving. What I need is a break in the weather." Dad glared at the wipers slapping rain around on the windshield.

"Well, the earth certainly is getting a spring cleansing," Mom said. "All the snow will be gone and forgotten before we know it."

"And they talk about Michigan weather being unpredictable," Dad grumbled. "I've had enough of Minnesota to last me a while."

"Maybe, Wisconsin will be better," Mom offered, back to her old cheerful self. "We'll be in Ashland soon. Why don't we stop and get lunch. I think we could all use a break."

"Well, I guess the kids could use a breather." Dad obviously was the one who needed a breather, but he'd be the last to admit it.

Lunch in a restaurant—now there was a treat to look forward to. For once, the shoe boxes were empty of sandwiches. Now we could have a real adventure, ordering off a menu. It was so exciting, I just knew I wouldn't have time to even think about getting carsick .

"Restaurant food, I suppose there's no choice." Eating anywhere but home was something Dad did only in an emergency. And, thankfully, we were in an emergency. I couldn't wait.

"There's the ore boats," Dad announced as we drove over the bridge from Duluth to Superior. "Better get a good look at them. It'll be a *long* time before we get back up this way again."

"It won't be *that* long," Mom said.

"Oh, yes it *will*." Dad's jaw set itself in a deliberately stubborn clench.

"How far to Ashland?" John decided to break up the argument before it started. "How long 'til we eat?"

"Yah, I'm starved," I chimed in.

"I think it's just another hour, or so," Mom answered.

"I'll never make it another hour," I insisted, "I'm already starving."

"Maybe we'd better start looking for a place to stop now. We're all getting pretty hungry." Mom couldn't stand the thought of her kids going hungry.

"Oh, they can make it a few more miles." Dad wasn't ready to stop. In fact, if he had his way, we'd probably just keep going until we had to stop for gas and then get right back on the road again until we arrived back home.

"No, we can't," I complained.

"I'm going to have a malted milk," my brother announced, "a nice big fat juicy hamburger and a malted milk."

"What's a malted milk?" I asked.

"It's ice cream, milk, and malt all mushed up in a special machine and you drink it through a straw. I think I'll have one, too." Dad licked his lips. Things were looking up.

"Well, I'm going to try one, too." If it had ice cream in it, it had to be good. I could almost taste it already.

"There's a truck stop." Mom pointed to a large blue and white sign that read simply, "TRUCK STOP - FOOD," and sat on a cedar pole outside a log cabin which looked like it had

been around since the seventeenth century. But who cared—
they had food. "Those truck stops always have the best food,"
Mom continued, "and this one's got a gas pump, too."

"Gas?" Dad did a double take. Mom had hit on the key
word. GAS. Now we'd only have to make one stop for food
and gas. Dad yanked the steering wheel right, pulled off the
road, and coasted in alongside the pump. "Fill 'er up," he said
to the teen-age boy who had hustled over to the car.

Dad paid for the gas, pulled away from the pump, and
parked the car near the entrance to the log cabin next to a
huge logging truck. The truck, piled high with a load of pine,
was covered with mud from the chains on its gigantic tires to
the chains on top of the logs securing the load.

"Geez, I wonder where that truck's been," Dad said as we
got out of the car and side-stepped the puddles to get to the
door of the restaurant.

It was easy to spot the driver when we walked into the
restaurant, as he was the only customer in the place. He was
hunched over his meal, shoveling food into his mouth as fast
as he could. I caught a whiff of a woodsy smell as we passed
his table and couldn't help staring at him. His grubby long
johns crept out from under his rolled up red flannel shirt
cuffs, the ear flaps of his black wool cap flopped over his
ears, and his old high-top leather boots were completely
crusted over with thick drying mud. He glanced up and nodded at Dad when we walked by, as if the rest of us were invisible. Dad gave him a quick nod and followed Mom and us kids
to a handmade log table across the room.

A hefty woman, slightly bulging out of her white uniform,
bounced out of the kitchen, grabbed a handful of menus from
the counter, and bustled over to our table. "How you doin'
there? My name's Beatrice, but you can call me Bea.
Everybody calls me Bea. That there's my boy Hank out there
pumping your gas. So what can I do you for today? We've got

homemade roast pork on special today. Comes with mashed potatoes, fresh green beans, and rice pudding." Bea, who looked like she'd been doing more than sampling the roast pork specials for years, handed each of us a menu and gave us a brilliant smile, happily unaware that the gaps left by missing front teeth were real eye-catchers.

"I don't suppose you have a high-chair, do you?" Mom asked hopefully.

"Well no, but I got a nice big cardboard box we can put right on that chair next to you for the little one." Bea flashed her spaces at little Connie. "Aren't you the little darling? We'll get you set in just a second." She bustled off to the kitchen and was back in seconds with a brown box. "Here, you go!"

"Oh, thank you." Mom, doing her best to be a good sport, tried to set Connie on the box, but my little sister didn't have any intention of sitting anywhere but on Mom's lap. "I'm sure she'll use it, later," Mom explained to Bea.

"Why sure she will." Bea, satisfied she'd done her level best to make us all happy, pulled out her pad and pencil and stood at attention, smiling patiently.

"I'll have a hot beef sandwich." Mom matched her smile. "And could you bring a small dish along with that."

"A small dish for the little one? Sure can do. But we ain't got any beef today. How about the pork?"

"That'll be fine." Mom didn't even skip a beat. Bea marked it down carefully on her pad.

"And you, sir?" Bea looked at Dad.

"No roast beef, hmm . . . well, I guess I'll just have the roast pork, then." Dad obviously had his taste buds geared up for a load of mashed potatoes smothered with beef and beef gravy.

"Two roast porks." Bea scribbled a number next to the first order. "And you, sir?" John jerked his head up when he heard himself called, "sir."

"A nice big juicy hamburger," he said with newfound authority.

"Grill's on the fritz, sir. Care for the roast pork?" Bea held her pencil poised and ready to hit the pad again.

"I guess," John said lamely. There went his heavenly hamburger. But he quickly recovered. "Have you got a malted milk machine here?" he asked, looking anxiously across the room toward the back of the rounded counter.

"We sure do!" Bea gave him a huge smile. "But it's broke."

"Broke? It's broken?" John couldn't hide his disappointment and Dad's face kind of fell, too. Since I didn't know yet what I was missing, I wasn't too upset, but I had been looking forward to both the malt and the hamburger.

"How about you, young lady?" It was my turn to get the big toothless flash.

"Oh, I don't know . . ." I'd had my order all ready, now I didn't know what to choose. I looked the menu over again, finally making a decision. "I'll have the spaghetti."

"Does it say spaghetti there?" Bea grabbed the side of my menu and peered at the place marked by my forefinger. "It sure does, doesn't it? Well, we ain't got any today. The roast pork's real good though."

"I'll have the roast pork." Who cared. We were all starving by now.

"I'll be right out with your orders." Bea threw the words over her shoulder as she hustled across the room, behind the counter, and back into the kitchen.

As soon as she was out of the room, my brother poked me under the table, trying to make me giggle. Dad lit up a cigarette and shook his head, while Mom, trying not to laugh, made herself busy getting Connie's coat and hat off.

In the meantime, the logger had finished his roast pork, walked up to the counter, and was waiting for Bea to come take his money. He rubbed his stomach, belched, and looked out the small window near the cash register. When Bea didn't return immediately, he walked over to the window, looked out and turned back, frowning, toward our table.

"You folks headed to Duluth or Ashland?" he asked, directing his question to the back of Dad's head, causing him to swerve in his seat.

"Just came from Duluth way," Dad answered tersely, immediately suspicious of the other man's motives. What business was it of his where we were going? Or where we'd been?

"Heading on down to Ashland?" the logger asked.

"Yah," Dad said with finality. The message was loud and clear, "Don't ask any more questions." But the logger either didn't catch on, or decided to ignore it.

"There's trouble on down the line," he said.

"Trouble, you say?" Now Dad was really getting suspicious. What was this guy up to anyway?

"You better get off US 2 when you get to the other side of Ashland and swing out of there on Highway 13." Just then, Bea came out to take the logger's money, interrupting the conversation.

Dad tried to conceal his worry at the logger's comments. It seemed to take Bea forever to get done with her business, but she finally handed the logger his change and as he pocketed his money, he took a step toward our table.

"I just come up through the Bad River Indian Reservation in Odanah and barely made it through with the truck. Whole place is flooded. You'll never make it through in that car of yours."

"Flooded, you say?" Dad was really getting tense.

"Never seen anything quite like it. The Indians are getting around in boats."

"Boats?" Who was this guy trying to fool anyway? Dad smothered a laugh, but his air of condescension was obvious.

"Where you headed in the long haul?" the logger asked, ignoring Dad's attitude.

"Iron County, uh, Michigan," Dad mumbled.

"I'm tellin' you, you'd better take the long cut home. Even if you gotta' backtrack, you'll be better off." The logger pushed his cap back farther on his forehead, looked down at Dad with a shake of his head, and started for the door. When he pulled the log door open, he turned back for a minute, gave us a last look and said, "*Boats*. They're getting around in *boats*."

"Takes all kinds," Dad laughed just as Bea sailed out of the kitchen, her hands and arms loaded with streaming plates of roast pork and mashed potatoes.

"But, Johnny," Mom said, "he says the Indians are getting around in boats."

"The roads may be bad from all this rain," Dad said smugly, "but I can guarantee you those Indians are not getting around in boats. Geez, what an imagination! Let's eat and then get the heck out of here and back on the road."

As soon as we had eaten our roast pork dinners, which were amazingly delicious, Dad tipped Bea for her trouble, paid our bill, and led the way back through the maze of water puddles in the parking lot to the green Chevy. Then, he headed down US 2 toward Ashland and Odanah.

"Lookit there, it's not even raining anymore." Dad leaned back, relaxed, and drove happily toward the Bad River Indian Reservation.

"I don't know why that man would have said all those things if they weren't true," Mom said, trying to think of a way to impress upon Dad we were likely heading for trouble.

"Oh, these guys get out in the woods logging and don't see civilization for months at a time. They get cabin fever, snort a little schnapps, and start dreaming up all kinds of things." The closer to home Dad got, the happier he became. "If you were out in the sticks all the time, you'd be in the same boat."

Boat. There was that word again. Mom squirmed uncomfortably in her seat. John and I sat up as high as we could in the back seat and stared out at the road ahead, hoping, by some chance, Dad was wrong and the logger wasn't just dreaming.

But there was nothing unusual to be seen—just the same old forests filled with trees along the sides of the road with the snow melting and running out into the ditches, until we got to Ashland where the main street buildings and signs offered a break in the boredom.

"There's a sign for Highway 13." Mom looked at Dad hopefully.

"Yah, I see it," Dad answered, driving right on by the arrow marked turn without even giving it a second glance as he sped on toward Odanah.

"We haven't met any cars coming from the opposite direction." Mom finally spoke up again.

"Well, it's the middle of the week and we're not in the most populated place in the world, you know. Everybody is probably at work, or at home." Dad said slickly.

"We're getting close," John whispered to me. "Look, there's one of those Indian shacks again. I still can't believe people live in those places." We looked into the soggy forest where a dilapidated one-room shanty sat, soggy and leaning under the branches of an old pine tree.

"There's another one," I said, staring at another run-down building. I thought about home again, and how much I missed it.

"We should be home in about three more hours," Dad announced, as if reading my mind. "I guess we'll make it by suppertime after all." He grinned at us in the rear-view mirror.

"Maybe, maybe not," Mom said staring in shock at the scene before us.

"There's water over the road!" John yelled from the back seat. "Can I use your camera, Mom? I've got to get a picture of this, or no one will ever believe it." Without waiting for a reply, John grabbed the black box camera off the back window ledge, lined up the sight in the viewfinder, and snapped a picture.

"We're going to have to turn around and go all the way back to Ashland." Mom was busy trying to figure out how to make Dad realize we had to turn back.

"Now, don't go jumping the gun," Dad ordered.

"Can't you see the water!" Mom was quickly losing her composure.

"Yah, I can see it." Dad slowed down and stopped at the edge of the water where we could all see it.

"You can't even see the road," Mom gasped. "We're going to have to backtrack, just like that man said."

"No, we're not gonna' backtrack, anywhere." We'd seen Dad like this plenty of times before. He was not going to change his mind. "We're just gonna' take our time, keep our wits, and get through this mess."

"But it's a real flood! Can't you see that?" Mom couldn't believe what Dad was proposing to do—though she knew him well enough to know he would not let a little flood stand in his way of getting home.

"What'll we do if we break down in the middle of this. Swim?" John was having a great time, snapping more pictures and imagining the worst. I wasn't sure how I felt. On the one hand I was with Mom—worried—but on the other hand, it was pretty swell to see the whole town under water.

"If we have to swim, we'll swim," Dad muttered. He took his foot off the brake, threw the car into low, and pressed on the accelerator as Mom closed her eyes and prayed.

"Boats!" I thought my brother's eyes were going to bulge right out of his head. "And there's people in them." It was true. The whole town was covered by water and many of the townsfolk were out paddling about in small rowboats. Some of them rowed from one house to another, others tied their boats to porches, got out, and stared at us in the old green Chevy.

"Well, then I guess we won't have to swim. We can catch a ride in a boat if we have to." Dad eased the Chevy slowly into the water where he guessed the road must be. As the water rose up over the tires, gushed halfway up the sides of the car, and flowed out in a foamy path behind us, no one said another word. Mom, clutching little Connie, and John and I all stared in wonder as, in stony silence, the inhabitants of Odanah watched us ride on by. Dad just clung to the wheel and drove with the calculated determination of a fox stalking a rabbit. The rabbit, in this case, was the other side of town and as we neared it, Dad rolled down his window and waved a triumphant good-by to a couple of boaters who were drifting along on the water in their front yard.

The car coughed, snorted, and chugged as we pulled out of the water and away from Odanah, but it didn't fail us. The old green Chevy, for all its problems, had held up in the worst of times.

It seemed like no time at all before we saw signs for Ironwood, Michigan. An inviting family restaurant on the outskirts of town caught Dad's eye. "I wonder if they've got a malted milk machine," he said. "Let's just pull in there and see." Dad making an extra stop when he didn't have to? This was the second miracle of the day. We all filed into the cozy little place and stood at the counter while Dad asked if they made malted milks there and when they told him they did, we each hopped on a stool at the counter and placed our orders.

I ordered chocolate and, once I figured out how to pull the thick stuff up through my straw, I knew I'd never tasted anything quite so wonderful. Full, snug, and satisfied, I slept away the next two hours to Stambaugh and, when Dad finally announced we were almost home, I woke, looked out at familiar sights, and knew I didn't want to leave there again for a long, long time.

From Michigan through Wisconsin, to Minnesota and back, the old green Chevy had remained faithful, carrying us to Grandpa's place for the funeral where we'd experienced the emotion and pain of burying Johnny and the relief of letting go of war. On our trip we'd met interesting people, watched Dad defy the elements, and encountered adventures we'd long remember. And while these unusual experiences were stunning and remarkable to us kids, it was time to return to the place where everything really started and stopped, where life—its puzzles, surprises, and difficulties—were met by the gentle, the brave, the wild at heart, the place where real miracles happened every day and hardly anyone ever noticed. That heavenly place called home.

Wallpaper Roses

"I think these rooms need a little magic," Mom said one day as she stood scrutinizing the dining and living room walls, rugs, and furniture. "I'm really tired of all this mauve. What we need is something new—something out of the ordinary—something exciting, elegant, enchanting."

"We could use a change," I agreed, trying to be helpful.

"Yes, we could. Let's go shopping!" she exclaimed, throwing on her coat and grabbing her gloves and purse.

"Wait for me," I called, grabbing my jacket and hurrying to catch up with her.

We drove down to "Monkey Wards," walked into the sofa section, and started the search, looking at colors, feeling fabrics, and sitting on every sofa in sight.

"May I help you?" A tall middle-aged man in a tight brown suit, semi-white shirt, and a head full of Wildroot Creme oiled hair had slipped up silently behind us—scaring us half to death.

"Oh no," Mom said, guiltily caught in the act of shopping without having first asked his advice, "we're just looking."

"That's a stunning item there, isn't it?" he went on smoothly, ignoring Mom's words.

"Actually, it's a little drab for my taste," Mom murmured, fingering the putrid putty-green sofa. "Too, uh, green, I guess."

"It's not green. It's *fern*." He sort of smirked as he looked down his snooty nose at Mom and me. "It also comes in *azure*. Have you seen the *azure*?" "Mr. Smooth" tossed his oily head, indicating we should follow. "It's right over here." He waltzed across the room, turned, and gestured grandly, like a ballerina, toward a sickly blue colored sofa.

I was hoping Mom would just up and leave the creep to his fern and azure sofas but, as usual, she was polite. She frowned thoughtfully and pressed her forefinger to her lips.

"Hm . . . too blue, uh, azure," she quickly corrected herself.

"Well, what color did you have in mind?" Mr. Smooth was becoming impatient with us.

"Well, I'm not sure," Mom admitted. "Something new and different. Something exciting—elegant."

Mr. Smooth folded his arms across the breast of his tight suit, cocked his head to one side, and gave her a discriminating look. Finally, having made some seemingly significant decision, he nodded to himself.

"You look like a woman of real class. A woman who can appreciate the finer things in life. I know exactly what you're looking for," he announced.

"You do?" Mom looked at him questioningly.

"Misty Rose," he said impressively. "Come with me." He led us past the other floor clerks, past the catalog sales desk, and through a massive doorway over which hung a sign stating, "Shipping and Receiving." He walked directly to a mauve sofa, stepped behind it and, facing us, ran his hand over the back of it. "Just arrived yesterday."

"Oh," Mom sighed, "it's perfect. You were right, it's exactly what I want. Misty rose!" I stood there with my mouth wide open, wondering if I should say something.

"Mom," I whispered finally, "that sofa is exactly the same color as the one we have at home." I watched my mother's face to see if she understood what I was telling her, but she just stood there, thoroughly entranced.

"No dear," she answered, "this sofa is misty rose, the one we have at home is just plain mauve. This is exciting, elegant, enchanting. It'll be just beautiful."

"Well we won't have to paint or get new rugs—it'll match everything that's already there," I said, shaking my head with wonder.

"Do you have another misty rose sofa?" Mom asked suddenly, throwing Mr. Smooth and me totally off guard.

"Surely there's nothing wrong with that one?" Mr. Smooth sneered.

"Do you have another just like it?" Mom demanded in a smooth sweet controlled voice.

"As a matter of fact, I . . . believe we do . . ." Mr. Smooth was getting fidgety, trying to figure what Mom was up to. He didn't like being surprised. He liked calling all the shots. It was fun seeing him squirm.

"Good." She beamed. "I'll take two."

"Two?" Mr. Smooth pulled out a wrinkled hanky, wiped his blotchy brow, and gulped audibly with relief.

"Is there a problem with that?" Mom asked icily.

"Oh no, Ma'am, no problem at all." Mr. Smooth coughed nervously. I was tickled to see him sweating. He'd been arrogant and rude. Now he was worried Mom might change her mind.

"Good. I'd like them delivered today." Mom snapped opened her purse, whipped out her checkbook, and started writing . . .

I thought Dad was going to have a heart attack when he came home and found the living room loaded with not one but two new sofas. He just kept pacing back and forth, looking at them and shaking his head.

"Why do we need two sofas?" he finally managed to get out.

"Because it's different, exciting, and beautiful," Mom explained. It made perfectly good sense to her.

"Exciting, huh?" Dad wasn't, by any means, convinced.

"And besides, the whole family can sit down comfortably at the same time," Mom said. Comfort. Now there was a word that made sense to Dad. Slick, I thought.

It took him a couple of days to get over the initial shock, but he finally went about his business and left the decorating to Mom.

"What do you think?" Mom asked, holding a wallpaper book opened to a muted mauve pattern.

"It looks just like what we've got," I told her honestly.

"Oh, do you really think so? Well, maybe just a little," Mom mused. It wasn't a little like what we had, it was exactly like what we had. It was mauve.

"I thought we were going to get something different and exciting," I commented.

"You're right, I did say that and this is really quite subdued," Mom admitted, flipping through the wallpaper book once again. "But I do love this misty rose." There was no point in telling her again that her misty rose was really the same old boring mousy mauve we'd had for years.

"I'm going to bring these samples back and find something else." Mom slapped the book shut and smiled excitedly. "Want to go along?"

"Sure, I guess," I said. Maybe I could urge her toward making a decision and the decorating could come to an end.

At Gambles Store, a sweet dark-haired lady invited us to sit right down and make ourselves comfortable. She then brought us a stack of sample books to browse through. Mom and I picked up the books, plunked ourselves down on an azure blue sofa, and pored over the pages.

"Look at this!" Mom said suddenly. She was pointing to a page covered with sprawling red, white, and pink cabbage roses. "Aren't they gorgeous?"

"Yah, gorgeous." I stared at her, surprised. "But I'm not sure they're right for our house."

"Why not for our house?" She looked at me quizzically. "You said you were tired of mauve, didn't you?"

I couldn't remember ever having said I was tired of mauve. I was tired of mauve, but I couldn't remember ever saying it. *She* was the one who was always saying she was tired of mauve.

"Well didn't you?" I could see Mom really needed an ally.

"I guess so," I replied, my eyes riveted to the rambling roses. They were wild wandering gypsy roses. A room full of them would make us feel like we were in the middle of a crawling cabbage rose patch.

"Now there, you see, these will be just perfect for perking things up a bit. You can almost smell them!" She pressed her nose to the page and I half expected her to find a fragrance there.

"Do they smell?" I giggled.

"They do to me," Mom laughed.

"Like magic, huh?" I teased.

"Just like magic," Mom smiled. "I know now exactly what we're going to do! Let's go home and measure."

"But Mom," I hesitated, "I think they're too . . . you know, too big, too bold, too . . ."

"Too beautiful?" Mom chuckled. "Don't worry. They'll be just perfect."

I slipped quietly in through the back door, careful not to let it thud behind me. From the kitchen, I peeked into the dining and living rooms. There stood Dad, bending over the wallpaper board, slopping wallpaper paste on to the backs of long rose-covered strips, and uttering epitaphs not intended for tender ears, while Mom stood on the step ladder, pushing paper into place, grumbling at Dad, and sweating bullets. I beat a quick exit to the back yard where it was safe.

The place was torn up for three days—wallpaper, paint, covered furniture everywhere. It was pure torture, trying to maneuver my way from one room to another and this I did only when absolutely necessary. Mainly, I just stayed out of everyone's way.

"Coralie," Mom sang out the back door.

"Coming," I hollered from the back yard where I'd been practicing red hot peppers with my jump rope. I threw the rope down and ran to the house.

"Wait 'til you see!" Mom's eyes were twinkling like shiny little stars. "Everything's back in place, the painting and papering is done, and the rooms are ready. Well, come see for yourself."

All the tools, paint, and scraps were gone. From the kitchen, I could see the north wall of the dining room and it was painted white. White? What had happened to all those rambling roses? How had they disappeared? I'd seen Mom and Dad hanging the strips?

I took a step closer, peered around the kitchen archway to the front rooms, and ventured inside. I was speechless. Only the west walls had been papered with roses. The rest of the walls were painted white. The new sofas were neatly placed, one against the roses and the other against a soft white wall. Sunlight streamed through the windows, creating a misty pink glow. Misty Rose? There was not a hint of mauve left in the room. The striking sprays of lush rambling roses—pink, white, and red—spread across the western walls providing a stunning garden-like setting. It was exciting, elegant, enchanting.

"What do you think?" Mom asked.

"It's beautiful!" I exclaimed. "I love the roses. You can almost smell them."

"Just like magic?" Mom laughed.

"Just like magic," I agreed, "and the sofas—the sofas aren't mauve anymore."

"Oh, honey, those sofas never were mauve. They were always misty rose. You just couldn't see it until now." Mom's Gemini eyes sparkled with success.

Mom and Connie enjoy the misty rose magic.

The Model A Adventure

It wasn't that our family was exactly falling apart. But without a car to take us on our travels together, we had lost one of our strongest connections. We went our separate ways—grumbling. Something had to be done. And fast!

Back before the old Chevy finally broke down and Dad had to sell it for parts, we were a happy family. Each Sunday, we'd go to church, come home for a full course dinner, and then pack ourselves into that green automobile to travel the width and breadth of the Upper Peninsula of Michigan—or at least as far as the car could safely go in an afternoon and still get back home without breaking down.

When we were in the car ambling along, we really got to know each other. Mom and Dad would tell wild wonderful stories about when they were kids and got into trouble with their folks. Mom would tell about calling her brothers sassy names, running as fast as she could, then falling headlong into the rain barrel. Dad would tell about his brother and him getting caught smoking behind the barn and how his dad taught them a lesson by making them smoke black Italian cigars until they were green in the face.

They reminisced about their high school days. Mom talked about the fun she had with her pals the Turpeinen sisters, Evelyn and Viola, how they spent hour after hour singing, playing the accordion, and planning theatrical programs.

Dad's favorite high school memories were of his seasons on the Stambaugh High School football team and winning the U.P. Championship. Even though we kids had heard the stories dozens of times, we reveled in every word. We loved the stories, but most of all we loved being together.

With Dad's underground shift work in the Hiawatha iron mine, the family didn't all get together much during the week, so we made up for it on Sunday's—adventuring in the Chevy. Dad taught us how to spot wildlife—partridge, white-tailed deer, and porcupines. Mom taught us the in's and out's of berry picking or how to survive the bugs, brush, and brambles and still successfully fill our metal pails with raspberries, blackberries, and blueberries for canning and pies.

We traveled to Agate Falls near Trout Creek where the view was breathtaking and the steps so steep and slick from the spraying falls we had to hang on for dear life, or get washed away.

We visited the sisters, Hulda, Hilda, Hilma, and Hilya, and Mom's other Finnish relatives in Ontonagon and White Pine and met cousins we kids didn't even know existed. My brother John taught my little sister Connie and me songs from his high school glee club concerts. Then we changed the words around until we giggled so hard we couldn't sing another word.

Dad drove us through an abandoned Indian village at Lac Vieux Desert, *old deserted fields*, where still stood the ancient remains of tribal homes—strange looking lean-tos which had been created by pulling the tops of several side-by-side growing trees into bow-shaped arcs, lashing them to the ground, and covering them with roofs of sod, mud and branches.

He drove us to Pentoga Park at Chicaugon Lake to visit the Ojibway Indian Burial grounds, where each grave was marked by a miniature wooden building resembling a doghouse with doorways on each end. We learned these houses were hallowed to the Indians—that they believed their spirits lived on within them. In the mystical quiet of the forest, we filed solemnly past the deserted resting places, praying the Ojibway spirits were not angered by our presence.

At Horserace Rapids near Crystal Falls, we sat daringly on the flint-like cliffs and hung dangerously over the mountainous edge, watching and listening with dread and fascination to the rushing river far below as it gashed its way through rocky ridges and disappeared into the forest. We made Mom so nervous we thought she'd never let us go back, but she always did.

We traveled to Gibbs City, a once thriving boom town, where iron ore and gold had been discovered back in the 1800's—where all that remained were a few buildings and the ghosts of long ago lumberjacks. We passed through tiny towns like Covington which consisted of one tavern, one gas station, and three churches and thought how lucky we were to live in metropolitan Stambaugh, Michigan—population 2500.

As we meandered our way back home each Sunday evening, we felt snug and satisfied. It wasn't just the excitement of our adventure, it was knowing we'd shared it with each other. We felt the love of Mom and Dad and their love for us. Nothing could take the place of those tender travels together.

Then, the Chevy was gone.

Dad had put in an order for a new car back in 1947, but nearly two years later there was still no car. All across the country, automobile production was down—World War II had taken its toll. Parts and goods just weren't available. We would have to wait.

Mr. Lindahl from the Chevy garage in Iron River, Michigan promised by the end of summer we'd have, not a 1947 or 1948 model, but a brand spanking new 1949, maroon, Chevrolet Fleetline, top-of-the-line automobile.

But that meant waiting all spring and summer. No Sunday rides. No special times together. It was hard to believe we were stuck without transportation for the first time in history, but unhappily we had to admit it was true. We felt grounded, penalized—prisoners.

Something had to be done to solve the problem.

One day, late in winter, Dad came home from work and said to Mom, "I've got a lead on an old 1929 Ford Model A. Think I'm gonna' go out and take a look at it."

"An old Model A? What will people think?" Mom always worried about things like that.

"Oh, for crying out loud," Dad muttered. But he was too excited to let anything change his mind. Turning to me, he asked, "You wanna' go with me, take a little hike? Use up some of that pep you've got stored up?"

"How far is it?" I wanted to know what I was in for. Everyone in the family knew Dad's idea of a little hike could mean hours and hours of walking.

"Oh, not too far—couple miles, I guess. We'll just hoof on over the bridge, up around the mines, and a little past the golf course. Won't take us long at all." I could tell he really wanted me to go along to keep him company.

"Sure, I guess," I answered quickly. Being with Dad was always fun, even if you did have to use up all your pep.

So Dad and I put on our warm winter jackets, scarves, and mittens and started off on our trek. We walked past the river, red with iron ore; past the mines, even redder with piles of iron ore looking like miniature mountains; and past the golf course. I hoped we were getting close.

"How much farther?" I was puffing away, keeping up with Dad, who at 6' 2" could cover a length of ground with little effort in no time at all.

"Down this road," Dad said as we turned south past the golf course. "It's supposed to be the last house on the left."

Of course, this was no real answer since there was no way of telling, from where we were, how long the road was. So I just muttered under my breath and kept on going.

Dad was having a great time. He was really excited about this car. I didn't know what to think. I really missed the times together in the old green Chevy and so did everyone else in the family, but there was respectability to consider. I knew this was what Mom was thinking. What would she do if we brought home a rickety 1929 Model A? Would she ride in it?

After what seemed like a century, we finally arrived at the back door of the home of a fellow called Jhalmar Gustafson. Dad knocked and Mr. Gustafson came out, buttoning up his long black coat. I was hoping he'd invite us in out of the cold for a minute, but he didn't. He walked right over to his garage and opened the door. I couldn't believe my eyes. The garage was spotless—clean as a house. There sat the Model A.

I could feel Dad's excitement mounting as he looked over the car. It needed a paint job—the black was looking a little rusty, like everything else in Iron County, but as Mr. Gustafson showed off the engine, I knew Dad would buy the car if he could.

"It's a beaut," Mr. Gustafson said earnestly.

"Yah. It sure is a beaut," Dad echoed.

"Tires are good," Mr. G. said.

"Yah, they look pretty good."

"Engine's like new—clean as a whistle."

"Yah, clean as a whistle."

"Only twenty-five bucks." Mr. G. decided to get right to the point.

"Twenty-five bucks, you say?" Dad was playing for time.

"So what do you think?" Mr. G. asked, trying to figure Dad out.

"Well, I don't know." Dad was stalling.

"Got another fellow coming over tomorrow." Mr. G. went in for the kill.

"Hmm. I haven't got twenty-five bucks today. Don't get paid 'til Friday." Dad let the cat out of the bag—we didn't have any money. Mom would have killed him!

"Well, you gotta' have twenty-five bucks, or no car." Mr. G. was putting the screws to my dad.

"I'll have it. Friday," Dad said. And then, with inspiration, he pulled out a five dollar bill and waved it in the air. "How about I give you five now and twenty at the end of the week?"

Mr. G. stroked his mustache thoughtfully and squinted an eye at Dad. He wanted that five dollar bill. Dad wanted the car.

"Okay, it's a deal, but you can't take it with you today. You'll have to bring the rest of the money Friday. Then you can take the car." Mr. G. was no fool.

"Okay," Dad said, "it's a deal! Now, I'd like a receipt for my money." Mom would have been proud!

"Okay, bring the girl and come on into the house while I write you a receipt." Mr. G. led the way into his kitchen.

"Oh, and don't forget to write the balance due on that receipt," Dad called after Mr. G as he disappeared into another room. Mom would have been very proud!

Though the hike back home was long, it was to be the last for a long time to come. Dad walked from the mine over to Mr. G.'s after work on Friday, paid for the car, and drove it home. Proud as a peacock, he brought Mom out to look at it.

She took a long silent look at the old car. I held my breath, hoping she wouldn't burst his bubble.

She looked that old car up. She looked that old car down. Then, from the corner of my eyes, I could see her eyes slide back and forth, scrutinizing the old-fashioned running board, the rust spots, and the funeral parlor black interior. I could almost taste the tension.

Finally, Mom looked away from the car and stared, instead, off into the distance . . . She seemed to be in another world. What was she thinking about? How we'd look riding in that old Model A? What the neighbors would think? Or was she thinking of all those berry pies we'd been missing? Or hanging on the cliffs at Horserace Rapids? Or visiting the relatives in Ontonagon?

I could feel Dad holding his breath—just like me.

At last she turned to us. There, in her eyes, was a wonderful magical glow.

"Now we can go adventuring again!" she exclaimed. I was very very proud of her!

Coralie with cousin Hulda on one of the trips to Ontonagon.

The Vanishing Wilderness

"Okay, if we're gonna' go, let's go," Dad said as he got up from the dinner table, bused his dishes to the kitchen sink, and headed for the back door.

"We'll be right there," Mom called after him. "You kids hurry on out. I'll be right behind you. You know how your father hates to wait."

The sweet smell of chicken gravy, mashed potatoes, and early June peas lingered lusciously in the kitchen. Mom scurried about cleaning up the last Sunday noon dinner dishes while John, Connie, and I ran to catch up with Dad.

He already had the engine running on the old Model A and was seated impatiently behind the wheel. The three of us climbed into the back seat, grabbed our favorite spots, and wound down all the windows to let in the warm July breeze. It was a beautiful day for a drive.

"Where are we going?" I asked excitedly.

"Oh, I don't know . . . where would you like to go?" Dad asked.

"Let's go somewhere different," I suggested.

"Let's go somewhere we've never been before," John said.

"I wanna' go somewhere different, too," piped up my little sister Connie.

"Somewhere different, hey? Well, let's see what your mother wants to do," Dad said. "If she ever gets here." He strummed his fingers on the steering wheel.

"I'm ready," Mom sang happily as she hopped into the car.

"Where would you like to go?" Dad asked.

"Oh, I don't know," she hesitated, "let's just amble along the back roads and see where they take us." Mom didn't really care where we went. She just loved going anywhere at all.

"Okay, I've got an idea." Dad shoved the stick shift into first gear and we pulled away from the curb.

"What?" I asked.

"You'll see." Dad was looking pretty smug as he shifted into second.

"Where are we going?" I persisted.

"Yah, where?" John asked.

"Yah, where?" Connie, the copycat, said.

"Yah, where?" Mom started giggling. We were off to a super Sunday start.

"Well, first we're gonna' head over to Crystal Falls and then I've got a surprise for you." Dad opened the old car up. Full throttle ahead.

"Oh, I know where we're going," Mom said slyly.

"Sure you do. Now don't go telling." Dad gave her a big wink.

"Aw c'mon, Mom, tell us," John pestered.

"Tell us, Mom," I harped.

"Tell us, Mom," the copycat repeated.

"Dad's taking us back in time," Mom replied brilliantly.

"That's right," Dad said mysteriously.

"What's that mean?" John asked.

"Yah, what's that mean?" I repeated.

"Yah, what's that mean?" Connie said.

"Quit saying everything I say." I gave my little sister a look that could kill.

"You, quit saying everything I say." John narrowed his eyes and stared at me with a sinister look.

"All right, you kids, settle down," Mom said, trying hard to keep a straight face.

"The whole darn bunch of you better cool down or we're gonna' turn around and head back home," Dad warned.

"She started it," I yelled, pointing at Connie.

"She started it," John yelled, pointing at me.

"She started it," Connie shrieked, pointing at Mom.

That was too much. We started squealing and laughing and poking at each other. The old Model A, grinding away down the highway, was practically bouncing from our boisterousness.

"I said, pipe down!" Dad was getting annoyed. "Take a look at where you're going and maybe you'll learn something."

I put my hands over my mouth, but it didn't do much good. The laughter just kept spurting out through my fingers.

"Oh, *h'yar* we set like *bards* in the wilderness, *bards* in the wilderness, *bards* in the wilderness . . ." John started singing hillbilly style and strumming an imaginary banjo. "*H'yar* we set like *bards* in the wilderness, waitin' for somethin' to eat."

It was one our favorite songs. Foolish. Funny. Fantastic. I hooted and hollered, "Sing it again."

Connie stood right up on the back seat and yelled, "Sing it again."

"*H'yar* we set like *bards* in the wilderness . . ." John started to sing again.

"You think you know about wilderness?" Dad silenced us with his sudden seriousness. "I don't think you do."

"Sure we do." I started giggling all over again. "Anybody who lives in the U.P. knows about wilderness." This sent everyone into fits of laughter. Everyone, except Dad.

"You know about living in Stambaugh, Michigan in a nice little neighborhood, with a nice big yard, in a nice white house with all the modern conveniences available. That's what you know. You don't know what it's like to live in a log cabin in the middle of nowhere and go to sleep at night, looking up at the stars through the rafters in the roof."

"Huh?" Who was he talking about? Abe Lincoln? "Is this a history lesson?" I spouted.

"Well, yes, I guess you could say it's a history lesson," Dad answered.

"Pioneers!" John thought he had it all figured out.

"Pio-what?" Connie asked.

"Pio-neers," Mom instructed, "the first people who came to this country, from other countries, and settled here."

"Yah, settlers," I said smartly. "They traveled out west in covered wagons." I'd seen it all in the movies.

"Not all the pioneers in this country went out west," Dad said. "Some came to the U.P. like my folks."

"Grandma and Grandpa Cederna?" I'd never thought of them as pioneers.

"That's right." Dad nodded. "My dad came to this country in 1898. He was only twenty years old. In fact, you kids might have grown up in Australia if it hadn't been for a quirk of fate."

"Huh?" Boy, this was news to me.

"When Grandpa Cederna was just a young fellow, he planned to go to Australia and start a farm. He wanted his kids to grow up in the wilderness and he'd heard that there was plenty of land and good farming there. So he left his home in Poggiridenti, Italy and found his way to the ships that were sailing for new lands," Dad said.

"What happened," John asked curiously.

"Well, the ship to Australia was full up. In fact, if Grandpa hadn't been so determined, he might have had to go back home again, but he found out they were offering jobs in the iron ore mines in Upper Michigan. So he decided to take a chance and got passage on a ship to America," Dad answered.

"Wow!" I thought how nifty it would have been to live in a country where kangaroos leapt around the back yard.

"Wow!" Connie repeated.

"So, anyhow, that's how we came to be born here. Grandpa came to the U.P. in 1898, went to Mansfield, Michigan on the Michigamme River near Crystal Falls, and got a job in one of the mines. He got hold of a small piece of land, started a little farm, and then he sent for Grandma." Dad was enjoying his captive audience.

"Your Grandmother came all the way across the Atlantic Ocean by herself," Mom added, "without knowing another soul on the ship."

"Really?" I was impressed. "She sure was brave."

"Yah," Dad continued, "you had to be brave in those days. Anyway, she and Grandpa were some of the first settlers in Mansfield. They stayed at the Fauri Boarding House in Crystal Falls until they moved into their own little log cabin."

"You lived in a log cabin?" I asked, surprised.

"Sure did," Dad answered proudly.

"What was it like, living way out in the sticks like that?" John asked.

"Well, we didn't have any electricity, or phones, and being so far out, there was always the danger of forest fires, but it was the best place in the world to live. We always had plenty of chow, vegetables from the garden, fresh fish and venison, rabbit, or partridge all year 'round. And we had goats and a milk cow. Ma used to make the best cheese. We never went hungry, that's for sure," Dad said.

"What did you do for fun?" I asked.

"Oh, all kinds of things. What we kids liked most was when Ma and Pa would take us to one of the big blueberry patches. We'd stay there all day, eating and picking. Next day, Ma would start baking pies and canning for winter."

"That's what you did for fun?" I thought it sounded like a lot of work.

"Is that what—?" Connie started.

"Shh," I warned her, "listen to Daddy."

"Shh, yourself," John said.

"Oh, for crying out loud," I griped.

"Listen to your father," Mom ordered.

"That's what we did for fun all right. Kids today don't know what's fun. Fun isn't just playing with toys or buying something new. Fun is sitting on a rock, looking up at the sky and watching the clouds roll on by. Fun is running with the wind blowing in your face, or skipping rocks across a river. That's fun.

"We kids had a great time. We used to run barefoot in the fields, playing tag, catching grasshoppers, and chasing butterflies. Then we'd head down to the water and go splashing around in the river. Even going to bed at night was fun. I'd lay there, all snuggled up, listening to the river rushing by and think about how lucky I was. I'd look up at the rafters and stare at the stars right through the splits between the logs." Dad didn't usually get nostalgic.

"How come you had to leave?" John asked.

"Well, the family was growing and Pa got offered a better job than the one he had—over at the old Dober Mine in Stambaugh, some twenty miles away from Mansfield. It was no easy decision, but the job paid plenty and he and Ma figured they could find another place where they could still do their farming."

"So you all drove over to Stambaugh?" John asked.

"Well, not exactly. You see, we didn't have a car," Dad said.

"So how did you get there?" John asked.

"Yah, how?" I glared at my little sister so she wouldn't imitate me again.

"Yah, how?" Connie asked.

"This is the best part of the story," Mom said enthusiastically.

"It's no story," Dad stated adamantly. "It's all true. I remember it, like it was yesterday. I was four years old when Pa told us we were moving. Boy, I hated to leave that wonderful wilderness. And I wondered how Pa would get us all over there."

"All?" I asked.

"There was Pa and Ma, my sisters Mary, Santina, Victoria, Serena, Celia, Elna, my brother George and me. And that wasn't all. We had a cow, pigs, goats, chickens, and even some cats that had to be moved. Well, Pa thought about it a while, and sure enough, came up with the answer. He made arrangements with the railroad to take us to Stambaugh." Dad continued his saga.

"The railroad? You mean you rode on a train, way back then?" I asked.

"Yah, we rode on the train all right. In a box car. Pa loaded all the kids, the animals, and the furniture into a box car," Dad chuckled.

"A box car?" I gulped.

"A box car. We just piled right in behind a long stream of iron ore cars and away we went. We got as far as Crystal Falls the first day, stayed there at the Fauri Boarding House overnight, and then traveled on to Stambaugh the next day." Dad smiled and shook his head at the memory.

We'd been so caught up in Dad's reminiscence that we hardly noticed passing through Crystal Falls. We were already on the other side of the city and in unfamiliar territory.

"Is that where we're going? Mansfield?" I asked.

"We're in Mansfield," Dad laughed. "Now all I've got to do is find that old log cabin." He seemed just like a kid, he was so excited. "I think it might be down this road," he said, turning onto a narrow gravel trail.

We drove down the trail, staring out at all the fields, the willowy brush, and great old pines that grew here and there. But there was no log cabin.

"Are you sure you're on the right road?" Mom asked.

"Of course I'm sure I'm on the right road," Dad snapped uncertainly.

"Maybe it's over that way." I pointed to where the road forked to the right.

"Well, I suppose it could be." Dad lit up a cigarette. He was getting edgy.

"Or maybe it's over there." John pointed to another fork in the road that led to the left.

"Hmm." Dad took a long drag on his cigarette and inhaled deeply. "I know where it is. I must have missed the turn a mile or so back." He turned the Model A around in the field while we all held our breath, hoping we wouldn't get stuck way out there in the middle of nowhere.

Soon we were clanking along back over the trail we'd just traveled. I hoped he was right this time, but I had a feeling he still wasn't really sure where the log cabin had been.

"There's the road," Dad said triumphantly as he turned down yet another old trail. This trail led into, around, and through more fields—fields of wild wheat growing golden in the summer sun. On we went, all eyes searching, but not a single building could be seen anywhere. Finally, we came to the end of the trail. There was nowhere to go, but back.

Dad stopped the car, let the engine idle, and looked off across the gently waving fields of wheat. He was silent, lost in thought. The Michigamme River, its sweet swampy smell rising and flowing into the open windows of the car, could be heard gently rushing somewhere off in the distance beyond the scented pines that lined its banks.

"It was right here. I'm sure of it," Dad said quietly. "Nothing left now but the wilderness."

"Such a shame," Mom murmured.

None of us kids said a word—we were all too painfully aware of Dad's disappointment.

"Well . . . this is the way it should be," Dad finally said. "Too much of our wilderness is vanishing these days. The Indians knew enough to cherish the earth—move on before they used it all up. But these days people move in, take over, and ruin the land. Even though there's nothing left of the old homestead now, it's better this way. It's peaceful, just the way the Lord intended."

"Yes, peaceful," Mom agreed softly.

"Peaceful," John said quietly.

"Peaceful," I whispered.

"Peaceful," Connie whispered in my ear.

I looked at my little sister and couldn't help smiling. Everything's peaceful here, I thought, looking out across the wild wheat to the great pines, white birch, and firs that harbored and hid the waters of the Michigamme. The chirping of a thousand crickets, the call of a chickadee, the rushing of the river blended to create a soothing song, a melody of memories.

I imagined I could see a little log cabin in the distance, a milk cow grazing nearby, and a small barefooted boy in blue coveralls, running across the open field following the flight of a yellow butterfly. His face shone with the sweet simple innocence, the joy, the zest of youth. As he reached out to grasp the escaping butterfly that dipped and danced and fluttered toward freedom and the blue heavens above, he smiled. Then he turned on his sturdy little grass-stained heels and raced off toward the banks of the magnificent Michigamme—vanishing into the wilderness.

Mom and Dad, Carrie and John Cederna,
taught us about adventuring.

Fireworks

The crack of dawn came crashing through my bedroom window, jolting me out of a dead sleep. Thunder! Bolting out of bed, I stumbled to the window, yanked up the yellowed shade, and—expecting the worst—was relieved to see the early morning sun beaming down. A large red-breasted robin silently hopping over the sparkling dew-covered green grass cocked his head toward the ground, pecked into a warm wet hole, and tugged until he hauled out a hefty wiggling worm. Nothing else stirred.

I pulled my nose away from the window, hurried into the long skinny closet at the end of my bedroom, and grabbed the hanger holding my new red, white, and blue sailor blouse and striped shorts just as another ear-splitting blast broke over the neighborhood. For a second, the whole house seemed to shake.

What a day this was going to be! I thrust the blouse over my head, tugged on my shorts, and snapped my white sandal straps in place around my ankles. Then, sailing like a shot down the stairs, past Mom and Dad in the kitchen, and out into the back yard, I looked up and down the block, searching the alley, street, and neighboring back yards, trying to figure out where the sounds had come from.

But the neighborhood was still. There wasn't a soul in sight. Disappointed, I turned back toward the house, but was stopped short by a spattered crackling of small explosions erupting from the alley, near Saco Johnson's place.

Mr. Widas, across the street, exploded out of his house like a stick of dynamite and ran toward the sound, shaking his fist and yelling, "Whaddaya think you're doing? You'd better get out of there or I'm gonna' call the cops!"

There followed a scuffling of gravel in the alley as two teenage boys took off on their bikes at high speed, hollering back, "Your mother wears long underwear!" and, "Mind your own business. It's a free country!"

Freedom! Firecrackers! The Fourth of July! I hightailed it back into the house to see what time we were leaving for the big parade in Iron River.

"What was all that noise out there?" Mom frowned. She was standing at the stove simultaneously frying bacon, stirring up scrambled eggs, and spreading bread on the broiler pan to stick in the oven to toast.

"Firecrackers!"

"Who was setting off firecrackers?" Dad, who had already finished his breakfast and was ready to go outside, looked at me as if I'd been the one making all the racket.

"I don't know. Couldn't see them. They took off on their bikes." I was pretty sure it was the Rivard brothers, but I wasn't about to tell on them. We kids had to stick together.

"Well, whoever set them off woke up the whole neighborhood," Mom said, pouring a big bowl of egg-mix into a sizzling frying pan.

"What time are we leaving for the parade?" I asked anxiously.

"Probably about nine, quarter to," Dad said as he went out the back door.

"Can I light the sparklers now?" I knew I had to wait until after the parade when we got out to the picnic at Chicaugon Lake, but what the heck, it was worth a try.

"Not until we get out to Chicaugon Lake," Mom said.

"Can we cut the watermelon?" The watermelon came after the parade—we had a regular routine on the Fourth of July and I knew that perfectly well.

"Sit down and eat your breakfast." Mom pulled the broiler pan out of the oven, flipped the bread, and pushed it back in to finish toasting.

"Do we have to wait?" No sense giving up that easily.

"Yes, we have to wait." She scooped up a man-sized serving of scrambled eyes, a few strips of bacon, and pulled the broiler out again. Buttering two hot pieces of toast, she set the whole works in my place at the table.

I hopped into the breakfast nook, dove into the eggs, bacon, and toast and washed them down with a glass of Ovaltine. "Have we got any crepe paper?" I asked, wiping away my milk mustache with the back of my hand.

"There might be some in one of those boxes in the basement," Mom said. "Don't talk with your mouth full."

"I'm not," I said, grabbing another piece of toast, chewing and gulping as I talked. "Gotta' trim my bike."

"Mind your manners."

"What manners?" I giggled, swishing the last bit of toast around in my mouth before swallowing.

"Heaven help us," Mom mumbled to herself as I trekked out of the kitchen.

In the basement, I found an old box overflowing with odds and ends—ribbon, paper doilies, and two ancient rolls of pink crepe paper left over from a long ago Boy Scout bake sale for which Mom, a former Den Mother, had made the decorations. The crepe paper smelled a little musty, but it still had plenty of stretch.

Cramming down the lid of the box, I raced back up the wooden steps and outside with my treasure. The old blue Zenith bike, which previously had belonged first to my sister Corinne, then to my brother John, and now to me, looked a little forlorn laying in the grass where I'd let it fall. But I planned to fix that.

I picked it up, booted down the kickstand, and unraveled the rolls of crepe paper. Then I wound the crepe paper in and out of the spokes until it covered the entire inside of each wheel. There was just enough left to tie two long streamers from the grips of the handlebars. I stood back, admiring my handiwork.

"I'm going to take a spin around the neighborhood," I yelled in through the screen door as I booted up the kickstand, jumped on, and pedaled up toward the potato field—certain I looked as stunning as a star acrobat straight from the Big Top.

"All decked out for the Fourth, hey!" Charlie Polich called as I rode past his driveway where he was lathering up his car then splashing away the suds with a long black garden hose. "You should be riding in the parade."

"Maybe I will—next year. Watch this," I called back, showing off by taking my hands off the handlebars and planting them firmly behind my head, as I whizzed by, weaving in and out across the newly tarred center line. "Nifty, hey?" Concentration. Split second timing. That was the key . . . my front wheel swerved slightly.

"Be careful!" he called back, but I just gave him a big broad grin and continued all the way down to the corner in front of Mr. and Mrs. Jenks' house before putting my hands back on the grips and making a U-turn.

No cars in sight, I pedaled as hard as I could, bringing the bike up to full speed, then slipped down to sit on its U-shaped bar. Coasting, circus-style, feet resting on the handlebars, down as far as the Martini's house the old bike finally ran out of steam and started to wobble dangerously. Like a jack-in-a-box, I shot back up in the seat, grabbed the handlebars, and grinned confidently at Mr. Martini and "Froggie" Conta who were standing in Martini's driveway watching me, mouths agape.

What a day! The popping of firecrackers echoed down through Dober Location from Stambaugh, a mile away up on the hill. I could hardly wait for the parade, the watermelon and sparklers, and finally the fireworks planned for after dark.

My brother John was just coming out the back door, when I coasted into the yard. "Look, no hands!" I yelled, jumping off in midstream as my bike sailed past me and made a crash landing.

"Yah, and you're going to have *no bike* if you keep that up," he yelled back.

"How do you like my snazzy pink wheels?" I scampered on over to the bike where the front wheel was still spinning from the fall, grabbed the ribboned handlebars, and pulled it back up. "Pretty foxy, hey?"

"For a grease monkey. What have you been doing? Playing with your bicycle chain?" He scratched his stomach with one hand, patted his head with the other, and hopped on one foot, squealing like a monkey.

"Huh?" I looked down at my hands. My fingers were covered with thick black grease. I darted in the back door, hoping Mom wouldn't see me as I headed for the bathroom upstairs.

"What have you gotten into? Just look at your new shorts," Mom gasped. She never missed a thing.

"Oh, no!" The patriotic stripes on my new shorts were crisscrossed with black oily streaks.

"You can't go anywhere looking like that." She gave me an exasperated look. "I don't know what you're going to wear, but you'd better get changed."

"And hurry it up," Dad said. Just my luck—he'd chosen that minute to come back in from outside. "We've gotta' get going right now if we want to get a parking place. You wanna' miss the parade?"

"No!" I raced upstairs and into the bathroom, looked at myself in the mirror, and saw that not only were my fingers and new clothes greasy, but also my face, arms, and legs looked like I'd been changing tires in a gas station. I turned on the water—full-blast—then snatched the bar of Ivory soap, lathered my hands, and scrubbed, but the grease wouldn't budge.

"Are you about ready?" Dad's voice boomed up the stairway.

"I can't get this off," I yelled back.

"Try Dad's mining soap. It's in the basement," Mom hollered.

"The basement? Geez!" Dad was already having a fit, worrying about being late. Now I had to go all the way down the basement. I tore down the stairs, through the kitchen, and down the basement steps where I grabbed the gritty bar of special soap Mom used for scouring rusty iron spots on Dad's mining clothes, flew back up to the bathroom, and started to scrub furiously.

"Time's a-wasting!" Dad hollered from the dining room.

"I'll be right there," I hollered back. Face, hands, and legs now rosy red and tingling, I stripped off my new clothes, threw them in a pile behind my bedroom door, and pulled on the first thing I could lay my hands on.

"Are you coming or not?" Dad yelled from the bottom of the stairs. "We're leaving!"

"I'm coming, I'm coming," I gasped, clipping down the stairs at top speed and trying to catch my breath as I trailed out to the old Model A behind the rest of the family—in my old faded yellow blouse and rumpled green shorts.

"Where did you get those clothes?" Mom's neck craned around from the front seat to stare at my shorts.

"Out of the ironing basket," I mumbled.

"Well, you can't go downtown looking like that," she said. "We're going to have to go back in and iron those things."

"No we're not," Dad said, starting the old car. "We've had enough hold-ups for one day. Either we leave now, or we're just gonna' have to forget all about the going to the parade."

"Well, rub your hands over those wrinkles, and maybe they'll smooth out," Mom said, anxious as the rest of us to get to Iron River.

"C'mon, 'Lizzie,'" Dad coaxed as he revved up the motor on the old coughing car and we clanked away from the curb, clattering down Nineteenth Street, heading for Iron River. "Don't know how long the old girl's gonna' last," he mumbled.

"Look at the horses!" I squealed from the back seat, pointing to a small group of men and women decked out in fringed leather jackets, neckties, western hats, chaps, and boots, and riding their palomino ponies toward town.

"Now there's transportation you can really count on," Dad joked.

"At least the old Model A doesn't leave road apples on the street," John laughed.

"Apples? I don't see any apples," my little sister Connie said.

"They're not for pies," Dad laughed.

"Huh?" We all giggled as she stared at the horses, watching their rumps sway and tails swish, trying to figure out what we were talking about.

"Horse stuff." John pointed to the droppings on the road ahead.

"Oh!" Connie caught on to the joke and laughed.

But I was too caught up with watching the women in their Western wear to laugh for long. Silently, I studied the silver studs on their costumes, leather fringe rippling on their jackets, and the hand-tooled artistry on their pointed toed, high-heeled boots. "Can I get a horse someday?" I asked. I'd been pestering Dad about it for years.

"We've got no place to keep a horse. You know that." Dad gave the answer practically by rote. "And even if we did, horses need a lot of special care. Lots of work, having a horse."

"If she took care of a horse the way she takes care of her bike, it'd be deader than a doornail in a week," John giggled.

"You're such a twirp—"

"That's enough out of you, Coralie," Mom interrupted.

"Talk to him. He's the one who's always getting away with murder." I glared at my brother, but he just kept on smirking at me.

"I said, that's enough," Mom said.

"You kids quite your beefing. Geez, these horses are slower than molasses in January," Dad grumbled, pulled the Model A out and around the horses, and veered west off Nineteenth Street. "We'd better take the cut-off over to Selden Road and by-pass all this traffic."

He drove down the hill near Grandma Cederna's house, across the Iron River bridge, and up the hill past the Hiawatha Mines. But it seemed everyone else in town had decided to by-pass the traffic, too. When we turned north onto Selden Road, there were cars everywhere, moving slowly toward the main street of Iron River, still about a mile away.

"Everybody's gotta' poke around all the time." Dad slapped his hands on the wheel of the car and swerved out to pass a new green Ford in front of us, but another car was coming from the opposite direction. He cranked the wheel and swerved back in behind the fancy Ford, but by now the driver was banging on his horn, making a terrible racket.

"Every nut in the county must be out today," Dad griped.

"I guess he thinks he's some kind of "Big Shot" with that flashy new car," John said.

"Well, that Big Shot's got his brains in his back pocket." Dad glared at the fellow in the Ford. "Look at that car he's driving. It's a Ford, for crying out loud."

"What's wrong with a Ford? The Model A is a Ford, isn't it?" I asked.

"Yah, this is a Ford all right, but this car was built back when old Henry and the boys knew what they were doing. You buy a Ford today and it falls apart before you get it home from the garage. The guys at the mine are always talking about it. That's why we're getting a Chevy. Best car in the world. Chevrolet." Dad smiled smugly.

"If it ever comes in," John said.

"Seems like we've been waiting for years," I added.

"We have," Mom said. "It's hard to believe we ordered that car way back in 1947 and here it's already 1949."

"And 1949 is half over," Dad snorted. "At the rate things are going, it'll probably be 1959 before it gets here."

"Well, we knew it would take a long time, what with production down after the war," Mom said. "Anyway, Lindahl's Chevy Garage promised we'd be the first to get ours when the new models finally started coming in. I'm sure the waiting will be over any day now."

"It had better be. We were supposed to have it by the Fourth at the very latest," Dad said.

"We're going to miss the parade if they don't hurry up," I complained. We were getting closer to the downtown area of Iron River, but the line of cars ahead snaked along at a snail's pace.

"Everyone in town must be out today," Mom said brightly. "Just look at all the cars."

As the long line moved lazily onward, Dad saw his chance to break free and swerve into a side street. "We're bound to find a place to park somewhere around here," he said.

"We're going to have to walk a mile to get back to town to find a good place to stand and watch the parade," I griped.

"Something wrong with your legs?" Dad heckled.

"No, I just don't want to miss anything." I was getting more impatient by the second. All the excitement was going to happen before we even got out of the car.

"We're not going to miss anything," Mom said. "There's a parking place, Johnny." She pointed to a space Dad was already backing into.

"Let's shake a leg," Dad ordered, jumping out of the old car, slamming the door, and leading the way downtown toward the anxious crowds of people grouping along the storefronts of Main Street.

"Hey there, Johnny." A rosy-cheeked, somewhat short and stout fellow called to Dad.

"Hey, Stubby!" Dad called back as we passed.

"Playing hooky from the mine?" A young dark-haired fellow teased as we walked by.

"Hey, Smoky, how's it going? I'm off 'til tomorrow night." Dad slowed down, but didn't stop. He called over his shoulder, "What about you? I thought you were supposed to be working today?"

"Aw, quit pulling my leg. You know I'm on vacation this week," the young man laughed.

"Here comes Big John, himself," a stocky middle-aged man called out, grinning, poking the guy next to him and pointing at Dad. "Did they close the Hiawatha down, or what?"

"Hey, Porky, who let you out?" Dad grinned, walking tall among his pals, greeting one after another as he led us to the front of the Miner's State Bank where we finally stopped.

"Who were all those guys," I asked.

"Oh just some men from the mine," Dad said, as he saluted yet another fellow with the flick of his forefinger. I wondered if they were all Chevy men.

"Geez Johnny, I just can't get away from you, can I?" Dick Trombley, one of Dad's best buddies from the mine sauntered up. Laughing, they gave each other a hardy handshake and slap on the back.

"Thought you'd be out at the lake fishing already," Dad said. "What's the hold-up."

"Can't miss the parade," Dick said. "Hey, Marge, look who's here!" His wife Marge and daughter Carol turned and waved from the curb.

"Yah, I guess the Fourth wouldn't seem like the Fourth without the parade," Dad laughed.

"So today's the deadline, hey?" Dick said. "Any word on the new car?"

"Nothing." Dad pulled a smoke out of his shirt pocket. He'd discussed that topic today once already, and once was enough.

"I thought you were supposed to have the new Chevy before the Fourth," Dick went on, ignoring Dad's unwillingness to talk about it.

"We were," Dad replied, lighting up the Lucky.

"Well, I hope they get a move on or your new car is gonna' be out of date by the time it gets here." Dick was getting a big kick out of razzing Dad.

"Like I said, there's nothing we can do," Dad repeated through a cloud of cigarette smoke.

"They're coming!" John yelled. The low rumble of drums, base horns, and trombones along with the shrill sharp sounds of trumpets vibrated in the distance, echoing off the hills of Stambaugh, through the valley along the river, and up again along the pavement of downtown Iron River.

I strained to see past the crowds of people. Up to now, their nervous chatter had been just a low buzz as they milled along the sidewalks waiting, but with the surging sounds of the band approaching, their voices swelled to a wild and spirited roar.

Kids ran alongside the curbing in front of the crowd, squealing and teasing each other, while parents hollered at them to get off the street. But mostly, everyone's eyes were fastened to one focal point, the spot just in front of the Jack O'Lantern Bar where the street leveled out from a small hill rising from the river's valley. Here is where the first sight of the parade would be visible. Here, as in previous years, would appear the local high school marching bands, the American Legionnaires, the VFW, the Cub Scouts, and a bevy of local beauties on the backs of convertible cars, pick-up trucks, and flat-bed trailers.

"Here it comes!" My brother John pointed down the street to where the tip of the American Flag came rising into view.

"There's Mario," I yelled to my brother as the VFW flag bearer, flanked by an honor guard, approached. Mario Contardi, one of our Dober Location neighbors, and two other men stood tall, strutting their stuff, proudly presenting the stars and stripes. Behind them, followed a group of VFW members in white shirts with dark pants and ties, moving forward in military precision.

"Hey, Mario!" someone in the crowd hollered as he passed in front of us, but he looked straight ahead, solemn and strong in his role.

"Look!" Mom said, pointing to the float which followed the VFW group. "Isn't that beautiful?" A brand new black truck, as slick and shiny as a panther, crept forward pulling a flat-bed trailer trimmed with red, white, and blue crepe paper streamers and hand-made tissue rosettes. Three pretty teen-age girls in long shiny pink, blue, and yellow prom formals sat on rosette covered risers, waving to the crowd. The sign on the side of the truck said, in thick black letters, "Iron River Business Men."

A pack of Cub Scouts, looking flushed in the face, trotted along behind the black truck, trying to keep in step by staring at each others feet. Their Den Mothers marched alongside, trying unsuccessfully not to frown under the heightening sun.

Peals of laughter could be heard just down the way, and in seconds I saw why. A grotesquely tall Uncle Sam staggered along the street, causing the giddy crowd of gawkers to gasp each time he stopped to sway and bend in mid-air.

"How does he do that?" I stared in astonishment at the teetering figure in red, white, and blue.

"Stilts, Birdbrain," my brother John replied.

"Don't call me Birdbrain," I warned.

"Watch the parade, you two," Mom admonished, but her words were drowned out by the approaching Iron River Marching Band, their drums thump-thumping, their trumpeters blasting away in dedicated bravado a lively rendition of *Onward Christian Soldiers*.

In the wake of the marching soldiers tramped a hilarious band of buffoons. A man dressed up as a woman bounced along, the lopsided bodice of his costume—plumped up with a pair of grapefruit—rolling, bobbing, and pitching as he walked. He led a crew of colorful kids dressed as hobos, wearing wide circles of red lipstick on their cheeks and smudges of black coal on their foreheads, and carrying tattered, patched packs on long sticks slung over their shoulders.

Behind them on a bright red leash pranced a cocker spaniel with a huge blue bow tied on his collar. He was led by a redheaded, freckled-faced girl dressed in a long flowing white gown fastened around the shoulders and waist with a gold colored rope. She wore a shiny paper silver crown on her head and carried a blue wand made of wood with red crepe paper flames tacked to one end. I guessed she was supposed to be the Statue of Liberty. I wasn't sure who the dog was supposed to be.

Next came the Legionnaires. They were all dressed in navy uniforms except for one feeble old fellow who wore a brown belted jacket over jodhpurs and a hat that looked like it belonged on a Canadian mounted policeman. Crisscrossing his chest was an amazing set of munitions belts. Glassy-eyed, he looked a little wobbly as he walked, but he spryly saluted the crowd with one hand while, with the other, he waved a World War I banner.

"I wonder how many parades that old codger's seen," I heard Dad say to Dick.

Then began the entourage of floats—vehicles lavishly covered with colorful tissue flowers and long trailing crepe paper streamers driven by local businessmen. Sleek convertible cars and pick-up trucks carried hand-waving, taffeta-gowned girls with aching plastic smiles plastered on their faces. A band of musicians, riding high on a wide-bed trailer labeled, "Hillbilly Heaven," pulled by a Cloverland Construction Company truck, plunked away on banjoes, strummed guitars, and flexed accordions, grinding out the *She's Too Fat For Me Polka*. Behind the trailer, tied with string, tumbled a dozen tin cans tinkling out their own tunes.

"Look at the clowns!" my little sister squealed. Clowns on tricycles, in wagons, and on roller skates wheeled by, blowing shrill, ear-piercing whistles at each other. A gangling twosome, two guys dressed up like a trained bear and its trainer, danced a dizzy jig, every so often rushing and charging at kids on the curbing. A buxom Little Red Riding Hood, arm-in-arm with the Wolf, sashayed along behind, throwing paper-twisted seafoam kisses from her crepe papered basket to the same kids who were trying to avoid the lurching bear—creating a mad scramble in the middle of the street.

The Stambaugh High School Marching Band tipped their instruments high and performed a fanfare for the Western riders and their palominos we'd seen on our way to the parade. No longer just ambling along, the horses trotted in formation, snorting and blowing when guided to stop, back up, and turn in unison. Drawing up the rear and stealing the scene scampered three clothespin-nosed clowns pushing little red wheelbarrows into which they cringingly shoveled "road apples" that plopped along the way.

"Get a load of that." Dad and Dick were laughing like a couple of nuts. "Pretty hard to top that!"

"Well, get a load of that car." Dick, still hooting, playfully punched Dad in the arm, as a sleek new black Ford cruised by.

"You couldn't give me one of those things." Dad punched him back.

"Me, either," Dick danced out of reach. Here were two dyed-in-the-wool Chevy men at work. "Lookit there." Dick stopped laughing and gawked at the next entry in the parade. "Isn't that the new 1949 Chevy?"

Dad's jaw dropped when he saw the beautiful new maroon top-of-the-line Fleetline Chevrolet gliding by—Mr. Lindahl, himself—smiling and nodding at the crowd, looking smart and sassy behind the wheel of the classy long-line beauty.

"Hey, Johnny, you see that?" Dick asked, still staring at the Chevy.

"Yah, I see it all right." Dad's face had gone stark white, then red. His temper sizzling, he looked like a rocket ready to go sailing off across the sky, exploding in a loud blast of fiery streaming color.

"Well, what do you think?" Dick still couldn't take his eyes off the snappy number.

"I think someone's gonna' answer to me about this," Dad growled.

"Huh?" Dick looked at Dad in surprise. Just a second ago they'd been laughing and having a good time.

"That's my car!"

"Geez, Johnny, you're kidding. I mean, that's not your car, uh, is it?" Dick was bewildered.

"Oh, that's my car all right. I gotta' go." Dad was furious now as he watched the maroon boat sail down the street out of sight, a single white streamer—the same shade as those flashy whitewall tires—flowing from its antenna.

"Go?" Dick stared at Dad.

"Yah, I'll see you at work." Dad said, nodding at Mom to follow.

"We've got to go," Mom announced, concern written all over her face.

"But the parade's not over—" I whined.

"This parade's over for us," Dad said, as he broke through the crowds of people huddled on the sidewalk and forged his way down towards Lindahl's Chevrolet Garage three blocks away.

"That was our car, wasn't it?" Mom said, panting to keep up with him.

"Yah, that's our car all right."

"What's going on?" she asked.

"That's what we're gonna' find out."

Dad's adrenaline was at an all time high as we rounded the last corner and arrived at Lindahl's Chevy garage, sweating— Mom and us kids from the rising heat of the day, Dad from his own stirred up anger. Dad didn't stop in the reception area of the garage, he just barged in through the automobile entrance, nearly sprinted down the hall, and charged into the main office. There was no one there.

"I guess he's still out riding around in our car." Dad paced up and down the room, studying the bold advertisements for the new 1949 Chevy and getting hotter by the second.

"Why hello!" A cheerful voice burst into the room. It belonged to Mr. Lindahl. I sure was glad I wasn't in his shoes.

"What can I do for you?" He thrust out his hand to Dad. "John Cederna, isn't it?"

"You got the name right." Dad ignored the extended hand, folded his arms across his chest, and delivered a double whammy. "Now let's get the rest of this situation straightened out."

"Situation?" Mr. L's smile sagged slightly, a nervous twitch catching the corner of his mouth, making it quiver.

"Yah, situation. When did my car come in?"

"Your car is on order, Mr. Cederna." Mr. L had all he could do to keep his feet planted in one spot—the rest of him was squirming like a nightcrawler yanked from its hole.

"You think you can parade all over town in my car on the Fourth of July and me not find out about it?" It looked like we weren't going to have to wait until dark for the fireworks to start.

O-oh, say can you see by the dawn's early light . . . The anthem just sort of popped into my head.

"Oh, the maroon Fleetline," Mr. L said smoothly. He was working hard to get a grip on his nerves.

"That's the one—the one with the nice white sidewall tires. That's my car and I want it."

. . . *What so proudly we hailed at the twilight's last gleaming . . .* I couldn't get the tune out of my head.

"I'm afraid there's been some mistake," Mr. L said. "That car belongs to the person ahead of you on the waiting list."

"Oh, and *who* might that be?" Mom asked. The fur was going to fly now! "You told us, *we* were the first ones on the waiting list."

"Well, actually my brother-in-law was first on the list for *that* car."

"*That* car was ordered by us back in 1947." Mom gave him a withering look.

"Yes, yes I remember you ordering your car." Mr. L was losing his bearings now and starting to sweat as much as we were.

"Like my wife said, you told us we were first in line for that car." Dad jumped back into the act.

"For *that* car—the one you ordered. This car has a radio. I'm pretty sure you didn't want a radio." Mr. L groped in his pocket for a large white hanky which he brought out, rolled into a ball and used to mop his forehead.

"Don't give me that baloney," Dad spouted.

. . . *And the rockets red glare* . . . This was better than any old fireworks display. And I had a front row view of the action.

"Now, now, I'm sure we can work this thing out. We're in the business of pleasing our customers, you know." Mr. L gave his forehead another long wipe, thrust the damp hanky back into his pants pocket, and gave us all an uneasy smile.

"That car's bought and paid for. And it's mine." Dad's voice had been steadily rising in volume. Now it dropped to a dangerously low pitch.

. . . *The bombs bursting in air* . . .

"Let me just take a peek at your order. I'm *certain* we can work this thing out." Mr. L did a little dance around his desk on his way to the file cabinet. He pulled out the middle drawer, flipped through a number of folders until he found Mom's and Dad's order, then pulled it out and studied it intently. "By gosh, you *did* order a radio, didn't you?"

. . . *Gave proof through the night that the flag was still there. . .Oh, say does that Star Spangled Banner yet wave* . . .

"I *ordered* a 1949 Chevrolet."

"You sure did and I'll tell you what I'm going to do. I'm going to call first thing tomorrow morning to find out exactly what's happening with it."

"Maybe," Dad paused for effect, "your brother-in-law should have that car after all."

"What?" Mr. L's eyes just about bugged out of their sockets.

Dad was going in for the kill. Giddy, I clamped my teeth tightly together so I wouldn't giggle. For once, it wasn't me in trouble.

"Maybe, you'd just better mail me a check." Dad smirked.

"But, Mr. Cederna—" Mr. L's hanky had magically come out of his pocket again and he was dabbing his upper lip and forehead with quick little jabs.

. . . O'er the land of the free . . .

"Maybe, I'm just gonna' take a walk down the block to see the Ford people. They had a heck of a nice car in the parade today." With that Dad tossed his head, motioning us to follow, and as he sauntered toward the door—the family traipsing behind him in single file—he looked just like the Pied Piper.

"We're *never* going to get our car, now," Mom muttered, but Dad just held his head a little higher and headed out the door.

"The car's not here right now." Mr. L tripped over his toes trying to catch up with Dad. "My brother-in-law took it out for a spin, but look, Mr. Cederna, I'll call you just as soon as I can work out the details."

"Call me at the Ford garage," Dad called over his shoulder.

. . . And the home of the brave . . .

"Just call us at home," Mom mouthed to Mr. L who gratefully acknowledged her words with a grey-faced grin.

"Johnny, you know you don't want a Ford," Mom said to Dad as we trudged up the street. "You know how you feel about Fords. You're always talking about how they don't hold up."

"Oh, don't worry. We're not getting a Ford," Dad snorted.

"You mean you were just bluffing?" Mom asked.

"Well, he was trying to bamboozle me, wasn't he?" Dad asked.

"I don't know—" Mom was trying to figure out how to save the day, but, for once, she was at a loss.

The crowd was still breaking up after the parade. Perspiring people thronged to hot cars and hot cars swarmed toward dusty roads leaving town. Everyone was heading home to pick up their sparklers, firecrackers, and picnic baskets before leaving for the local lakes to cool off.

Dodging people and cars, we hiked back to the old Model A—now hot as an oven—crawled inside, and kept our mouths shut. Had Dad played his cards right? Or was his bluff going to backfire?

"If we have to order a Ford, it's going to take forever to get it," Mom said, finally breaking the silence as we traveled home on Selden Road in the long caravan of cars creeping along and honking their horns.

"I don't think we're gonna' have to worry about that. Everything's gonna' be just hunky-dory." But Dad didn't sound nearly as convinced as he had when he was shooting the sparks at Mr. L.

"I hope you're right," Mom sighed, fingering the peeling black paint on the old Model A outside her rolled down window. Dad didn't answer.

"Last one out's a rotten egg!" I yelled as we pulled up alongside the curb outside our house.

"Beat you to the watermelon," John taunted as he vaulted out of the car three steps ahead of me.

"I'll bet I can spit my seeds farther than you can!" I yelled as he burst in the back door.

"Beat the pants off you!" he yelled back, letting the screen door thud in my face.

"Over my dead body!" He was going to have to do some really slick spitting to beat me.

"Watch out, you two. One of you is going to break a leg one of these days!" Mom cut herself short and hurried to answer the ringing phone. "Hello?" Mom said into the black receiver. "Yes, he's here. Just a moment, please. It's for you," she mouthed to Dad.

"Who is it?" he mouthed back, to which Mom gave a shrug and handed him the receiver. "Hello?" We all stood, watching and waiting, as Dad didn't get many phone calls unless he was being called to the mine on an emergency. "Today? No . . . we've got plans. Yah, for the whole day. Tonight? No . . . we've got plans for tonight, too." It couldn't be the mine calling. When the mine called, Dad dropped everything.

By now Mom was waving madly at Dad, trying to get his attention, trying to get him to tell her what was going on. Finally, Dad put his hand over the receiver and looked at her.

"Who is it? What do they want?" she asked.

"It's Mr. Lindahl himself," Dad said. "He wants us to come back down to the Garage and talk. I told him we've got plans and we're not heading back downtown now."

"Maybe he wants to give us the car." Mom was wide-eyed.

Dad turned back to the phone, took his hand off the receiver, and said, "No, we're not gonna' come back into town now. Like I said, we've got plans. We're heading out to Chicaugon Lake like everyone else in town. And when we're done there, we're gonna' to see the fireworks. We're gonna' be busy all day."

There was a short pause while Dad listened to Mr. L. "No we're not gonna' be home. We're leaving just as soon as we carve up this watermelon and the kids have their seed-spitting contest." Mom glared at Dad for making that last remark, but he didn't notice. He simply hung up the phone, drew open the kitchen utensil drawer, and pulled out the filleting knife Aunt Hannah had sent him, from Finland, for Christmas.

"I think we should go," Mom said. "I think you should call him back and tell him we'll be there in a couple of minutes. The watermelon can wait and so can the picnic. But this car business can't wait much longer."

"Look," Dad said, carefully slicing the watermelon down its middle, "I've already been to the Chevy Garage today and I'm not going back. If he wanted to talk to me, he should have done it while I was there."

"I hope you're not cutting off your nose to spite your face," Mom said, nearly causing Dad to lose his grip on the knife as he finished carving and fanning out the melon pieces.

"I'll be outside," Dad announced, rinsing the knife, drying it, and returning it to its Elk-engraved leather sheaf.

"You kids take that watermelon out in the back yard. I don't want it slopped all over the kitchen. I don't want to have to start cleaning when we could be out at the picnic."

But we were already out the door, a hunk of sweet pink melon in each hand. At the edge of the garden, we stopped, filled our mouths with pink cool juicy bites, and stored the black slippery seeds in our cheeks like chipmunks until they were filled to overflowing, then blasted them out across the rows of carrots and beans, one by one.

"No fair. You're standing over the line," I yelled at my brother. But just then I happened to look up and see a maroon Chevy, that looked an awful lot like the one in the parade, drive slowly past the front of our house. "You see that?" I asked John, wiping my face with the back of my hand.

"What?" he asked through a mouthful of seeds.

"That car." I pointed, with dripping fingers, to the street just beyond Auntie Sep's back yard.

"Geez, there's our car again." John caught sight of it just before it disappeared. "Boy, Dad's going to be mad if he finds out they're still driving around in it."

"Dad!" I yelled as loud as I could, without letting the seeds spill out of my cheeks.

"Huh?" He came to the garage door and stood looking at me questioningly.

"I think we just saw Mr. Lindahl riding past in our car," I sputtered.

"Past here? You think so?" Dad stepped out of the doorway and looked down the street. "Which way did he go?"

"Toward Caspian, I guess. We couldn't see him anymore once he passed by Auntie Sep's house," John said. "You think he was trying to rub it in that he's got our car?"

"Hard to believe he'd do a thing like that," Dad said. "Still you never know."

"There he goes again!" I nearly swallowed my seeds when I saw Mr. L in the Chevy again, traveling the same route he'd taken just two minutes before. This guy was really looking for trouble.

"Where?" Dad craned his neck to see the car, but once again it had disappeared past Auntie Sep's back yard.

Suddenly, from behind the garage flashed a glint of red-wine metal and we were dumbfounded to see the Chevy easing its way toward the old Model A parked alongside the curb.

"I don't know what this guy's trying to prove, but he's about cooked his goose," Dad muttered under his breath as he strode toward Mr. L and the sassy Chevy. "What's up?" Dad roughly placed one hand on the roof of the car above the window and leaned in toward the culprit in the driver's seat.

"Had a little trouble finding your place. Your house number really #13?" Mr. L said, trying to create a pleasant mood.

"Yah, it's house #13 all right," Dad growled to which Mr.
L gave a nervous laugh. "So what's up."

"How'd you like to spend the rest of the Fourth in your
new Chevy?" Mr. L said with a brilliant smile.

Dad jerked his hand off the roof, smoothed out his invisible hand-print, and stared down at the sparkling white
sidewall tires. It was impossible for him to conceal his excitement.

"Can't have our customers unhappy, you know!" Mr. L
said brightly.

"Or going to the Ford Garage," John chuckled in my ear.

"Think you can give me a ride back to my place" Mr. L
continued, "in your new car?"

"In my new car?" Dad was trying to be nonchalant, but he
wasn't convincing anyone that this was not a major event. "I
think we could manage that."

"Just a couple of papers to sign and you'll be all set. Won't
take but a couple of minutes."

Mom, too, had come out of the house when she heard Mr.
L drive up. She stood there beaming at him, the new car, and
us.

"A couple of minutes," she said, "I don't think that'll be a
problem." I was kind of wishing she'd rub it in about a couple
of minutes being nothing compared with a two-year wait, but
as usual Mom was letting bygones be bygones. "Go wash up
those watermelon hands," she said to us kids.

"And make it snappy," Dad said, happy as a lark. "We've
got some business to take care of."

In our own private parade, we drove Mr. L back to his
Chevy Garage, thanked him for his efforts, and headed back
home through the now empty streets, past the all but silent
mines, to a deserted Dober Location where we picked up the
picnic baskets, sparklers, and continued on our way to the
Iron County picnic at Chicaugon Lake.

With the smell of "new car" tickling our nostrils, we sailed along with a newfound sense of independence and anticipation, knowing it was a day we would long remember—a red-letter day from dawn to dusk. The afternoon's pleasures of sparklers, swimming, and the sweet smell of potato salad, like the ice of the purple popsicles my brother John purchased for my sister Connie and me at the WigWam concession window, melted away all too quickly.

Evening slipped into place and, like a jewelry peddler's treasured stash, brought with it an indigo sky inlaid with a gold crescent moon, set with silvery stars, and spattered with a carnival of colors splashing from the shooting rockets of our community's Fourth of July display.

As the flashing sprays of gem-like fireworks burst in brief brilliance over the iron mining shafts, the rolling hills, and abandoned ore pits, we wanted to reach out and catch the dazzling explosions of light before they, too, disappeared. But we could only tuck them away in our hearts as we watched—breathless—encountering both a feeling of farewell and a sense of excited anticipation. The 1940's, soon to pass with its memories of war, recovery, and rebuilding, were nearly behind us, while the promise of the 1950's lay just ahead, tempting and tantalizing in its possibilities.

We waited for over two years for the 1949 maroon Chevy!

Dad's Dream

"We're going out to Hagerman Lake to look at a couple of forties next Sunday," Dad announced one evening after work. He'd been talking about buying land on a lake and building a summer cottage for several years.

Mom and Dad were thrilled. John and Connie were thrilled. Me? I was convinced it was a plot, masterminded by the experts, to keep me away from civilization. All the action in Iron County—swimming, sun-bathing, and swooning over boys—was taking place at Pentoga Park on Chicaugon Lake or Bewabic Park on Fortune Lake. Even Sunset Lake and Ottawa Lake attracted families for swimming, boating, and picnicking. But nobody, who was "anybody," spent time at Hagerman Lake. It was practically in another state. The Wisconsin border lay only three miles down the road. If Mom and Dad bought land on Hagerman, my future was doomed.

"Let's go!" Dad hurried us out to the car and slipped smoothly behind the wheel of our beautiful new 1949 maroon Chevy. John, Connie, and I climbed into the back and Mom took her place in the front seat, sliding easily across the slick multi-colored fabric upholstery. I closed my eyes and let the scent of "new car" tickle my nose. I still couldn't believe we owned this luxurious automobile. It was great having a brand new car, yet I couldn't help noticing how mournful the old black Model A looked, sitting there empty alongside the curb, as we pulled away.

"Two families, the Vassars and the Djupes, already have cottages out there at the end of the road, but it's pretty isolated. The land is high above the water with a beautiful view and plenty far away from the public beach, so we won't be bothered by people hanging around the place," Dad said.

Far from the public beach. Of course, it would have to be. But then, what difference did it make? Nobody ever went to Hagerman Lake public beach anyway.

"Why can't we buy a place on Chicaugon Lake?" I just had to ask.

"Why can't we buy a place on Chicaugon Lake?" Dad mimicked. It really made him furious when I brought up the idea. "You know why," he said testily. "The whole point in having a cottage is get away from it all—go out into the wilderness where you can really learn about the woods. Maybe do some hunting and fishing. But the main thing is to get away from the rat-race."

I *liked* the rats—and the race, but Dad's preference was a fact of life. And it was cut in stone.

"You know how your dad hates picnicking at public beaches with all those people around," Mom reminded.

"That's right. I don't want to smell someone else's cooking when I'm out in the woods. When I'm out in the woods, I want to smell the woods," Dad snorted.

"There aren't any kids out there. There won't be anything to do," I complained. I just couldn't leave it alone.

"There'll be plenty to do out there," Dad said with finality.

Where the paved road turned left toward the public beach, we took the gravel road that forked right.

"This is a dead end road," Dad announced proudly.

"Dead end. You can say that again," I mumbled.

"You've got a lot to learn." Dad glared at me in the rear-view mirror.

We drove to the end of the road where there was a brief turnaround just above Vassar's cottage, then drove back several hundred yards.

"This is it," Dad said as he stopped the car. "Let's get out and take a look."

We all piled out of the car and stood in the middle of the road, staring. The forest leapt up around us like a thick green wall. Everywhere we looked there were sprawling trees, bristly brush, and tall billowing ferns. It appeared impenetrable. Somehow, even though I should have known better, I'd always pictured our cottage built on a neatly landscaped lawn that led easily to a sandy beach. Talk about a dreamer—Dad would never have considered owning such a place.

"C'mon," Dad encouraged, "let's walk down to the lake."

"You can't even see the lake," I said.

"Not from here. That's the beauty of it." Dad was in his glory.

He led us down the hilly pathless forest to the top of another hill, a steep hill that led finally to the lake below. There was no road, no trail, no steps—nothing but trees.

"Watch your step now," Dad said clinging to one tree at a time, lowering himself down to the brief shore of the lake.

"Be careful," Mom advised as she followed right after him, dragging my little sister Connie and trying not to gasp as her feet almost slid out from under her.

"Go ahead. If you make it, then I'll know it's okay for me to come, too," John joked.

"Very funny." I gave my brother a gruesome look and began the descent. The soft silty soil felt like grease under my shoes, but I grabbed onto the trees as I'd seen Dad do and made it down to the shore, John right on my heels.

"Look at that water." Dad's eyes glistened just like the thousands of little waves that sparkled in the sun. "See that land there?" He pointed out across the water to what appeared to be the other side of the lake. "That's an island owned by the state of Michigan. No one can build there, so we don't have to worry about that."

I sure wasn't worrying about that. What I was worrying about was the so-called beach. It was nothing but rocks, millions and millions of rocks. Large green slime-covered rocks, probably dating back to pre-historic days, I figured. How were we ever going to swim here?

"There's nothing but rocks," I complained. "How are we supposed to swim here anyway?"

"All you've got to do is pick those rocks and throw them up on shore. There'll be sand underneath," Dad said.

"I'll bet," I grumbled.

"Lookit there, lookit there, lookit there!" Dad whispered ecstatically. "There's one of the eagles Bert Djupe is always talking about. Watch it circle. Geez, it's gonna' dive right down there and pick up a fish. You kids better watch this— not too many places around here where you can see something like this. Boy, oh boy, oh boy, this place is unbelievable."

Unbelievable, that was one word for it, I thought, but I watched in awe as the eagle circled closer and closer to the water, dipped swiftly to the surface, and flew away carrying a large wriggling fish.

"You see the size of that fish?" Dad turned to John.

"Yah, we could get in some real fine fishing here, Dad," John said excitedly.

Just then a low mournful yodeling sound echoed across the water. For a moment, I felt like we were trespassing.

"What's that?" I asked.

"Ducks," Connie said, pointing to a family of black and whites swimming off across the water.

"Loons," Dad corrected, sighing from pure pleasure, "crazy old loons. They sing a song all their own—like nothing you'll ever hear anywhere in the world. Just listen to that sound. They'll tell you a story you'll never forget."

"Look—they're disappearing," Mom said.

"They're just diving under. They'll come up in another place. Just keep your eye on the water," Dad said. And sure enough, in seconds, they popped up in another area of the lake.

"Boy, this is the life." Dad was now absolutely exuberant. "Well, let's crawl back up and take a look at the other side of the road. We'll own both sides of the road, if we buy this place."

Going back up was even more difficult than coming down but, by sheer determination, we all made it up the steep embankment to the top of the first hill.

"We could put the cottage right here," Dad exclaimed. "It's a natural setting. Look how the land kind of flattens out for just a piece and then starts rising uphill again. You won't be able to see the cottage from the road and we can clear away enough trees so we can see the lake from the cottage. Look at that." Dad pointed back to the water. "That's west. We'll have the sunset every evening. When we're done working we can just sit around, relax, and look at our own private sunset."

"We'll never be done working," I grumbled to myself.

"Well, let's have a look across the road." Dad started the climb and we followed, one by one.

"This is all virgin timber," Dad boasted as he led us back past the parked Chevy, across the road, and onto the other half of the property. It was impossible to walk through the forest without getting snagged, scratched, or slapped by prickly pines, branches, and brush. And it was hot. Gigantic deer flies descended upon us like the plague. And mammoth mosquitoes. We were under attack from all sides.

"Isn't this just dandy?" Dad said gleefully.

Dandy? We were getting beaten back by the brush, bruised by branches, and eaten alive by alligator-jawed flies.

"Just dandy," Mom said brightly. The bugs weren't bothering her.

"Great for hunting," John added.

"I like it out here." Little Connie was as nuts as the rest of them.

"We'll never be able to swim with all these bugs around. And it's too hot." I was the only sane person left in the pack.

"The lake will cool you off," Dad laughed, "and the wind will blow away the bugs."

Now that was something to look forward to, I thought grumpily.

"Look," he called to me, "fungus!"

Fungus? Great. Life was really looking up. I fought my way over to where Dad had made his discovery. On the side of an ancient tree grew immense fungi, creamy white crescents with brown ridged edges that clung like clamps to the bark.

"Here." Dad broke one away from the tree, and handed it to me.

"Uh, thanks," I mumbled, taking the cool moist growth in my hands. It had a pleasant feel to it. It was solid but with a soft, spongy outer layer. Cool and moist, the smell was unique, musty and mysterious.

"You can be an artist, just like the Chippewa's," Dad said.

"What?" I asked.

"Indian art." Dad snapped off a brittle branch about the size of a pencil, took out his jackknife, and sharpened one end.

"Indian art?" This actually sounded interesting.

"You can use that fungus to write on like a piece of paper. And here's a pencil." He handed me the sharpened branch.

I took the branch and wrote my name in the soft spongy layer of the fungus. It jumped right out at me—brown, bold, and clearly defined. "Wow, it really works!" I exclaimed.

"Sure, and when it dries, you'll have a piece of art that'll last for years," Dad said. "Okay now, I want to do a little more scouting further in, so the rest of you might want to go back to the car. It could get a little rough going."

Rougher than this? I decided not to ask. I'd entertain myself with the fungus and keep my mouth shut—for a while anyway.

John grabbed a couple more fungi off the tree, sliced off a few more small branches, and led Connie and me back to the new Chevy. While Mom and Dad continued exploring, the three of us sat on an old log near the car, drawing.

Under my name, I wrote the date, July 7, 1949, and in large letters, HAGERMAN LAKE. Then, inspired with thoughts of Chippewa Indians, I drew fir trees and a deer with spidery antlers. Sepia against the creamy smooth fungus, my scratchings looked amazingly like pictures of Indian drawings I'd seen in books at school.

"Boy this is really fun," I said without thinking. I looked up quickly, hoping no one had heard me make this admission.

"Don't let Dad hear you," John teased. "If he doesn't hear you complaining, he'll think you've lost all your marbles and then we'll have to send you off to the funny farm."

"We're all gonna' end up in the funny farm if we buy this place," I shot back.

"You kids ready to go?" Dad's voice came from somewhere within the jungle of trees.

"I don't want to go yet." Connie was intently laboring over her fungus, determined to finish her drawing of an Indian teepee.

"Don't worry," Dad said, stepping out onto the road, Mom right behind him, "we'll be coming back here a lot."

I looked up at Dad and gulped. I could see my complaining wasn't going to do any good. His eyes were shining like sparkling sunbeams striking the morning dew. I could tell from the emotion in Dad's eyes, the lilt in his voice, the strength of his stance as he reverently surveyed the new domain that our lives were about to change. It was obvious what the future held.

"This place is gonna' be our second home." Dad's words danced across the gravel road, drifted through the flourishing forest, and disappeared down the hill toward the hidden lake. Dad had discovered his dream.

"Swell," I said under my breath. Dad's dream was going to be one long miserable nightmare for me. My life would consist of blazing trails through savage brush, throwing green slimy rocks onto a forgotten shore, and being devoured by demonic deer flies. My friends would forget I had ever existed. I'd probably never see the beach at Chicaugon Lake again. I was destined to die an old maid.

The Dream Unfolds

The day after our safari into the "jungle" along Hagerman Lake, Dad contacted Guy Cox, the real estate lakeside developer. I kept hoping some miracle would make Dad change his mind, but within a week we became owners of lake property.

"First thing we need is a well," Dad told Mom. "Gotta' have water out there. Guy Cox tells me there's an underground spring running through the property, but I've gotta' figure out how to find it."

"I'm sure all you have to do is dig a hole and there'll be plenty of water," Mom said cheerily. She was busy pulling dishes, pots, and pans out of the cabinets, packing them into boxes, and stashing them away for use at the lake. "We're going to need some better dishes at home. These old things will work just beautifully at the cottage. And we can always just wash them in the lake."

"Cottage?" Dad wiped some imaginary sweat off his brow with a clenched fist, but then just shook his head and managed a smile. "First, we need water for drinking."

"Of course, dear, I know that." Mom gave him a long look. "Like I said, all you have to do is dig a hole and you'll find water." She was now attacking the dishtowel drawer, folding, and packing towels and tablecloths around the dishes. "We're going to need silverware, too . . ." Mom added thoughtfully.

Dad stood watching her, dumbfounded. I thought he was going to blow his top, but he didn't. He was too enamored of his new dream and realized Mom was just as excited as he was—even if she was a little ahead of the game.

One evening after work, Dad came home from the mine, laughing.

"The Finlander says he can tell me exactly where to dig my well," Dad told Mom—tongue in cheek. "He's crazier than a hoot, but I told him to come on out and see the new property, give it a try."

"Give what a try," Mom asked curiously.

"His water-witching stick." I thought Dad was going to keel over with laughter. "Bill Lahti said he can take a willow stick, go witching with it, and it'll tell him right where I should dig. Says it works every time."

"Now don't go making fun of him." Mom, always trying to set a good example for us kids, bit her lip to keep from giggling.

"Boy, I've got to see this," I said, conjuring up a colorful image of what I imagined water-witching looked like.

"Johnny," Mom said to Dad, "why don't we invite Bill and Lena out to the lake for dinner. They can be our first guests. I'll make pasties and we can have a picnic. Won't that be fun? I'll call Lena tomorrow."

"It'll be fun to see the Finlander do his water-witching, that's for sure," Dad said gleefully.

"Good, then it's set," Mom said. "I'll see if they can come after work some night this week." She was already pulling out pans and checking her flour supply.

"Boy, I can't wait to see this," I said.

Mom called Lena and she said they could come Thursday, two days away. I could hardly wait. On Thursday, I hung around the kitchen, keeping an eye on the clock and watching Mom whip up the pasties. Mom rolled out several rounds of dough and made a pile of ground meat, diced potatoes, onions, and some finely chopped carrots on one half of each round.

She sprinkled salt and pepper and a few dabs of butter on top of each pile of stuffing, pulled the empty half of the round over the mixture, and crimped the edges. Then she slapped the crescent-shaped pasties onto a cookie sheet and popped them into the oven.

At four o'clock Dad came home from work and Mom, Connie, and I were ready to head for the lake with the picnic supper.

Lena and Bill followed us out to the lake and we all climbed down through the brush, ferns, and trees to the proposed cottage site. Dad had already started working the land. He had uprooted the trees growing in the middle of the site, yanked them out with his pick and shovel, and set a few stakes in the ground.

He'd brought an old wooden cable home from the mine which, set on its side, made a perfect picnic table. For chairs, he sawed one of the large uprooted trees into sections that were just the right height and width for stools.

"You're gonna' have a pretty nice place here, Johnny," Bill said. "All you need now is some good drinking water. You got any willows around here?"

"Up over the hill," Dad said. "C'mon, I'll show you."

"Gotta' pick out a good sturdy willow with a perfect fork in it," Bill, the water-witching authority, pointed out and away they went.

Mom and Lena gabbed about Aunt Rosie and Uncle Toivo, and other mutual relatives and friends, while they set a white tablecloth decorated with wildly feathered red roosters on the cable-table. They set out white rose-rimmed plates, old silverware, and plain white paper napkins. Then came bottles of Orange Crush and a bottle of beer for Bill.

"I've got coffee in a thermos and date bars for dessert," Mom said, placing a large bottle of ketchup in the middle of the table, "so as soon as the men get back, we can eat."

In just a few minutes, Dad and Bill returned. Bill carried in his hands a forked willow branch, the perfect water-witching rod. He was beaming. "My dad showed me how to find water when I was just a kid," Bill said nostalgically, "and I've been doing it ever since. Want to get started now?"

Mom gave Dad a meaningful look that said, "It's time to eat."

"Looks like the food's ready," Dad said, nodding at Mom. "Let's have some chow first."

"Sure, I don't want to get you into trouble with the boss." Bill gave a big hearty laugh as the two men plunked themselves down on the log stools in front of the red-roostered tablecloth.

Mom, Lena, Connie, and I perched on our logs and Mom served up the pasties, still hot from the oven at home. I took a bite of mine and was amazed at how scrumptious it tasted. Was it my imagination, or was the crust actually lighter, the potatoes, meat, and onions tastier, the ketchup tangier than it had ever been at home?

"Boy these pasties sure are great," I exclaimed, looking up at Mom just in time to catch her and Dad sneaking each other a quick smile. The thrill they felt at entertaining their first guests at the lake was contagious. I felt myself puff up with pride. This, after all, was my place, too.

We made quick work of the pasties, guzzled our Orange Crushes, and Bill polished off his bottle of beer.

"Can't beat those pasties—taste twice as good out in the wilds, hey?" Bill patted his blue coveralled belly with pleasure, politely tipped his blue and white striped cap at Mom, and grabbed his willow stick. "C'mon Johnny, we gotta' get down to business, right now."

"Okay," Dad agreed, following Bill and his willow to the clearing in back of the stakes. I turned on my log to watch the show.

"Okay, okay," Bill said nervous with excitement, "you gotta' hold this thing just right or it won't work." He grasped the two forks of the willow in his thick paw-like hands so that the stem stuck straight out in front of him. "See how I hold this?" Bill looked right into Dad's face to make sure he was paying attention. "Tight. You gotta' keep the witchin' stick taut, but you can't hold it so tight that you force it up or down. When the stick finds the water it'll let you know."

"Uh huh." Dad had willed himself to hold a serious expression, but it was pretty hard for him to hide his skepticism.

"Nothin' here," Bill said. "We'd better go up the hill a ways." They started up the hill and I followed. Bill kept walking slowly back and forth across the hill but the stick just stayed taut. "Boy, oh boy, Johnny, you might have a problem here," he said shaking his head.

"Well, maybe I'm just gonna' have to dig a hole. There's gotta' be water down there somewhere with the lake so close," Dad said.

"Let's go back down by the stakes," Bill instructed. "Maybe that's where your water is. Maybe you're gonna' have to figure out another place to build your cottage."

Dad's skepticism was quickly turning into impatience. He'd already had enough of this water-witching stuff and he wasn't changing his building site for any reason.

"Can I try it?" I asked.

"I suppose you think *you* can find water," Dad snorted.

"I just want to try it," I replied stubbornly.

But Bill wasn't ready to give up his willow stick. He was walking back to the table—slowly. Deer flies were dive-bombing his head, but he kept his hands firmly on the stick. This was a man filled with determination.

Dad and I glanced at each other, wondering where all this was going to lead, when suddenly the tip of Bill's willow started to bob up and down. The closer to the table he got the faster and harder the willow's stem bobbed. It was fascinating.

"He's making it do that," Dad whispered to me.

"Move that table!" Bill shouted to Mom and Lena.

Mom, Lena, and little Connie jumped up from their logs, grabbed the side of the cable, and tugged with all their might, pulling the cable away from the bobbing willow and making the Orange Crush bottles, the ketchup, and the dishes dance.

"This is it!" Bill, grinning from ear-to-ear, his hands white-knuckled with exertion, and the willow dipping like a dizzy duck, stopped right where the cable had been. "Hey, Johnny! Here's your water!" Bill yelled, finally letting go of his grasp on the willow stick.

"Now, can I try it?" I asked, impatient to see if it was just a hoax or if the willow really did bob on its own.

"Okay." Bill was reluctant to give up his crowd-pleasing trick-stick. "Here's how you hold it." He started to show me, but I'd been watching him like a hawk. I knew exactly how to hold it.

"Like this?" I grabbed the forks of the willow so the stem pointed straight out in front of me. Then, I carefully turned my closed fists outward to keep the branch taut and walked slowly in the opposite direction. I wanted to follow the same path Bill had traveled just to see if the stick would work for me, too.

"You got a good hold on it?" Bill called after me.

"Sure," I hollered back.

Nothing was happening. Just like Dad, I was convinced the whole show was a spoof. I turned around and inched my way back toward the spot where the table had stood. And, suddenly, the stick went wild, bobbing and dipping just as it had for Bill. It had a mind of its own and was tug-tug-tugging down on my hands and wrists.

"It works! It really works!" I yelled to Dad who stood watching, arms folded—amused. "Try it, Dad," I squealed. "It really works!"

"No, that's okay." Dad shook his head. He had no intention of digging a well where the table belonged.

"Gosh! This is really something!" I handed the water-witching willow back to Bill.

"Yah, never fails." Bill chuckled like a chipmunk. "But I don't think your Dad's convinced. Johnny, I tell you, that's where you gotta' dig your well."

"We'll see . . ." Dad said. But he wasn't laughing anymore. He was stroking his chin and staring at Bill, me, and the empty spot where the cable had served us as a dinner table. I'd never seen Dad look so puzzled. Then he strode over to the cable, grasped the top, and pulled. "Let's get this back in place, hey!" he demanded.

On Saturday, Dad was packing the old Model A with tools when I rode into the yard on the old blue Zenith bike.

"What are you up to?" Dad called.

"Nothing—just practicing riding with no hands." I hit the brakes, dropped my feet to the ground, and leaned over the handlebars.

"How about you take a ride out to the lake with me?" he asked.

"Oh, I don't know . . ." I didn't really feel like going out *there*.

"Oh c'mon," Dad urged. "You got anything better to do?"

"I guess not. I've got a new mystery book from the library I was going to read." I knew Dad wouldn't like this, but I did NOT want to go.

"So take it along. You can read out at the lake same as you can read here, you know," Dad chuckled.

"Yah, I guess." There was no arguing with that logic. "I'll get my book and be ready in a flash," I said, letting my beat-up bike clank to the ground.

Armed with a jug of water and saltines for snacks, Dad and I pulled out of Dober Location and sped, in the "old clunker," as Dad now called the Model A, out to Hagerman Lake.

When we got there, I scooted out of the Model A, skipped over the stakes, and skidded down the hill to the shore, my mystery book quickly forgotten. Pulling off my shoes and socks and rolling my jean legs as high as they would go, I wiggled my toes in the water and decided to brave the rocky beach. The cold clear water lapped at my ankles, tickling my knees and spraying the cuffs of my jeans. The slippery rocks were hard under my feet, but as a soft cool wind swept my face, I giggled with sheer delight.

"Guess I might as well get started," I told myself as I reached into the water, scooped up several large rocks, and pitched them on shore. Up on the hill I could hear Dad sawing and pounding purposefully, while somewhere in the forest a woodpecker hammered happily away. Just off shore, I heard the low cry of the loons and turned to see a whole family sail slowly by. There was nothing like this at Chicaugon Lake, I thought as I pitched one scoop of rocks after another out of the lake.

"Can you come up here for a second?" Dad hollered down to me.

I scrambled out of the lake, slipped my wet feet into my shoes, and high-tailed it up the slick side of the hill.

"Give me a hand with this cable," Dad barked. "Gotta' get it out of the way."

"Out of the way of what?" I asked, pushing the cable-table toward Dad as he pulled, maneuvering it away from its original spot.

"The well, of course." Dad looked at me and laughed like I was some kind of a half-wit. "This is where I've gotta' dig the well. This is where the water is."

"Right," I replied, resisting the temptation to remind Dad that he'd said he didn't believe in the Finlander and his water-witching stick . . .

We thought Dad was going to kill himself that first summer. When he wasn't working one of three rotating shifts in the mine, he was working at Hagerman Lake. All he did was work.

He dug the well by hand, beginning with a shovel, digging a hole just large enough for him and his ladder—which he constantly elongated—to descend into the depths of the earth. When he completely disappeared below the surface of the land, I came over to the hole and looked down at the top of his head—worried.

"Aren't you scared you won't be able to get out of there?" I asked.

"Hmph. You gotta' do what you gotta' do to get the job done," Dad answered, his voice muffled by the wall of earth encircling him.

Using a small scoop attached to a rope which he painstakingly filled with the last spoonfuls of soil before reaching water, he finally finished digging. Then, at last, he ran the lines for the pump. And we had cool crystal clear water for drinking.

After the well was done, there were a million more projects to do before he could start building the cottage and he planned to do them all himself. Where the other new buyers on the lake hired a bulldozer to come in and blaze out a road, Dad decided to take each tree down himself—by hand. Everyone, including his closest cronies, thought he was crazy, but Dad stuck to his guns.

"No sense pulling down every tree in sight. I'm just gonna' take down a few necessary trees. Bringing in a bulldozer to tear up the land is just plain crazy. Ever seen the mess they make? When I'm done, you won't even be able to tell we're missing a couple of trees. We'll just have a good usable road so we can get in and out," Dad said firmly.

"Ready to go?" Dad asked almost every day. I no longer asked where—there was only one place we went anymore.

"Let me grab my bathing suit," I'd say and off we'd go.

While Dad was working on his road project, I'd pull on my bathing suit, grit my teeth against the cold and slime, and wade into the lake. Sliding and stubbing my toes on the slippery rocks, I was determined to get down to the sand Dad had promised was there.

From where I worked, I could see the eagles' tree-top nest far away on the big island. Often, I'd see the eagles circling the lake—fishing. I'd stop my rock picking and watch in fascination. I began to feel a kind of proud ownership in the eagles. They were *my* birds, on *my* lake.

And the loons swimming out from the islands, singing their tribute to the day, thrilled me with each new greeting. I copied their calls as best I could and attempted to commiserate with them. It must have been obvious to the black and white birds that I was no threat to them, for they continued to swim close to shore—curious to get a look at the new kid on the lake.

The days flew by like greased lightning. Dad and brother John struggled with trees while I wriggled my fingers under rocks, loosened, and hefted them out of the water. On Sundays, Mom cooked dinner and toted it in the car to the lake where we all sat around the newly positioned cable-table and shared time.

"Let's go to Wisconsin!" I begged when it was time to leave for home. The novelty of living only a few miles from the Wisconsin border and being able to travel there in just a few minutes was tantalizing.

"Yah, let's go home through Wisconsin," John and Connie chimed in.

"And stop in Nelma for ice cream cones," Mom said.

"I suppose we can do that," Dad laughed.

Our roundabout trip home through Wisconsin was the highlight of the day. In Nelma, which lay just three miles west on M-73, we stopped for bottles of Coca-Cola, Oh Henry candy bars, or double-dip chocolate ice cream cones. Savoring our treats, studying the countryside, and watching for wildlife, we ambled south on M-73 through Alvin, turned east to pick up M-139, then north through Tipler back to Michigan and Dober Location.

"This is the life." Dad shook his head as if he were afraid he'd been dreaming. And when he was sure he wasn't, he repeated, "This is the life. Almost too good to be true."

Sitting in the back seat of the car, next to the warmth of my little sister Connie, licking my cone, and watching the world go by, I begin to see he was right. I wasn't going to *tell* him that—just in case I changed my mind—but there was no denying the happiness I felt.

When autumn arrived, Dad and I drove out to the lake every evening after work and school. We'd drive slowly out to Hagerman, watching for birds. Night came quickly to the forest in the fall so there was little time to accomplish much, but we always managed to complete some small project. Dad's dream was beginning to unfold.

Dad had been dreaming of building a cottage on Hagerman
Lake for years.

Lullaby of the Loon

When the first snows of winter stormed across Iron County, swept the lakeside, then swirled and whistled through the forest spreading sprawling drifts over the cottage site, Dad took pencil and paper, disappeared into the basement at home, and drew up a floor plan for the cottage. He designed a kitchen with a large picture window overlooking the lake, a generous living room with a fireplace and three more picture windows, and bedrooms with built-in bunks—full-size—so there would be plenty of room when my sister Corinne and her family arrived for summer visits from Chicago.

The road still passable, he drove to the lake, and walked— plunging purposefully on snowshoes through plush mounds of white to the back of his forty. Eyeing a few select pines he would use for building, he sawed them down, loaded them into a homemade trailer he'd concocted for just that purpose, and brought them to the sawmill to be cut to his specifications.

While Dad took care of business at the sawmill, I waited in the car, rolled down my window, sniffed the sweet scent of sawdust unfurling through the icy air like an alluring French perfume, and listened to the blades twist, grind, and whine as they turned out smooth slick slabs of lumber.

When Dad had done all he could, except wait for spring to return, he decided to try his hand at ice fishing. He built a black tar-paper shanty large enough for four people. From a pal at the mine, he got the name of an old Indian in Watersmeet who carved and painted rapalas, life-size wooden lures for attracting Northern Pikes, drove sixty miles round-

trip to put in his special order, and drove back again two
weeks later to pick it up.

"You want to go ice fishing?" Dad asked, one Sunday in
January.

"I was planning to go ice skating," I answered, anxious to
get to the rink at the Stambaugh Recreation Center and meet
my friends.

"Well, what makes you think you can't skate at the lake?"
Dad asked. "You could have the biggest ice rink in the county.
All you gotta' do is take a shovel and clear it off."

"Really?" I could easily visualize Hagerman Lake as one
gigantic ice rink. All I had to do was run the shovel back and
forth a few times. I could see myself gliding gloriously across
the ice, pushing Dad' snow shovel, and effortlessly whisking
away dusty white snow. It sounded simple. And fun. I skated
at the regular rink every day. This would be something new
and exciting. "Okay!" I said, bundling up in my black wool
snowpants, black and white plaid wool jacket, and red fringed
"babushka."

While Dad worked at cutting a large square fishing hole in
the foot-thick ice and getting his shanty situated and stabilized,
I put on my sister Corinne's hand-me-down white figure
skates, grabbed the shovel, and made a path several yards long
through the snow to the ice. But it wasn't as easy as I'd
thought it would be. The foot-deep snow was heavy and hard
to move. Back and forth I went, struggling to push the snow
out of the way, but when my leg muscles started to lock and
sweat begin to roll off my forehead, I stopped to consider
what I'd accomplished. Not much! The lake was gigantic. In
comparison, my rink looked like a three-cent postage stamp. I
looked over toward Dad, now sequestered in his shack, and
wrinkled my nose. It wasn't hard to figure out that I'd been
duped again. While my girlfriends were in town practicing
figure eight's on slick new ice, playing tag with the boys, and

squealing above the loudspeakers, here I was at Hagerman Lake.

Just then a loud blasting boom exploded across the lake, shattering the silence. I felt the ice under me shift and my insides tremble. Dad flipped open the flap on the shanty and bailed out like a paratrooper.

"Geez, what was that?" I yelled, scared.

"You hear that crack?" Dad yelled back.

"No kidding! What the heck was it anyway? I've never heard anything like it in my life," I hollered.

"Just the ice shifting and cracking, I guess," Dad answered after a moment's hesitation. "All this open space makes everything echo and sound twice as loud." He stood next to his shanty, stretched his arms, and looked out across the great white lake, once again quiet and calm.

"You sure this ice is safe?" I asked skeptically.

"This ice is over a foot and a half thick! You see me trying to cut through for a fishing hole?" Dad threw back his head and roared with laughter.

"Sure," I sulked. I'd been hoodwinked into coming out to Hagerman again. Now, I was getting teased and I didn't like it.

"So how's the ice rink coming?" Dad was still chuckling as he walked over to take a look.

"Okay, I guess—pretty slow going," I answered.

"Well, you got a good start," Dad said. "You keep coming back every weekend and you can make it a little bigger each time." He grabbed the shovel and made several wide sweeps, easily widening my little rink. Then he stuck the shovel in a snow bank. "There, now you've got some room to skate."

In just a few minutes he'd opened the rink up for some real skating. I slid ecstatically over the ice, turned, and skated backwards dreamily looking off across the lake, imagining every flake of snow had been shoveled away, and that I was costumed in a bright apple red flared skating dress, whirling, waltzing, gliding with grandeur across the great expanse of Hagerman Lake accompanied by a thousand strings sweetly singing Strauss' *Tales of the Vienna Woods.*

"Thanks!" I waved at Dad as he climbed back into the shanty. Dipping and dancing in duet with the soothing serenade, I hummed the romantic tune, lost in my winter wonderland . . .

When spring rolled around, Dad completed the road and was able to drive the Model A and trailer down to the cottage site. He hauled his lumber and stacked it, ready for use. He bought brick for the fireplace and neatly stacked it, too.

"We've got to have a bathroom out there," Mom demanded. "I don't care what else has to be done, the next project has got to be a 'place to go!'"

Dad didn't argue. He just got out his digging equipment again. Before long, we had a outhouse, complete with a fancy homemade knotty pine seat. The new wood smelled fresh and aromatic. It seemed there was nothing to complain about until a gigantic black furry-legged spider startled me half to death one day.

"He was as big as my fist," I yelled to Dad. "I'm not going in there any more!"

"Don't be silly," Mom said.

"I'm not being silly," I griped.

"Don't worry about it," Dad said. "If you don't bother the spiders, they won't bother you."

"Just close your eyes," Mom added. "Don't look and you won't have to be afraid." Now there was some sound advice.

I came up with my own solution to the problem by leaving a flashlight in the outhouse, flicking it on upon arrival, and flashing it into every nook and cranny until I could make my departure.

Dad borrowed a cement mixer and he, John, and a couple of buddies poured a concrete slab for the foundation of the cottage. Then, Dad began, in earnest, to build the home of his dreams. When I wasn't in the water pitching rocks, I ran errands, fetching water, toting tools, and dragging scraps of wood out of the way.

"Dad!" I scrambled half-way up the hill from the shore. "The loons are back! Hurry!"

Dad was in the middle of framing in the cottage, but he stopped pounding, walked quickly and quietly to the top of the hill, and looked down. The loons had come unusually close to shore.

"Quite the singers, aren't they?" Dad chuckled.

"Uh huh," I smiled, letting the thrilling sound of their call rinse my soul like a rapturous rain.

I had to admit Hagerman Lake was a lot better than I'd thought it would be, but I still missed spending time at the beach with my pals. I decided to ask Mom what she thought.

"I'd really like to go to Chicaugon Lake, but I don't want Dad to feel bad," I said. "Hagerman's okay, but I miss my friends."

"Well, why don't you ask Dad if you can bring your friends to Hagerman to swim?" Mom suggested.

"You think he'd let me?" I asked.

"I don't see why not, but you'd better talk to him about that. He's got a lot of projects going on right now and may not want to have a lot of kids around while he's trying to get things done," Mom continued. "But, go ahead and ask him. The worst thing that can happen is he'll say, 'No.'"

Actually, the worst thing that happened is that he said, "Yes." I invited two of my best friends out to spend the day at the lake. I *told* them the beach wasn't sandy, that there weren't any steps down to the lake, and that there wasn't any grass to lie on and sunbathe. But they didn't listen. From the time we got there, until the time we left, all they did was complain.

"There's no sand!" Judy stuck one toe in the cold water and started whining. "How can you stand it out here? All those slimy rocks!"

"It's not so bad once you get in," I told her. "It used to be a lot worse. You can see from the shore, I've pulled hundreds of rocks out. My dad says there's sand underneath."

"I wouldn't bet on it," she grumbled, grimacing as she finally plopped the other foot into the water and began to wade out further. "Egads! There are bugs all over this place!"

"Once you get in the water, they don't bother you much and there's usually a breeze that just blows them away," I said, trying to be patient.

"I think I'll just skip the water for now and lay in the sun. Where do you sunbathe?" Diane asked, flicking her towel at a deer fly.

"I don't lay in the sun out here. There isn't any sun out here—I mean, the trees are in the way. But my Dad is going to clear the shore and plant grass so we can put our towels down and lie there," I explained. "It's going to be sensational."

"There's nowhere to lie in the sun?" Diane asked in disbelief, totally missing everything else I'd said.

"C'mon, let's just get in the water and swim," I urged.

We finally did spend the afternoon swimming. After a while they adjusted—somewhat—to the rocky beach, the bugs, and shadowing trees, but it was obvious they had no idea how hard I'd worked to clear the rocks off the beach. It wasn't half as bad now as it had been when I'd started. They had no appreciation, or interest, in the forest, the lake, or all our hard work. And when I pointed out how swell it was that the place was on a dead-end road and isolated—we even had islands, eagles, and loons—they just stared at me strangely.

The cottage began to take the shape of a beautiful summer home, the picture windows granting a spectacular view of the lake. The entire interior was finished in knotty pine and Dad artistically designed a scalloped trim that bordered the ceilings in each room.

When Dad built the fireplace, I asked if I could bury treasure between the inner bricks just as Nancy Drew had done in a recent mystery book. He thought it was a great idea, so I sat down the evening before and wrote a brief history of our life at the lake. I wrapped the papers and some old cracker jack charms in a lavender felt tie-string purse, dropped it into the designated spot, and Dad covered it over with brick and mortar.

"Someday, someone will find this," I told Dad, "and they'll know all about us."

"You might be two hundred years old by then," Dad joked.

"Yah, I know, but the important thing is that I did it—left some history behind," I insisted.

Another winter came and went, spring passed, and the glow of summer was upon us again.

"We need a boat," I told Dad, repeatedly.

"Yah, we really need a boat, Dad," John agreed.

"You don't need a boat right now," Dad told us. "There's plenty to do out at the lake besides go riding in a boat."

"We *need* a boat," John and I persisted.

"Okay, okay, I can see you kids aren't gonna' be satisfied until you have that boat," Dad said, finally giving in to the pressure.

The next Sunday we all packed into the car, drove to Florence, Wisconsin, and then on to Iron Mountain, Michigan where we bought a robin's egg blue rowboat with long wooden paddles. We took it out to Hagerman Lake the same evening, piled in the whole family, and went for a boat ride. Finally, we could explore the area. We rowed along the shore down near Djupe's cottage and worked our way in and around the tiny islands there.

"Listen to all those frogs," Mom said.

There must be a billion of them, I thought. It was dusk and the frogs were croaking away.

"Shh . . ." Dad warned. "Look over there."

Just off shore, in about a foot of water, stood a huge buck, drinking. John stopped rowing, silently hooked the tips of the oars over the edges of the back seat, and let the boat drift. The buck didn't seem to see us and slipped into the water.

"He's swimming!" I whispered in astonishment.

Dad gave me a glaring look that said, "Be quiet," and I held my tongue, while we watched the deer swim slowly across the small bay where he turned, gave us a momentary glance, and ambled slowly into the forest.

"Sure am glad we got this boat," Dad said. John and I gave each other a knowing look but didn't say a word.

It was a perfect evening. When we returned to shore with the wonderful new boat, the whole family decided to take a quick swim. As soon as we got into the lake, Mom and I dived in to get used to the water. Then, as we watched Dad and John cautiously dipping their toes, shivering from the first contact with the water, and trying to adjust to the temperature, we were overcome by the irresistible urge to shower them with icy water. Squealing and giggling, we sent wild splashes of water spiraling over them until they were soaked. We tried to make our getaway, but too late. They caught us, stole our rubber bathing caps, and dunked us under the water.

"You're getting my hair wet," I shrieked.

"Too bad," they hollered. It was their turn to laugh. "Now we're the bathing beauties!" They each put on a bathing cap and jumped up on shore.

"You look like a couple of idiots," I yelled.

Mom, her hair dripping wet and laughing hysterically, leapt out of the lake and ran for her camera.

"Smile!" she shouted and snapped a picture just as Connie decided to get into the act, strike a silly pose, and stick out her tongue . . .

Dad built wide wooden steps, with railings, down to the lake. It was hard to believe that we'd ever made it up and down so many times without them.

Then, he built a retaining wall along the shoreline, using thick timbers to shore up the thousands of rocks we'd pitched on shore. He built it high and wide enough so we still had plenty of room to keep adding more rocks. Eventually he'd fill it in with soil and plant grass.

Next, he designed a boathouse at the end of the retaining wall. It had a little door that swung upward on a chain and pulley. Dad showed me how to unlock it, push the boat out when I wanted to go rowing, and pull it back in when I was done.

The boat opened a whole new world to me. Whenever I didn't have to help Dad with a project, I'd pull out that robin's egg blue boat and row away to the islands. Here amidst the pink petaled water lilies, I'd sit and listen to the call of the loons, the croaking of the frogs, the slapping sound of the water against the boat. Breathing the cool moist rocky smell of the lake, I wondered why I had once complained so much about the place . . .

I pulled the boat up into the boathouse, thrust down the door, and snapped the lock shut. Then I walked back along the rocky shore to the bottom of the steps.

I stood alone on the shore of Hagerman Lake, looking off past the gently rippling waves toward the large island. The morning was overcast and still. Listening to the almost silent sounds of the lake and forest, I thought about life and love and miracles—dreaming of the past, the future, and far away places. Someday my world would change and broaden—I would be far from this quiet peaceful place. I yearned for that time to come, yet my heart held fast to the lovely lake.

A low mournful loyal call beckoned from the small island bay, bringing me back to my surroundings. The longing lullaby of the loons rose up from their hidden nesting place, echoed across the waters, and touched me. I felt a oneness with the bird and its mystically melodious song. I knew no matter where I went in life I would carry with me this song, the scent of the lake, the spirituality of the forest—for here would always lie my roots—my soul.

"Ready to go?" Dad called from up on the hill.

"In a minute," I called back, lingering, not wanting to leave.

"Gotta' head for home early today," Dad said.

"Okay," I turned and slowly climbed the steps.

"Kind of dragging your feet there today," Dad remarked, a smile in his eyes.

I nodded in answer.

Dad had already packed away his tools. He was due to work the afternoon shift. We got into the Model A and clamored up Dad's winding road. Neither of us said a word as we drove out to the main road.

"Kind of quiet today, hey?" Dad said suddenly.

"Uh huh," I answered. I guessed he meant me and the lake.

"Maybe you'd like to bring along a pal with you tomorrow?" Dad suggested after a thoughtful silence.

I thought about it a minute. But I could hear them complaining about the deer flies, the beach, the rocks.

"No," I answered, "I'm going to take the boat out tomorrow and row over to the small islands in the bay where the pink and yellow water lilies grow. They should be in full bloom by now and maybe the turtles will be out sunning. There must have been a million of them out on the lily pads last year at this same time . . . and, who knows, maybe I'll even spy the loon's nest—this year."

"Okay," Dad said doubtfully, "if you're sure."

"Yes, I'm sure," I answered without hesitation. Somewhere along the way, I'd forgotten about how important being at Chicaugon and Fortune Lakes had been. I still went there once in a while with my friends, ogled boys, and had a good time. But things had somehow changed.

Dad smiled to himself as we drove home in silence, each of us wrapped in our separate dreams—the lullaby of the loon lilting in our hearts.

Brother John, Dad, and Connie cutting up at Hagerman Lake.

Mom's Dream

"Let's go, or we'll be late." Dad paced the kitchen floor, waiting for Corinne, John, and me to get ready to leave for church. What Dad meant by late was being less than a half hour early for Mass at St. Agnes Parish in Iron River. We were never late.

As a child, Mom had been raised in the Finnish Lutheran Church in Copper Country, but as an adult, she'd been so busy with us kids she hadn't gotten around to joining the church in Stambaugh. When Dad and we kids, all Catholics, started off to regular Sunday Mass, no one thought to ask Mom if she'd like to go, too. After all she "belonged" with the Finnish people at the Finnish Lutheran Church. Didn't she?

"See you later," I called to Mom and little Connie as I hurried out the back door, patting the ermine tails on my white rabbit fur hat before pushing my hands into my matching fur muff.

"Keep your coats buttoned. It's freezing cold out there," Mom called after us.

The Sunday ritual had begun. While Dad and the three of us kids went off to kneel on padded pine planks to pray, Mom knelt on the kitchen floor with pail and brush to scrub. While we sat stiffly in upright wooden pews, gathering food for our souls, Mom peeled potatoes, stuffed the chicken, and baked bread, peas, and brown gravy for a big Sunday noon spread. By the time we heard the homily, picked up the Milwaukee Sentinel Sunday "funnies," and returned home bursting hungrily through the back door, the kitchen was spotless while pots and pans simmered and swelled with fare for our family feast.

Ravenous for mashed potatoes and gravy, none of us noticed the hunger in Mom's eyes.

"How was it?" Mom asked excitedly.

"About the same as usual," Dad said absentmindedly.

"What was the sermon about today?" Mom persisted.

"Money." Dad snorted irreverently. "He said we should all support the weekly Bingo games at the parish."

"And there's a big drive on to send money to the missions," John said.

"Yah, to the missionaries who work in the jungles," I piped up, proud to show I'd been paying close attention to the sermon. "He also talked about leopards!" I found the bible passages about leopards fascinating.

"Lepers—not leopards—geez, what a dope," John giggled. "Don't you know anything?"

"I know what I heard." I scowled. I could feel my face turning bright red, as I suddenly became aware of my mistake.

"All right, you two, you just came from church," Mom admonished. She turned to Corinne. "What did you sing?"

"We sang the same old hymns, *Oh Lord I Am Not Worthy*, *Holy God We Praise Thy Name*, and someone in the choir sang a solo, *Ave Maria,* at offertory," Corinne replied politely.

"Yah, John's girlfriend played the organ and he kept looking at her all through Mass." I gave my brother a sly look.

"Oh, for crying out loud! What a brat! She's not my girlfriend," John snapped.

"You could have fooled me," I snickered, sneaking behind Mom's back to stick my tongue out at him. Now I was satisfied. I'd paid him back for that lousy leper crack.

"You didn't miss a thing," Corinne told Mom. "It was just the same old Sunday stuff."

"Oh," Mom said disappointedly.

"We saw your chum, Marguerite DeRocher," Dad said, referring to Mom's best friend from high school. "She said to tell you, 'Hi.'"

"You saw Marguerite . . . oh, I wish I'd been there!" Mom said, now even more disappointed. Mom seemed to think going to church was some big deal. Every Sunday she'd meet us at the door with all those questions.

"Let's eat," Dad said, putting an end to the questions, never for a second realizing Mom was forming a dream—a dream built on wishes—wishes that were as yet only silent puzzling prayers.

Then one Sunday, our lives changed. Totally.

Dad paced the kitchen floor, smoking his last cigarette before church. John stood around in his neatly pressed brown pants, white shirt, and tan jacket. Corinne and I raced from one mirror to another, getting our clothes and hair just right.

"Everybody ready?" Dad yelled, giving John an all-knowing male glance.

"We're ready," Corinne and I gasped as we bolted into the kitchen in our freshly ironed dresses and good coats.

"Ready," Mom said, stepping into the kitchen. We turned in unison to stare at her. Smiling, she held Connie by the hand. Connie was all dressed up in a new blue dress, coat, and hat and Mom looked like she'd just stepped out of one of the pages of the Alden's catalog. She was dressed to the hilt in a new bright red plaid dress, black suede shoes, and her short dyed grey muskrat coat. To top it all off, she wore a classy wide-brimmed black felt hat with two exotic striped feathers that looked like they were growing right out of the hat band. She looked sensational.

"You're coming to church with us?" I asked in astonishment.

From under the brim of her new bonnet, her laughing blue-green Finnish eyes danced with delight. "I just have to turn the burners off on the stove." Still clutching Connie's hand, she marched over to the stove, gave each pot of steaming food one last swift stir, and sent the lids jangling back into place.

"Well, let's go." Dad may have been in shock, but he wasn't going to let that make us late. The rest of us just stood there tongue-tied. The Finnish lady was going to the Catholic church and she wasn't even going to do it unobtrusively.

Once we arrived at St. Agnes church, Dad led us upstairs to the choir loft where we always sat. We filed into "our" pew and knelt down to pray. I tried to concentrate, but kept sneaking looks at Mom and Dad. I wondered what they were thinking. Dad, his Italian profile appropriately austere, was concentrating intently on the center altar, focusing all his energy on that one particular place. His eyes never wavered.

Mom's eyes darted curiously from one thing to another, taking in the majesty of gold encrusted crystal chandeliers hanging heavily on thick black chains from the cathedral ceiling; the lustrous rays of light that poured through spellbinding stained-glassed windows grandly portraying the figures of St. Peter and the other apostles; the painted pastel statues of the Blessed Virgin Mary, St. Joseph, the adopted father of Jesus, St. Francis of Assisi, the animal lover, and St. Theresa, the "Little Flower"; and the artfully painted ornate red and gold embellishments symmetrically adorning and enhancing each detailed crevice and corner of the cream-colored plaster walls.

I followed Mom's gaze down the red carpeted central aisle of the church, to the walls just above the pews where the mysteries of the Stations of the Cross were swathed in vibrant color and captured inside rugged oak frames, and to the people who one by one entered, genuflected toward the altar, then seated themselves in one of the massive pine pews. Mom studied each new person with interest, until her eyes were drawn to the crucifix above the central altar laden with tall white candles set in gleaming gold candlesticks, and came to rest on the figure of Jesus. She stared silently for a moment, then clasped her hands, and closed her eyes. Her lips moved silently in prayer.

With an introduction, regal and resonant, the organist brought the massive organ to life and us to our feet. As the choir began to sing, *On This Day, Oh Beautiful Mother*, I grabbed a black *St. Basil's Hymnal* and followed the words. Mom looked over my shoulder and hummed softly along with the choir.

The following Sunday, it was announced that because there was not enough room at St. Agnes Parish in Iron River for all the people from both Stambaugh and Iron River, the Bishop had decided another church must be built. The Stambaugh people would have their own parish. During the time the new church was being built, we would have to endure temporary quarters in the Stambaugh Recreation Center, a log building with fieldstone fireplace, used mainly for community activities such as parties, receptions, and meetings.

Dad was not happy. No one from Stambaugh was happy. Except Mom. Mom was ecstatic about attending church anywhere. And so our family, along with all the other Stambaugh families, reluctantly left St. Agnes Parish to attend Mass in the confines of the log structure never intended for such events as Sunday church services.

Mass became a long painful event. Some of the ladies of the newly ordered Stambaugh Catholic Church got together to sew and stuff kneeling pillows to protect our sorry shins from the wood plank floor, but there was nothing they could do to make the wooden folding chairs more comfortable. Where Sunday Mass previously had been a kind of exciting escape from the regular routine of the week, now it was quickly turning into a kind of torture session for us kids and Dad.

But for Mom it was absolute heaven. People had begun to take notice of her and her lovely voice. Mrs. Kofmehl, an elderly gentlewoman, stopped Mom one Sunday as we were leaving the Recreation Center. She introduced herself, welcomed Mom to the parish, and suggested that she should consider joining the choir that was now forming.

Mom agreed to come to one of the choir's practices and give it a try. The following Sunday, Mom and eight other people, including Mrs. Kofmehl, formed a small concert choir. As they began to sing the Latin words to the Mass, Mom at first seemed a little shy, but I guess she was just warming up because by the time they got to the second hymn, Mom's voice rang out loud and clear. I couldn't believe what a beautiful voice she had. Somehow, I'd never noticed. Sure she often sang to us in Finnish, if we were sick or just wanted to hear some of the old songs, but this was different. We were in the midst of a throng of people and Mom was leading the whole group.

A few months later, Mrs. Swanson, the choir director, announced to the little choir that her husband was being transferred to another city and the family would be moving. "The church," she said, "will have to find a new director." She looked directly at Mom.

"I couldn't possibly do it," Mom told Mrs. Swanson. "I just couldn't."

Not long after Mom became the choir director, the building of our new church, Blessed Sacrament Church, was completed. The congregation gladly left the Recreation Center and moved on in. The choir no longer had to use a piano for accompaniment as we now had our own oak pump organ, antiquated though it was. Miss Vella Manning played the organ and, when Mom told her I took piano lessons, she said she'd be glad to show me how to play the organ, too, so I'd know how to use the correct stops, pump, and play at the same time.

When first I sat down at that little organ and struggled with the stops, pumps, and keys, I never dreamed what lay in store. It all came about when Diane Blood, organist for the newly formed Junior Choir, could not attend choir practice. Marie Anderson, the co-director of that choir, contacted Mom and asked if I could fill in, just for one rehearsal. I said, I'd give it a try. And that was just the beginning.

Loretta Kofmehl took Mom under her wing. She invited her to a variety of church meetings and functions besides Sunday Mass, brought her literature on becoming a Catholic, and encouraged her to take adult religion classes. She told Mom, if she became confirmed, she could be a full-fledged member of the Catholic Church. She would need to be baptized in the Church, receive her first holy communion, and have her marriage to Dad "blessed." Then, all she needed to do was be confirmed and she would be a bona fide Catholic.

Across the street from Blessed Sacrament Church, at Nelson Park, I waited with my little sister Connie for Mom, Dad, and brother John. I'd promised Mom I'd keep my mouth shut about the day's activities. It was nobody's business. But how often do you get to tell people that your mother and father are getting married for a second time?

"My Mom and Dad are over in the church right this minute getting married," I bragged to my friend Jeannie Baker. "Mom's becoming a Catholic so she and Dad have to get married again. My brother's the best man."

"That's nice," Jeannie said. "Your family will probably get even bigger now, just like mine." There were ten kids in

Jeannie's family. I wondered what she meant by that statement.

"What do you mean?" I asked curiously.

"Oh, Catholic families always have bigger families than
Protestants," Jeannie said knowingly.

"Really?" I wouldn't admit that I hadn't the slightest idea
of what she was talking about.

Daily Masses were held each morning at 7:30 A.M. and the
church needed someone to play the organ and sing. I was
eleven years old and Mom decided that we could do the job as
a team. I'd play the organ and she'd sing.

"Every day? I've got to go to church every single day?" I
looked at my Mother in disbelief. I hadn't done anything
wrong. Why was I being given this kind of sentence?

"Someone has to do it," Mom said firmly. "It might as
well be us. We owe it to the Lord. I know it'll be a sacrifice,
but I'll be there with you."

And she was there with me. Every single day. Until the
morning of the Great Canasta Tournament on January 23,
1951.

The Great Canasta Tournament

The wild winds of January swirled vengefully around our house at 13 Nineteenth Street. While gales of white swept the yard, clouded the windows, and whistled through the trees, I woke to Dad's voice calling me awake. "Time to get up for church."

It couldn't be morning already. I didn't want to open my eyes, but the icy cold air in my bedroom brought me full awake. Chilled to the bone, I slipped out from under the covers and wriggled out of my flannel pajamas and into my favorite white blouse, grey corduroy jumper, and warm wool red cardigan sweater. I pulled on my grey wool socks and brown and white saddle shoes, tied them, and crept downstairs. It was January 23, 1951 and outdoors a whining U.P. winter storm gathered momentum.

"Mom's not feeling too good this morning," Dad said, standing at the stove, bathing the fried eggs he was cooking in scalding hot bacon grease. "She wants you to go to Mass alone. I'll drive you there, pick you up, and take you to school when you're done." Sliding the eggs over to one side of the fry pan, he hastily cut two thick slabs of homemade oatmeal bread, and dropped them, too, into the spattering bacon grease. Turning the bread rapidly, he finished fixing his favorite meal. "There," he said pleased, "sit down and eat. Gotta' have a breakfast that'll stick to your ribs." He slipped two eggs—cautiously keeping the yolks from breaking—and a slice of slightly seared, dripping toast onto my plate. Then he set out a separate plate stacked high with sizzling bacon.

"Alone!" Panic, hot searing panic, swept through my veins. "You mean play the organ and sing? By myself?" I reached over and grabbed three pieces of crispy bacon, rammed one into my mouth, and dropped the other two on my plate. Then I broke my egg with a crust of the toast, dabbed the crust until it was coated with yellow yolk, and stuffed that into my mouth, too.

"You can do it, dear." Mom wandered into the kitchen. Usually dressed and ready to go, she was still in her bathrobe. "Dad will drive you."

"You never said I'd have to do this job alone!" I said, suddenly feeling betrayed. "You said, we'd do this together." I took another large mouthful of egg, toast, and bacon and chewed nervously.

"I know, dear, but I'm not feeling up to it today. And I just know you can do it," Mom insisted.

"I've never sung by myself," I said, thrusting the last mouthful of bacon and egg into my mouth and wiping my plate clean with the last piece of toast crust I'd saved for that purpose.

"But you've been playing for me for a long time. You know the music better than I do. All you've got to do is sing along with the organ." She made it sound so easy.

"It's not that easy," I pouted, wiping my mouth with the back of my hand.

"I know it isn't, but please do this for me." Mom looked suddenly pale as she got up and left the room.

"All right . . . I'll try," I said, following her into the dining room. Mom always felt good. Seeing her like this made me worry. "I'll do the best I can."

"That's all the Lord ever expects from any of us," Mom said, trying, with difficulty, to smile.

I wiped my hands on a kitchen towel, then bundled up in my thick green wool coat, brown stadium boots, and red hat, mittens, and scarf which I wound several times around my neck and face to keep out the wind. Dad was already warming the car when I went out the back door and plodded down the snow covered sidewalk, fighting my way through the blustery wind.

"I just shoveled that sidewalk, but it didn't do much good. Snow's flying like crazy. It won't snow much longer though," Dad said. "It's getting too cold."

"Uh huh," I mumbled. I was sweating with fear. I slipped off my mittens and rubbed my hands on my coat.

"I'll be back to pick you up in a half hour," Dad called after me as I gave the car door a bang, raced up the steps to the church, and pulled open the heavy wooden door.

All I had to do was get through the next half hour, I thought. Maybe God, in His goodness and mercy, would strike me dead and I wouldn't have to go through with this singing after all. Maybe an earthquake would mysteriously occur—like a miracle—and the earth would swallow me up, relieving me of my responsibility. Maybe people would even think I was one of the great martyrs of the Church.

I sat down at the organ, placed my shaking hands on the keyboard, and began to pump with my feet. The old organ creaked and groaned, gasped and wheezed, and finally came to life. My back to the altar, I could look into a mirror positioned on the back wall to see when the priest entered and how the Mass was progressing. The bells rang and the priest walked out onto the altar, two altar boys following closely behind.

It was time to start. The possibility of an earthquake was looking more and more remote. Maybe I could drown out my voice with the vibrato of the organ. I played the first notes and the organ sounded softer than ever. I heard a tiny distant voice singing the words of *The Mass of the Dead*: "Requiem, in eternam . . ." It was me and I was singing. Alone. I had to sing louder. I forced my lips to form the words, my diaphragm to expand, and my vocal chords to project the sound out over the congregation. I managed to get through the Kyrie.

"Dominus vobis cum," the priest chanted.

"Et cum spiri-tu-tuo," I chanted back.

I was doing it. I was sweating. But I was not going to die after all. I was going to get through it.

As soon as Mass was over I pushed all the organ stops back in, tucked away the wooden bellows, and slapped shut *St. Basil's Mass of the Dead*. Then, I flew down the stairway from the choir loft to the main seating area, down another flight of stairs to the outer door, and nearly knocked over sweet old Mrs. Brunell who was slowly working her way out of church on arthritic ankles.

"Was that you singing up there?" she asked brightly.

"Uh huh," I replied shyly. I must have sounded like a real idiot.

"You sounded just like your mother." She smiled. "She's not here today. Is she all right? Did she have the baby yet?"

"Not yet," I said, giving her a little smile of thanks before I ran for the door.

Just like Dad had said, the snow was settling down and the air was becoming even colder. It was a typical January day in the U.P. I ran for the warm car where Dad was waiting to take me up the hill to school.

"I need fifteen cents for hot lunch money," I told Dad as I jumped into the car. "I hope they're not having that awful bean soup," I mumbled to myself.

Neither of us mentioned the singing. Dad didn't get involved in Mom's "choir business." He just took out his little coin purse, found a dime and a nickel, and handed them to me. It took us less than five minutes to drive to school.

"See you tonight," I said, one hand on the door, ready to slam it shut.

"Not tonight, you won't," Dad said, "I've gotta' work the night shift. Won't be home until morning."

"Well, see you tomorrow then," I slammed the car door and ran, rushing to reach my classroom before the last bell rang.

Somehow the school day dribbled on by and, at last, it was time to walk home. I pulled on my green coat, snaked my scarf around my face and neck, pulled on my mittens and boots and trudged on down the long hill to Dober Location. The snow had stopped but the wind, icy and insistent, whipped and whirled wickedly around me. I pulled my coat tighter and pressed on toward home.

The house welcomed me with a blast of soothing heat, the spicy smell of Italian spaghetti, and Mom's voice calling me from the living room.

I couldn't hear what she was saying, so I just yelled as usual, "I'm home!"

"Well? How did it go?" Mom walked into the kitchen, smiling. She wore her homemade two-piece green maternity dress and looked like she was feeling just fine.

"Okay," I answered, "but I hope you can go with me tomorrow."

"I'll bet you did a beautiful job." Mom sounded both pleased and excited. "I've made your favorite dinner."

"Yah!" I loved spaghetti, but Mom hardly ever made it when Dad was home. He, the Italian, didn't care for most Italian foods. When I teased him about it, he explained his family was from a province where cornmeal dishes such as polenta were popular, but spaghetti, ravioli, and other pasta-type foods were never even heard of.

"I thought you should have something special today," Mom said.

"Thanks, Mom." I hung my outdoor clothes in the shed, dished out a generous serving of zesty spaghetti, and settled myself into the breakfast nook to enjoy my feast. Next to the nook, Mom sat on a wooden stool Dad had built for her to use to reach the food stuff on the top shelves of our kitchen cabinets. Since she could no longer fit into the breakfast nook, it was the perfect place for her to perch.

"Aren't you going to eat?" I asked, shoveling spaghetti into my mouth.

"I had a little something earlier," Mom said. "I haven't been too hungry today . . . you know this baby's overdue. I've been having pains off and on, all day. I called the doctor and he says today will probably be the day. But I don't know . . ." Suddenly she clutched her arms around her middle and took a deep breath. She held on like that for several seconds, then relaxed and laughed. "Guess this baby is just going to takes its good old sweet time."

"You okay?" I asked, concerned.

"I'm fine," she laughed. "It's this baby that's having a problem."

"Well as long as you're so fine," I said, "how about we play Canasta." Mom and I had an ongoing tournament to see who could win the most games of Canasta. We were usually so close it was hard to tell who was really winning.

"Oh, I don't know honey, I probably wouldn't be able to stay in one place long enough to play cards."

"Some excuse," I taunted.

"I didn't say I couldn't beat you!" It looked like Mom might pick up the challenge.

"Beat me? Ha! Who won the last game?" I teased.

"I did!" Mom exclaimed.

"I don't think so," I insisted.

"That's right, you did, didn't you," Mom agreed, "but I won the one before that. All right I'll make you a deal. We'll play one game and it'll be a play-off game."

"The Great Canasta Tournament! Okay, get the cards out! I'll get out of my school clothes," I yelled as I flounced away up the stairs to change into my flannel shirt and blue jeans.

By the time I got back downstairs, Mom was sitting at the dining room table, shuffling the cards. I took a seat across the table from her.

"I want to watch." Connie climbed up on a dining room chair next to me.

"Cut, to see who goes first." Mom offered me the double deck.

"Right." I turned over a five of hearts.

"You're already behind," Mom giggled. But then she cut to a four of clubs.

"Ha! Ha! Who's behind now?" I scoffed.

"Doesn't mean a thing." Mom grabbed up the cut cards, blended them into the double deck, and placed it in the middle of the table.

"My deal." I smirked.

We were barely into the first hand of the game when Mom started breathing heavily. She clutched her cards to her chest. "Ooh, oooooh," she whimpered.

"No whimpering allowed in this game. Play cards," I hollered, which made her giggle right in the middle of an "oooooh."

"You cut that out," she managed to say through her giggles.

"You're not getting out of the game that easily," I told her.

"This hand's over. I'm out," she announced, laying out her cards in a grandiose gesture.

"You're just making all that noise to try to throw me off my game," I said.

"I am not. Quit making me laugh so much," she squealed.

"I can't help it if you're laughing. You're the one who's acting goofy. Not me," I giggled.

"You're both goofy," Connie said, clapping her hands. "Goofy, goofy, goofy."

That sent us all into peals of laughter.

"Maybe I'd better quit," Mom said, trying to sound serious. "This is a lot of activity for me tonight. Maybe I should be getting ready to go to the hospital."

"You can't quit now. You're ahead. It wouldn't be fair. You do want to win fair and square, don't you?" I badgered.

"All right. We'll try one more hand and see what happens," Mom agreed.

Nothing much happened during the next hand except that I won and now Mom and I were almost tied. Mom won the third and fourth hands and I won the fifth and sixth. We had about one more hand to go, when suddenly Mom leapt up from the table and gave a long groan.

"Maybe you'd better call Dad at the mine and have him come home," I suggested.

"No, it might be a false alarm and I don't want to bother him at work." Mom got her breath back, straightened up, and sat back down at the table. "Go ahead and deal another hand. I'm going beat you. And don't make me giggle any more."

"Don't worry, I won't." I dealt out another hand and Mom started to hoot as she looked at her hand. She started laying down red three's. She had three of them which gave her an extra 300 points and if she got the fourth, she'd get an extra 800 points. She would definitely win with that score.

"I wish you wouldn't act so silly," I said in a disapproving way, pretending I was the parent.

Mom couldn't resist the temptation to start giggling all over again. But just as she was doubling over with laughter, she shot up off her chair again. "I'd better call a cab!" she hollered.

"A cab?" I looked at her in amazement. We never ever rode in a cab.

"What else am I going to do? This baby's not waiting any longer. By the time they found your father down in the tunnels, it would be too late for him to get here to drive me." Mom was still humped over as she walked to the phone, picked it up, and asked the operator to ring Vic's Taxi Service.

"It's 10 o'clock. The cab should be here in fifteen minutes or less." Mom was sounding a little worried.

"You're walking like a camel," I giggled, trying to take her mind off the situation.

"I told you to stop making me laugh," Mom screeched, as she made her way back to the table. "I can't even sit down."

"You'll do anything to get out of this game, won't you?" I hollered.

"Yah," Connie yelled, banging her hands on the table.

"I'm going to finish this game. And I'm going to beat you," Mom said, picking up her cards and taking her regular turn.

The play moved right along. First, Mom played. Then, I played. And we all listened for the cab to come. The three of us kept looking at the clock, but the seconds dragged. Not a sound could be heard outside. The wind had settled down to severe below zero temperatures. Nothing out there moved.

Mom got up from the table, and still carrying her cards with her, slipped her winter coat on. She went into her bedroom, came out with a small carrying case, and went to the window. Still there was no sound.

"Going somewhere?" I teased.

"The cab's here," Mom gasped. "I've got to go. Now!"

"But you can't go now. We've only got a couple of cards to play!" My giggling was out of control.

A loud heavy honking of the cabby's horn penetrated the January night.

"All right," Mom scooted back to the table. "Canasta!" she yelled, laying her concealed canasta, and game-winning hand, out on the table—just as the impatient cab driver honked the horn again.

"You won!" I bellowed.

"You bet I did!" she hollered over her shoulder as she walked out the front door and disappeared into the cold stark January night . . .

"Time to get up," Dad called up the stairway. "I'll drive you to church."

Church? I had to sing alone again. As I slipped out of bed and got my bearings, I realized that Mom had gone to the hospital the night before. I dressed as fast as I could and practically ran down the steps.

"You have a baby brother, born last night at 11 o'clock. His name is Jim!" Dad stood at the stove cooking breakfast. He was beaming. "Mom said to tell you thanks for all your help. She said it was the easiest birth she's had."

"Jim." I tried out the name and liked the sound of it. Mom's dream was coming true and I had a new baby brother to prove it.

Having a new little brother was exciting, but I was anxious to have Mom get home from the hospital, rest up, and come back to church with me for daily Masses. However, nobody told me that one baby brother leads to another . . . but I found that out on the opening day of bird season, October 1, 1952.

Opening Day of Bird Season

Mom's dream of glorifying the Lord grew in great proportions over the next years. Shortly after little brother Jim was born, she returned to her place at my side, Monday through Saturday, singing the daily Masses at Blessed Sacrament Church in Stambaugh. She directed the Senior Choir on Sundays and sang solos for all weddings and funerals with me at her side, playing the organ. On Tuesday nights we held choir practice and on the first Friday evening of each month, we supplied the music for Novenas. During Lent, we attended the Stations of the Cross on Wednesday nights. Then, during the months of May and October, which were the months of Mary, Mother of Jesus, we sang for special devotional services on Tuesdays and Fridays. On Monday nights, I got to do my own "thing" which was attending our Catholic Youth Organization (CYO) meetings in the church basement.

Mom's love of the Lord carried over into everything we did. Even when we took a trip to Iron Mountain, forty-five miles from home, to go shopping—or anywhere over ten miles from home—Mom had me take out the rosary so we could pray for a safe trip. Connie watched over baby Jim in the back seat while Mom drove and we all prayed out loud. Connie and I admitted it did seem to make the trip go faster, but we agreed Mom would never get away with it if Dad was with us. For Dad, praying was still intended for Sundays, in church. But Mom did manage to talk him into going to a church retreat with her early in 1952.

That summer, Mom started knitting mysterious little pink and blue garments. By fall, she was again packing her little overnight bag to go to the hospital. This meant that I'd be singing the Masses alone again, but this time I didn't mind so much. I had experience now, and besides, I thought that having another new brother or sister was really pretty exciting. I also figured that maybe, just maybe, I could talk Mom and Dad into letting me get a special permit to drive alone.

Well, the permit to drive was still down the road a ways. On the morning of October 1, 1952, Dad drove me to church, dropped me off, and hightailed it back home to pick up his lunch bucket and get to the mine.

"I don't think you'd better go, Johnny," Mom told him. "I think this baby is going to be born today."

"You sure?" Dad never took time off from work. As a shift boss in the mine, he felt there were no good excuses for missing work. If you were sick, you worked. If someone else in your family was sick, you worked. Taking off work was not acceptable, and he let every man, who asked for time off, know it. "I can't be missing work for nothing."

"I don't think this is nothing," Mom said.

Dad paced the kitchen for a while, finally picked up the phone, but quickly put it down again. "I'd better take a run over there. Check things out. Make sure the job's running right on schedule."

So Dad drove over to the mine, went into his office, and made arrangements to be off for the day. "I gotta' take my wife to the hospital," he told everyone. "I'll be back tomorrow."

Then he jumped back into the old Model A, rolled down the windows, and drove toward home. The autumn day was aglow with color. Scarlet leaves, like ruby jewels, still clinging to burgundy branches flashed like flames of fire while tangerine and topaz tinted leaves swirled in the sun, drifting lazily to the golden-hued ground. The hills above and beyond Selden Road, where the Hiawatha Mine rose rustily up toward the cloudless blue sky, teemed with heavenly hues of carmine, crimson, gold, and orange—inviting the eye to stare in breathless wonder and awe.

It was the opening day of bird season. Dad certainly hadn't forgotten the importance of the day, but knowing he had to work, had set aside thoughts of partridge pleasure until after the day shift was over. All of a sudden, he realized he was free of work responsibilities. He had the day off! He revved up the motor and raced for home. It was a perfect day for hunting. Maybe he didn't have to miss it after all.

"How soon do you think this baby's gonna' come?" Dad asked Mom, as he shot in the back door smiling from ear-to-ear.

"Well, I don't know. Pretty soon. That's all I can tell you." Mom looked at him dubiously. He was up to something.

"Well, how about we do a little hunting before I take you to the hospital?" Dad ventured.

"Hunting? Now? But what if we can't make it back to the hospital?" Mom blurted out. "Then what will we do?"

"Oh, heck, we'll make it back in time. We won't go out that far. You can pack your bag and take it along. That way you won't be stuck up there in that hospital any longer than you have to. Look at this weather. It would be an awful shame to miss out in it." Dad was as persuasive as a peddler when he wanted to be.

"Well, all right," Mom warily agreed. "It is a gorgeous day."

Dad bounded out to the garage, grabbed his shotgun and shells, and started up the '49 Chevy. No sense taking Mom out in the old Model A, he thought, patting himself on the back for thinking of her comfort while Mom came cheerfully trudging out the back door loaded down with her coat, purse, and overnight bag.

Just as Mom had carefully placed her baggage in the back seat, smoothed out her maternity dress, and managed to get situated in the front seat, she started to breathe heavily. "Here comes another one," she managed to get out.

"Hang on," Dad directed, "I gotta' get my hunting license." With that he left Mom gasping in the car as he vaulted out and bounded back into the house to retrieve his new license.

"Oh boy, what a day!" Dad sighed as he slipped back into the driver's seat. "We're gonna' have a great time."

"Let's not go too far out of town," Mom reminded him.

"Oh, we won't. I think we'll just take a ride out to the Smoky Lake Road. Those birds are gonna' be right out there sitting in the sun, waiting for us."

They hadn't gone far when Mom started gasping again. "Maybe we'd better not go anywhere. Maybe we'd better just go to the hospital."

"Roll your window down so you can get some air," Dad offered, being the perfect gentleman and concerned husband. "That fresh air will make you feel a lot better."

"Uh huh," Mom reached for the window knob, rolled down her window, and inhaled deeply.

"Isn't that air just great? Smell those pines?" Dad exclaimed. "Now keep your eye on the side of the road. That's where you'll see the birds. They'll be hiding right down there in the tall grass or under the trees."

"I know how to spot partridge." Mom shook her head but dutifully turned her eyes toward the side of the road.

"And don't make any noise, if you see one," Dad pulled over to the side of the road, slowed down, and began doing some serious hunting. Intent on birds, he didn't notice the car coming toward them or the two fellows in the front seat waving him down.

"Johnny, do you know those men?" Mom tapped Dad on the arm and pointed to the oncoming car.

Dad, who'd been daydreaming, nearly jumped out of his skin at her touch and, when he saw the car, he wished he could become instantly invisible. Instead he pulled to a stop— what else could he do?

"Hey, Johnny whatcha doin' out here? Thought you were on the day shift." Two of Dad's buddies from the mine were looking at him quizzically.

"I'm taking Carrie to the hospital," Dad said after a prolonged pause. "Oh." Dad's pals looked at each other knowingly. "Sure . . . See any partridge?"

"Partridge?" Dad asked—like he'd never heard of them.

"Yah, partridge. You know, *birds*."

"Birds?" Dad gave them an innocent look. "No, haven't seen a thing. Say, aren't you two gonna' be late for work?" Dad had gotten hold of himself and decided to turn the tables on these hecklers.

"Yah, sure. You betcha'. See ya' Johnny, hey?" they yelled as they drove off, poking each other in the ribs and laughing like a couple of idiots.

"Geez they're gonna' tell everybody I took the day off to go hunting," Dad griped to Mom. "No one will ever believe I got off work so I could take you to the hospital."

"Oh yes they will!" shouted Mom, grabbing onto the car door for support. "You're going to turn around and take me right now!"

"Right now?" Dad looked at her disappointed.

"Right now!" Mom clung to the car door, her eyes big as saucers.

"Right now," Dad agreed. "I'll pull into the first logging road we see and turn around."

"It had better not be too far." Mom who had been doubled over, pulled herself up to a stiff straight sitting position and tensely looked out the window—just in time to spot a partridge sitting in the grass alongside the road. "There's a bird," she whispered.

Dad jammed on the brakes, grabbed his shotgun from the back seat, and slowly opened the car door. He wormed his way around the car, pressed a shell into gun, and fired.

"You got him," Mom cheered, forgetting the hospital for the moment.

Dad walked back proudly to the car, dropped the partridge on the floor of the back seat, and slipped back into the front seat. "What a day! You sure you want to go back already?"

"Want to go back? Do you want this child to be born right out here in the woods?" Mom started to gasp and giggle at the same time.

"There's a logging road right up ahead," Dad pointed out. "Hold on honey, we'll be back in town in minutes."

My little brother Jerry was born minutes later, in Stambaugh General Hospital. Dad even carried Mom's coat, purse, and overnight bag into the hospital for her. But when he found out that he could visit with her and the bouncing new baby boy for only a short time after the birth, he did what any good proud new U.P. father would. He went back out hunting.

Our "gang" going off to church before Mom joined us.

Jim and Jerry, the new kids on the block.

One Step at a Time

"Grow up!" I used to hear often enough when I was twelve, but every time I tried to do just that, something or someone stood in my way, making me dodge, step back, side step, try again. It was like an intricate, challenging dance pattern and I always seemed to be out of step.

"Act your age!" I was told, but to me that meant making my own decisions, trying out new movements, meeting adventure head on. The rhythm was a complicated pattern of puzzling paces. I decided, in order to survive, I'd better learn to take one step at a time.

Mom gave me fifty cents, said she was heading for the domestics department, and left me on my own to shop at Newberry's Five and Dime. I went directly to the elegant blue velvet display case in the jewelry section and stared hungrily through the glass at the familiar rhinestone necklaces, bracelets, and earrings.

I was Lana Turner, swathed in a sleek shining red satin gown, wrapped in soft brown mink, and dripping with diamonds. A dozen long stemmed red roses in my arm, I stood on the steps of Metro Golden Mayer, graciously signing autographs and sending sweet kisses out over the crowd with my red, nail polished fingertips. Swept off through the throng of admirers by my agent, who escorted me to a long black limousine, I was chauffeured away to my home in the hills of Hollywood . . .

I waltzed over to the jewelry section and spent the next ten minutes studying the fake sapphire, emerald, and ruby rings, fascinated with every facet of hue, depth, and tone. For sixty-five cents I could own one of those beauties, but I wasn't sure if it was the right step to take just then. I still had seventy cents left in my pocket from the last shopping trip, but I didn't want to blow my whole wad on one item.

I wandered on down the aisle toward the front of the store and slowed to a stop in front of the glass bins of candy: hard candy in assorted flavors and colors, maple nut rolls, peppermint sticks, liquorice, and, of course, chocolates filled with creamy white maraschino cherry centers.

The sweet tantalizing scent of fruit and chocolate tickled my nose and taste buds, but I couldn't figure out how to make a purchase. Above the bins hung a large round silver scale shaped like a bowl and suspended from a Roman numeraled gauge by three slender chains, extending from an even larger chain hanging all the way down from the ceiling of the store. The silver links of chain, twisting and turning, invited the eye to travel upward to the embossed metal Victorian curlicues spreading out over the store's ceiling like an upside down magic carpet.

Mesmerized, I didn't see her approaching. "Can I help you?" Startled, I jerked my head down, took a step backward, and nearly tripped over a woman passing behind me. "Well?" the clerk said impatiently, snapping her spearmint gum and tossing her long red-blond hair with a quick twist of her head. "You wanna' buy some candy?" She was about eighteen years old, glowed with self-confidence and, while not necessarily a beauty, had learned to punctuate her features in a striking manner. Her hair, which I figured had received a little help from a Henna rinse, glistened like flames of fire under the soft white lights. Penciled in perfect little arches, her eyebrows emphasized blue-green eyes—pools of cool water in a deep dark sea. Her lipstick and rouge were the same bright pink color—wondrous water lilies floating on the surface.

Would I ever be old enough, or experienced enough, to fix myself up like that?

"Well, do want something, or not?" She was even more impatient now that I hadn't answered her first question.

I coughed to clear my throat, but nothing else came out. I wanted some candy, that's for sure, but I didn't know what to say. I looked back at the bin of cream-filled chocolates, but there was no sign or label to give me a clue. I decided to take a risk "How much are these?" I pointed to the chocolate creams.

"Depends on how much you want." She chewed her gum harder, rolled her eyes, and tapped her finger on the counter.

"How much would a small bag be?" It was a simple question. I'd have my sweets in seconds. My mouth watered.

"Look, we sell these by the pound. You want me to weigh some out for you?" She was definitely not going to put up with any more of my stupid questions.

I stared first at the Roman numerals, the bowl with chains, and then back to the chocolate covered temptations. It was too complicated. I was sure I'd make a mistake. "I changed my mind." I was blushing like a big red beet.

She gave me a scornful look, cracked her gum, and raised her penciled arches to a fellow clerk who had just stepped up to help another customer. I made a quick getaway down the aisle.

My ears were still burning as I fled the candy counter clerk to freedom. I'd find something else to buy, something plainly marked with a price. I ambled through the toy section, searching the shelves, eyeing the Bobbsey Twin books, sets of ball and jacks, pairs of trick magnetic Scottie dogs. Too childish. Boy, that was the last thing I needed—something childish.

I strolled past the greeting cards, gift wrap, and note paper, slowed down at the perfume rack where the fragrance of lily of the valley, rosebuds, and lavender wafted into the air, and finally stopped at the cosmetic counter. Lipstick! If only Mom would let me buy some. Finding several opened tubes of the stuff just lying on the counter, left there by others who'd tested the colors, I slipped the top off of a bright red stick, twirled the tube open, and stared at it longingly.

"Looking for some lipstick?" The Henna-haired clerk from the candy counter had slunk up silently in front of me. She leaned over the cosmetic counter, slid her yellow lead pencil smoothly into her hair and behind her ear, and shot me a sassy smirk. "Your mother know you're over here?" I hadn't noticed before that her green-hued eyes strongly resembled those of Grandma Cederna's barn cats. They leered at me from behind mascara laden lashes—cunning, crafty, challenging. "Well, does she?"

Without a word, I crammed the cap back on the lipstick as fast as I could, set it back in its place, and turned away. She was too much for me. I couldn't cope with an eighteen-year-old. I hurried to the other end of the store, only once furtively looking back to make sure she wasn't following.

My eyes darted up and down the walls, scanning the shelves for something special. I knew Mom would be back any minute and, if I wanted to take home a treasure, I'd have to make up my mind.

Then I saw them—magazines. *The Saturday Evening Post*, *Life*, *Woman's Day . . . Modern Screen . . .* My heart started to pound. On the cover of the latest issue was a full color picture of Linda Darnell and Tyrone Power, standing on the bow of an ancient ship. Looking off into the sunset, engulfed in a rapturous rose-hued blend of evening sky and sea, they were locked in a lover's embrace. It was absolutely dreamy. I reached over, picked it up, and flipped through the pages. They were jammed full of photos of movie stars, starlets, and filmmaking celebrities. Each page held a panorama of color, glitter, and gossip.

But what would Mom think? I placed it back on the shelf, studied the cover again, and the following words, "Learn to Fox Trot with Fred Astaire and Ginger Rogers," leapt out at me. In the upper left corner of the cover in a well defined black circle was printed the price, fifteen cents. I grabbed the magazine, whipped out my money, and looked cautiously around for "Miss Cat Eyes of Candy Counter Fame."

The coast was clear. I made a deliberate dash for the nearest clerk, an older woman who smiled sweetly at me, took my money, and held the magazine at arm's length, admiring the cover. "Don't you just love Tyrone Power? Isn't he dreamy?" she sighed. "Here, I'll put this in a bag for you."

"That'll be just fine," I said, trying to sound grown up, "and I'll take a pack of that gum, too," I added boldly.

"Beechnut gum, my favorite." The woman smiled again. "Would you like this in your bag or do you want to have a stick or two right away?"

"Right away. Thanks!" I gave her a nickel, returned the smile gratefully, and took the gum from her friendly little hand. I'd just been treated like a grown-up. With new confidence, I sauntered down yet another aisle, my brown bagged magazine tightly clasped in my hands, unwrapped a stick of gum, and popped it into my mouth. Then I began to chew in earnest.

"Ready to go home?" Mom slipped up behind me. She stopped dead in her tracks when she saw me, stood there staring, and gave me an awful look.

"Ready." I cracked my gum like the Henna-haired clerk had done.

"What is that in your mouth?" Mom gasped.

"Beechnut." I'd conveniently forgotten how Mom felt about gum chewing.

"Gum? Why in the world did you buy gum? You know how I feel about girls chewing gum. It looks very unladylike." Mom made no attempt to cover her obvious disappointment in me.

"I just felt like having some gum," I fibbed. How could I tell her I was trying to look grown up like the Henna-haired clerk. She would never understand that in a million years.

"If you think that makes you look grown up, you're wrong." Mom lowered her voice. It was uncanny how she always knew what I was thinking. "I used to think that same thing when I was your age, but now I realize it doesn't look very nice." She breathed a beat then continued, "If you're going to chew, at least keep your mouth closed and be silent about it."

"Right," I answered meekly. I wouldn't be buying any more gum. It wasn't worth it. If I couldn't snap the gum, what was the use of chewing it?

"What have you got there?" Mom said brightly, trying to change the mood.

"A movie magazine." I was in for it now.

"You spent your money on *that*?" Mom didn't sound too pleased. First the gum, now this.

"It's got a great article in it on learning to dance," I pointed out.

"Hmm . . ." was all Mom said. "Let me see that." She tucked her package under her arm, looked at the cover, and gave me an accusing look. I felt myself shrink at least two inches while I stood there waiting, barely chewing my gum at all. She opened the magazine, turning and scrutinizing each page carefully. I held my breath. Would she make me return it? I'd just die of embarrassment, if she did. "I guess it's all right," she said finally, handing it back to me, "but I hope you use better sense the next time we go shopping. You could have bought a Bobbsey Twin book with that money." Or a set of ball and jacks, I thought. Or maybe I should just have gone over to the baby department and bought myself a rattle. How could a girl grow up, when everyone around her kept trying to make her feel like a little kid? It was downright painful, that's what it was.

When we finally got home, I couldn't wait to get out of the car, race up to my bedroom, and pour over my very own new movie magazine. I threw myself on the bed, sprawled out on my stomach, and paged through it. The pictures were sensational. There were stars in ice cream shops where they'd been discovered by movie producers; stars lounging around their luxurious mansions, sipping iced tea at pool side; stars in jungle, desert, and wild west scenes from their recent box office hits. There were photos of starlets in glamorous costumes, bathing suits, and shimmering evening gowns. It was sheer heaven.

I turned my attention to the article on learning to do the Fox Trot. I read it over twice, studying the accompanying diagrams consisting of little black footprints, dotted lines, and arrows indicating the path of movement which formed a sort of squared box pattern. One step. Two step. Side step. Step together. Repeat.

I stood in front of my sister's old round mirror above her vanity table, held the magazine in one hand, and—looking back and forth from the page to my feet—tried to do the Fox Trot. One step. Two step. Side step. Step together. Repeat. I felt clumsy as an ox, but I was determined to learn the dance, no matter how difficult, or impossible, it seemed. I tried it again, but something was missing. Of course! Fred Astaire and Ginger Rogers didn't dance alone. What I needed was a partner.

Fox Trotting in the Forest

"I'm going over to Nancy's," I yelled to Mom in the kitchen as I raced—movie magazine in hand—past her, out the back door, and over to my friend's house, across the alley and two doors down.

"Come on in," Nancy's mother called through the screen door to the steps where I stood pounding. "Nan's ironing. She'll be done in a minute." I opened the door, stepped into the kitchen, and waited for Mrs. Gagne, who was washing windows with ammonia, to invite me to sit down. "You can sit at the table and wait, if you like."

"Thanks." I pulled out one of the four red padded chrome-based kitchen chairs tucked neatly under the table in the corner of the small sparkling kitchen, sat down, and hoped Nancy would hurry before I choked on the wafting waves of ammonia drifting about the room.

"You girls going to color today?" Nancy's mom wiped the two small windows above the sink with a damp soapy cloth, rinsed them, and dried them vigorously with a clean cotton towel.

"Color?" We'd spent many an afternoon sitting at the kitchen table with our crayons and coloring books. The good old days. "Uh . . . no, I don't think so." Be polite, I cautioned myself. How could I tell my best friend's mother we weren't babies anymore and were far too grown up for that kind of kid stuff.

"Mom's kidding you," Nancy laughed as she came into the kitchen, a white cotton ruffled blouse hooked on a black hanger, dangling from her forefinger, and smelling pleasantly of starch.

"Oh." I looked sheepishly at Mrs. Gagne who gave us both a big grin as she continued her attack on the windows.

"So what do you want to do this afternoon?" Nancy asked.

"I thought we'd see if we can learn to dance. I've got this great new magazine that shows you how. What do you think?" I opened the magazine on the table to the article on doing the Fox Trot.

"Fred Astaire and Ginger Rogers?" She leaned over my shoulder, looked at the page, and gave me a quizzical look. "Aren't they a little advanced for us?"

"It says right here even a beginner can learn, just by following this article and these steps." I indicated the diagrams.

"Just let me put my ironing away. We can go outside in the yard and give it a try," Nancy said.

In her back yard, we spread the magazine open on a newly painted green wooden lawn chair, poured over the dance diagrams, and stood side by side. Both sets of eyes on the directions, we tried out the steps. "One step. Two step. Side step. Step together. Repeat," we read aloud from the page.

"I don't think this is working," I said finally. "It says here to form a box. See the diagram. But it's so awkward."

"Maybe if we had some music . . ." Nancy suggested, giving up for the moment, flinging herself to the ground, and sprawling out like a rag doll on the green carpet of grass.

"We've got an old record player around our house somewhere," I offered. "Let's go over and see if we can dig it up."

After much searching, we finally unearthed Mom's and Dad's old blue portable wind-up victrola, along with about a dozen 78-speed records, hiding under a bunker of boxes in the basement. The victrola was covered with dust, smelled of mildew, and weighed about a ton, but we managed to carry it up the basement steps and out into the sunshine. We set it on a small wobbly white painted table we'd dragged out of the garage, took some rags, and wiped away the debris and cobwebs. Then we started sorting through the red and blue labels on the records.

"How about this one? *Tiger Rag* by Spike Jones?" I wound the arm on the old victrola until it wouldn't turn any further, set the record on the spindle, and placed the long silver arm holding the needle on it. Something that sounded like pots and pans clanging, whistles, and sirens started vibrating out of the old blue machine.

"What else have you got?" Nancy could hardly stop laughing. "This doesn't sound like Fred's and Ginger's kind of music."

"Here's one that says, 'Fox Trot' right under the title!" I said excitedly. "It's called *Moonlight on the Strand*." I took Spike Jones off the machine, placed it back in its yellowed jacket, and filed it in the record holder attached to the cover of the victrola. Then I put on the Fox Trot. The music blared out across the yard. "Let's dance," I yelled over the music. Side by side, Fred and Ginger, to the music we did our steps: One step. Two step. Side step. Step together. Repeat.

"Now let's try it together," Nancy insisted. "You lead, you're taller."

"I don't want to lead, just because I'm taller. You lead."

"Let's just take turns." Nancy put her arm around my waist and held out her hand.

"Geez, I feel like such a dope. Don't you?" I giggled.

"Sure, I do, but if we're ever going to learn this, we're going to have to do this now. Let's be sensible," Nancy, almost two years my senior, said with authority.

We both started—one step, two step, side step, step together—at the same time, tripped over each others feet, and fell on the lawn, laughing. "One of us is going to have to step backwards," I giggled. We hadn't thought of that.

We were just about to try again when the Contardi kids, Micky, Steve, and "Mugsy," ran to the white picket fence in their back yard across the alley, climbed up on the lower board, and leaned over watching, pointing, and giggling.

"You kids get out of there," Nancy yelled. "I'll be baby-sitting you tonight, so you'd better behave." She gave them a mean look, shook her fist at them, and they ran shrieking to tell their mother.

"Let's try it again," Nancy said. It was my turn to lead. I wound up the old victrola, set the needle on the record, and we started again. Just then a car horn honked heavily from the street out in front of the house. We looked up just in time to see a carload of high school boys driving by, smirking, waving, and whistling.

"I'm not doing this here," I said dropping my hand away from Nancy's waist. "Everybody in town can see us, if they drive by.

"They're gone now," Nancy pointed out. "Come on we've got to concentrate."

I started the record over again and took the lead. Strains of *Moonlight on the Strand* poured out across the yard. "Everybody in the neighborhood must be looking out their windows. I feel like a real drip."

"Ginger Rogers was a beginner once, too," Nancy philosophized.

"Oh no, here comes my Dad," I whispered. The old Model A came rumbling to a halt on the street, alongside the yard, where we were trying to dance. I hoped he hadn't seen us, but the big grin on his face told me he had.

"What have we got here?" Dad jumped out of the old jalopy, walked right over to the magazine, and picked it up off the ground. "Fred Astaire and Ginger Rogers? Which one of you is Fred?" Dad joked.

"We're learning to do the Fox Trot, Mr. Cederna," Nancy said pleasantly, ignoring the crack about Fred.

"Fox trot, huh? Red fox or grey fox?" Dad's eyes were dancing devilishly. He wasn't going to stop teasing us for ages—I could tell. We were in for it now.

"Oh Dad, c'mon," I begged.

"I've seen a lot of foxes trot in my day, but I've never seen any trot like that." Dad was grinning from ear to ear as he walked away toward the house.

"It's a dance, Dad." Why was I bothering to explain. "We're learning how to dance."

"Yah, I can see you two are headed right for the stage." Dad disappeared into the house, chuckling loudly.

"We're never going to learn how to dance. Not here. We've got to figure out a place where we can get some privacy," I said to Nancy.

"How do you think we're going to find any privacy around here? If you figure it out let me know. I've got to get home for supper." Nancy bounded off down the alley, her long dark braids bobbing behind her as she ran.

Who would ever have guessed Dad would be the one to come up with the answer to our problem?

"You want to take a ride out to the lake?" Dad asked on Saturday morning.

"I don't know. Nancy's coming over this afternoon. We've got some stuff we want to do," I told him.

"Well, ask her to come along," Dad suggested.

"I don't think she'll want to go."

"Sure she will. You two can take the old victrola out there, play your music, and trot around to your heart's content."

"Really?" Now there was a place we could find some privacy. There was nothing out there except the chipmunks, squirrels, and woodpeckers to see us make fools of ourselves. "Okay, I'll ask her."

When we got to Hagerman Lake, Dad eased the shimmying old Model A down the hill to the cottage, parked alongside, and unloaded his boards for building the steps to the lake. Then he set up two wooden sawhorses in the back of the cottage, laid a board over them, and set the old blue victrola from the back seat of the car on it.

"You'll probably have every fox in the county trying to get in on this dancing business," he joked.

"Dad!" I begged.

"I'll be out front, if you need me." Dad disappeared out front, leaving Nancy and me to our precious privacy. Except for a few dozen pesky deer flies, we spent the afternoon uninterrupted. We played *Moonlight on the Strand*, over and over, took turns leading the dance, and by the end of the afternoon felt pretty confident that we could actually do the dance out in public. If we ever got the opportunity.

Growing Pains

Nancy was waiting for me after school, a load of books in her arms weighted down further by her green metal lunch pail. "Isn't it exciting," she exclaimed, "Shirley, getting married?"

Our friend and my junior choir director, Shirley Cavadias, had met this cool guy named Chet, was getting married and, even though she was in her twenties, she'd decided to invite the whole gang of us younger girls to her wedding reception. She'd be wearing a gorgeous white gauzy gown, having a big church wedding, and hiring a band to play at the reception. And that meant dancing!

"Do you think your parents will let you go?" Nancy asked as we trudged down the hill toward Dober Location.

"I don't know. How about yours?" I shifted my books from one arm to the other.

"Oh, I'm sure I can work it out with them. My Dad will probably offer to drive us." Nancy was always so sure of herself. "I'll have my mom call your mom. Okay?"

"You betcha! See you tomorrow." I raced into the house to share my good news and see what I could do about getting permission to attend the reception.

"Shirley Cavadias has invited the whole Junior Choir to her wedding reception," I yelled to Mom as I shot in the back door. "Can I go?"

"Well, I don't know. Where is it? And when?" Mom looked up briefly from peeling potatoes at the kitchen sink.

"It's at the Verona Clubhouse in Caspian. Nancy's going to ask her Dad to drive us there and pick us up," I said breathlessly.

"I'll have to talk to Dad about this, before I decide," Mom replied.

"Dad? You've got to talk to Dad about this? He'll say, 'No' for sure. He thinks I'm just a little kid. He'll never let me go. Can't you just say it's okay?" I tried not to whine, but I felt my hopes of going with the gang falling fast.

Just then the phone rang. Mom answered, then a brief silence followed. Then Mom said, "Well, I don't know. I've got to talk to Johnny. I think the girls are a little young to be going to a wedding reception, unchaperoned." I winced at that, but perked up my ears, not wanting to miss anything. After another space of silence on Mom's end, she said, "Oh really? I didn't know she was going. Well, that does change things a bit. Let me see what Johnny says. I'll call you back." She hung up the phone and looked at me?

"Well?" I asked. The suspense was killing me.

"Nancy's mother says her dad is going to drive her to the wedding reception. And she said Mrs. Anderson, the other junior choir director, is going to be there, too."

"Then I can go?" I tried to see the answer in Mom's eyes.

"I told you, I have to talk to your father. We'll see what he says," Mom said with finality.

When Dad finally got home from work, he went right to the kitchen sink, rolled up his sleeves, and started scrubbing the iron ore dust from his hands and arms. Then he took the evening paper and went to the breakfast nook to sit and wait for supper.

"Dad, Mom's got something to ask you." I knew I should let Mom pick the time to ask him, but I just couldn't stand the waiting.

"Huh?" Dad put the paper down, folded it, and looked at Mom.

Mom rolled her eyes at me, letting me know I was not doing my cause one bit of good, then quickly covered for me. "Coralie's been invited to a wedding reception at the Verona Clubhouse in Caspian. Shirley Cavadias is getting married and she's invited the whole Junior Choir to come. Mrs. Anderson, the other director will be going along, so the girls won't be entirely on their own."

"Whoa!" Dad picked his paper up from the table and dropped it on the seat beside him. "When is this party?"

"Next month, on the eleventh. It's about four weeks away." I suppose I should have kept my mouth shut, but I just couldn't.

Dad looked me square in the eyes, narrowing his own in a kind vulture stare. "It's at night?"

"Uh huh." Dead in the water. There was no way he'd let me go out at night.

"And just what do you think you're gonna' do there?" The interrogation had begun. I was already in trouble and I hadn't done anything.

"Talk to my friends? Eat? I don't know—dance, maybe."

"Dance? With boys?" It seemed he had totally forgotten about helping us practice the Fox Trot at Hagerman Lake. I knew I was sunk.

"Well, no. I don't know. I mean I don't know if there'll be any boys there. I don't even know if we'll dance."

"You're too young to go out dancing." The subject was closed. "Maybe when you're in high school. Maybe." Dad picked up his paper and started to read. So that was that. I was crestfallen. I hadn't really thought he'd let me go, still I had held out hope. Now there was no hope.

"Bill Gagne has offered to drive the girls there and pick them up."

Mom, the miracle worker, was actually pleading my case. "Maybe it would be all right to let her go, under the circumstances?"

"Under the circumstances, I'd say she's too young to go dancing," Dad repeated.

"Geez, I don't even know how to dance. I mean, Nancy and I can barely do the Fox Trot. We'll probably just sit there all night and watch. There's nothing wrong with that, is there?" I said, an edge to my voice. I was living dangerously again, but I figured all was just about lost anyway.

"Well if you're just gonna' sit there all night, you might as well stay home. You can sit here all night." Dad gave a little laugh.

"It's not funny!" I was heading for worse trouble now.

"Watch your tongue." Mom gave me an exasperated look.

"It's just that all the other girls are going. They've got new dresses and some of them are even wearing nylons." Out of the frying pan into the fire.

"Nylons," Mom said surprised, "you didn't say anything about nylons."

"Well, I was going to . . ."

"Are we gonna' have supper around here tonight, or not?" Dad's patience had ended. The discussion was now definitely over.

I kept my eyes on my plate throughout supper, picked at my food, and slunk out of the room and up the stairs to my bedroom afterward. Then I put my head down on my pillow and felt the curse of hot tears forcing their way into my eyes. I didn't want to cry. Crying was for babies. Maybe I was only twelve, but I could act grown up enough not to cry. It was no use. The more I tried not to cry, the more I cried. I sobbed softly into my pillow until there were no more tears.

Next morning, Mom whisked me out of bed, fixed me cream of wheat for breakfast, and drove us both to morning

Mass. I didn't feel much like talking in the car, but I finally couldn't resist asking, "Did you talk to Mrs. Gagne, yet?"

"No, not yet," Mom replied, her eyes on the road. "I'll get back to her today. What was all this talk about nylons?"

"The girls who are going to the wedding reception are getting new dresses. Arlene's mother bought her a garter belt and nylons. All the other girls already have nylons."

"Well, they're all older than you, too." Mom's comment did nothing to make me feel better. Could I help it if I was one of the youngest in my grade. Was it my fault Mom started me in Kindergarten when I was only four years old and now nearly all the kids in my class were older than me?

"Some of them have been wearing nylons for over a year," I said stubbornly. I'd probably be eighty years old before I got a garter belt and my first pair of nylons.

"Why in the world would they need nylons?" Mom asked.

"Because white anklets and dress shoes look stupid together." Boy, if I had to spell that out, then we had a real problem.

"But you don't wear dress shoes every day," Mom continued.

"Nylons are not for everyday," I said impatiently. "They're for special occasions, like going out . . . or to church." I figured the mention of church would make a favorable impression on Mom.

"You girls are always in such a hurry to grow up. Before you know it, you'll be wearing nylons every day and wish you didn't have to worry about keeping your seams straight." Mom tried to make a joke of it, but I was in no mood. I gave her a dull look as we walked into church.

School was buzzing with the news of the wedding and reception. Everybody was talking about what they would wear, how they would fix their hair, and about dancing. Nearly everyone was worried about dancing in public. No one had done it before. Here, Nancy and I were a step ahead of the others, but then it would do me no good if I couldn't even go to the reception.

"So, has your mother decided if you can go, or not?" Nancy asked as we trudged down the hill after school. "Mom said she hadn't called her back as of last night."

"My Dad says I'm too young to go out dancing," I grumbled. "Even after he found out that your dad is driving, he wouldn't give in."

"Maybe he'll change his mind," Nancy said, trying console me.

"My Dad never changes his mind," I said firmly. "It would take a miracle for me to be able to go. See you tomorrow."

I watched Nancy walk down the alley to her house and wished I was thirteen, almost fourteen like her. Then, maybe Dad would let me go. "I'm home," I yelled as I walked in the back door.

"I have something for you." Mom was holding two small brown paper sacks and smiling. "Here, open this one first."

I put my books down on the kitchen counter, took the first sack, and opened it curiously. Inside, there was a flat box, about a half inch high, and the shape of a small stack of typing paper. I pulled it out, opened it, and saw a beautiful brand new pair of tan nylon stockings pressed perfectly flat and wound around a white cardboard insert.

"Oh, Mom, they're gorgeous!" I put my hand inside the top of one of the stockings, held it to the light, and knew I had never owned anything so luxurious.

"Now open this," Mom held out the other package. "The nylons won't do you much good without it," she laughed. Inside was a white garter belt which fastened at the waist and sported four garters with rubber buttons that hooked inside silver clamps. "Just a few words of wisdom," she went on, "always make sure your nails are filed and buffed so you don't accidentally pull a run in your stockings. Watch out for anything sharp, like pins or nails, and always keep your seams straight. Here I'll show you how to put them on." She pushed one stocking up on her arm, rolled it down to the toe, and said, "Start at the toe and work your way up. Slowly. Make this pair last. They're expensive."

I took the stockings and belt up to my bedroom, hitched the belt around my waist, checked my fingernails, and cautiously pulled on first one and then the other stocking. I caught a look at myself in the mirror. I looked absolutely ridiculous. But, once I was dressed up, the new stockings would make all the difference in the world. I felt practically grown up.

If only I could wear these to the wedding reception. What would make Dad change his mind about letting me go? I couldn't think of a thing. I carefully slipped off the nylons, now baggy where the creases had been, replaced them as best I could in their attractive box, and headed back downstairs for supper.

Dad was washing up for supper, when I stepped into the kitchen, and it made me mad just to see him standing there. He didn't have a thing to worry about in his life. Everything was just perfectly fine. Why should he care if I had a good time? Why should he care if all my friends were going to the big party and I had to stay home?

"Hi there." He gave me a big grin. Like I said, not a worry in the world. Boy, was I mad at him.

"Hi." I looked right past him and didn't say anything else. I was thinking maybe I'd never even really speak to him again.

"You want to go out to the lake tonight?" he asked.

"No." No, period. No, I didn't want to go anywhere with him. No, I didn't want to go anywhere with him—ever again.

"I'm just gonna' take a little ride out there and back. It'll be a quick trip?" Dad would be sorry he betrayed me when I needed him most. I'd make him pay. He'd miss me on his trips. He'd be sorry.

"No, I don't want to go." I couldn't bring myself to look him in the eye.

Just then the phone rang and Mom answered. "Coralie?" she said into the phone. "Well, I don't know. When? How long will you be? I don't know. I'll have to talk to her father. Let me call you back."

I stared at Mom after she'd hung up the phone, waiting to hear what it was all about. "Mrs. Holmes wants you to baby-sit tonight," Mom said to me. Then she said to Dad, "Her regular baby-sitter is sick and she's got a meeting she's got to go to."

"Well, I don't know." Dad frowned. "How late will she be?"

"She says she should be home by eleven o'clock. It's just down the street and she's really in a pinch. I think we should let Coralie go. She can call us if there's a problem."

"I suppose." Dad wasn't too happy. "But I don't want this to be a regular thing."

Mom called Mrs. Holmes back, told her I'd be over in ten minutes, and hung up. Baby-sitting! This was great. Nancy, and several of the other girls I knew, got baby-sitting jobs regularly. It was the grown up thing to do.

Ten minutes later, I knocked on the Holmes' front door, was invited into the house, and told the kids were already in bed and asleep. Mrs. Holmes eyed me up and down, showed me where the telephone was, said I was not to use it unless there was an emergency, and told me not to play the radio. She pointed to the sofa where the evening newspaper had been tossed upside down and suggested I sit and read. Then, she picked up her purse, and headed out the door.

Some fun I was going to have. I couldn't even play the radio. I sat on the sofa, gave the radio a longing look, and decided I'd better do exactly as I'd been told—read the newspaper.

I picked it up, turned it over, and was shocked and intrigued by the headlines. "World saddened by King George's death," "Elizabeth to become Queen," "British Monarchy passes on crown." I spent the next two hours reading the detailed account of King George's death, the chronicles of the British Monarchy, and a complete description of the lives of young Princess Elizabeth and her younger sister Princess Margaret and how they would be affected by the change in Elizabeth's new status as queen. It was all totally fascinating—a real live queen, just a little older than my sister Corinne. I wondered how the younger sister, Margaret, felt about not getting to be queen, just because she'd been born a few years later. It seemed pretty unfair to me.

Lots of things were unfair. I was sure I knew just how Princess Margaret felt. My sister was just like a queen in our family. She was married; had three beautiful kids, Cheryl, Lester, and Wendi; and was grown up. She lived in Chicago, looked like a movie star, and knew exactly what to say all the time. She never, ever, got blemishes on her face, got tongue-tied, or blushed. She was grown up and that seemed to be the key to everything. She could do exactly as she pleased and Mom and Dad thought it was just fine.

But me? Oh, that was a different story. Here I was old enough to have a baby-sitting job, but too young to go with to Shirley's reception. It was just plain unfair.

The next morning, I made myself a glass of Ovaltine, fixed myself a bowl of Pep cereal, and sat down to eat.

"So how's the baby-sitter?" Mom seemed full of good cheer this morning.

"Okay, I guess. Mrs. Holmes paid me a dollar for baby-sitting," I said proudly.

"So how did you like it?" Mom asked.

"Well, the kids were asleep. I couldn't play the radio, so I read the paper. Did you know that Princess Elizabeth is going to be Queen of England?" I took a hearty bite of my cereal, then gulped down what was left of my Ovaltine.

Mom looked at me with what appeared to be new interest, was silent for a moment, then finally said, "I didn't know you were interested in current events. You seem so grown up all of a sudden."

I didn't know what to say. I was so surprised to hear this from Mom, I just looked at her, tongue-tied.

"Dad and I were talking last night, honey," Mom continued thoughtfully. Oh great, now what kind of trouble was I in. "We think you're a pretty responsible girl." Responsible? Me? "Especially for your age." There it was, the age thing again. "Now, you're even going to be getting baby-sitting jobs . . . seems like just yesterday you were such a little girl."

"I'm twelve," I said like an idiot, as if Mom didn't know how old I was.

"Yes, twelve." Mom smiled. "So young and yet you'll soon be a teenager. Hard to believe. Well, anyway, your father and I have decided if you're old enough to baby-sit, you're certainly old enough to go to a friend's wedding reception."

"Really?" I couldn't believe my ears. Here I was ready to start World War III, and a peace pact was already in place.

"Dad says you have to be home by eleven, but it's okay for you to ride with Nancy and her dad. I already called Mrs. Gagne and told her." I pushed away my empty bowl, jumped up, and gave Mom a big hug. "Oh Mom, thanks!" I sure was lucky to have parents thoughtful enough to see I really was growing up.

I rushed over to the phone, gave the operator Nancy's telephone number, and waited excitedly for her to answer. "Nancy, we've got to brush up on the Fox Trot," I hollered into the receiver.

Dancing in the Dark

Before the big night finally arrived, Mom took me shopping at Kromm's Department Store. Upstairs in Women's Apparel, we found a beautiful pink and grey dress that fit perfectly. On the main floor in the shoe department, Mom and I had a brief argument about me not being old enough to wear high heels, but it was quickly forgotten when I fell in love with a pair of black suede flats with an interesting cut-out pattern over the toes. Finally, Mom let me pick out a card of three little gold animal scatter pins in the purse, glove, and novelty section of the store.

Sequestered in my bedroom, I held a dress rehearsal in front of the mirror. I tried on everything including the new garter belt and nylons, and after taking a long scrutinizing look, I decided I really did look a lot more grown up. I could hardly wait for the wedding reception.

The day of the wedding finally dawned. It was a Saturday that seemed to stretch on forever. I thought suppertime would never arrive, but it finally did and, as soon I'd finished eating and helping with the dishes, I made a bee-line for my bedroom, assembled my clothes on the bed, and carefully dressed. Then I went downstairs to show Mom and Dad how I looked.

"You look very pretty," Mom said, looking up from her crocheting.

"What do you think?" I asked Dad who was listening to the news on the radio.

"Pretty fancy." Dad wasn't about to say anything much about all this dressing up business, but I could see a little twinkle in his eye as he looked at the new me.

"Now, you know what time you have to be home? And you know what to do if you need us. Just call. Stay with the other girls, no matter what. Be polite . . ." Mom started listing the things we'd been over a dozen times already.

"I know, Mom," I groaned, grabbing my coat. "I'm going over to Nancy's. Okay?"

"Have a good time," I heard Mom say as I left the house and headed down the alley.

Nancy's Dad was already out in the black Nash with the motor running when I got there. "Get in," he called. "Nan's on her way out." So I climbed in the back seat.

A minute later, Nancy climbed in beside her father in the front and off we went, neither of us saying a word until he dropped us at the door of the Verona Clubhouse. Then we headed right inside and straight to the nearest restroom so we could look in the mirror. Nancy had a shiny new dark blue taffeta dress, a rhinestone necklace, and black suede shoes much like mine only without the cut-out patterns. Her dark shiny hair, which she'd worn in long braids for years, had been recently cut and curled. She looked smashing.

"I love your dress," I told her excitedly.

"I love yours, too!"

"Are my seams straight?" I asked nervously.

"Let me see." I turned around and pulled my hem line up over my calves. "They're fine. How about mine?"

"Fine." I nodded. "What have you got there?" Nancy had pulled a tube of lipstick out of her little black purse, opened it, and was preparing to apply it to her lips.

"Lipstick. You want to use it?" She put two dabs of dark wine-colored lipstick on her upper lip then drew a long narrow curve on her lower lip, capped the tube, and offered it to me.

"No, I'd better not, my mother would kill me. Doesn't your mother care?"

"Oh, Mom bought this for me. She doesn't mind if I wear lipstick." Nancy slipped the little gold tube back into her purse. "Well, shall we go in?"

"I'm nervous." My hands were cold and clammy, their telltale palms damp. "Aren't you?"

"Not really," Nancy said calmly. "We've got to start sometime." She led the way out of the restroom down a hall to the main room where long tables and chairs were set up all around the edges of the room, leaving the center of the wooden floor open and ready for dancing. In one corner of the room, there was a small bar where an older guy was stacking glasses, napkins, and sorting bottles, getting ready for the crowd. Across from the bar was a small makeshift stage built of risers. A bass fiddle, snare drum set, and black metal music stands, with the words, "CASPIAN BAND" stenciled in large letters on the backs, were set in front of empty chairs waiting for the musicians.

"Look, there's Mrs. Anderson and Arlene." I nudged Nancy and we hurried over to them, relieved to see someone we knew. The four of us found seats at one of the long tables, smoothed our skirts, and sat, looking anxiously around the room. A few people milled around the bar, visiting, but most of the guests hadn't arrived yet. We were early.

The air was thick with anticipation and tension. As the band members drifted in, went to their stations, and began tuning up, I thought I'd die of excitement. Before we knew it, we'd be out on the dance floor, dusting it off with our own rendition of the fabulous Fox Trot.

"Look there's Shirley," Mrs. Anderson whispered. "Doesn't she look gorgeous?"

Shirley and Chet walked into the hall. Shirley, her white wedding gown and veil unfurling about her, was still carrying her bouquet of pastel roses and white Shasta daisies with white silky streamers as she sailed over to our table.

"I'm so glad you could come. There'll be food in a minute, so fill your plates." She was beaming with a bridal brilliance we'd never seen before. We were held in the spell of her happiness. Chet, in black tux, followed silently along behind as she left our table and started making the rounds of the other tables, greeting guests who were now piling in by the dozens.

"Just think, someday, that'll be you, or me," I whispered to Nancy.

"Let's get something to eat, girls," Mrs. Anderson said, nodding her head for us to follow her to the long tables laden with plates, silverware, and bins of food. Sticking as close together as possible, we followed, single file behind Mrs. Anderson, watched how she filled her plate, then, for fear of making a mistake, copied her every move. None of us took much food. We were far too eager to think of eating.

We fiddled with our fingers, took small bites of our food, and watched nervously as the assembling band members took their places on the stage. The guy in front with the trumpet, tapped his foot, nodded at the drummer, and they began to play a rousing polka. The trombone, sax, and bass players joined in and the whole room started to vibrate. "We'll never be able to dance to this." I looked at the other girls and saw disappointment in their faces, too.

We sat glumly through two more loud boisterous polkas, wondering just how long they would go on. But when they finished, the trumpet player took out his hanky, wiped his dripping forehead, and gave the other players some kind of a sign. Before we knew it, they had lapsed into a new tune— slow, mellow, and romantic. Shirley and Chet got out there in the middle of the dance floor and waltzed in wide beautiful circles, sometimes looking into each other's eyes, and sometimes just staring blindly off into space as if they were the only people in the place. We sat there spellbound, watching them sway to the music.

"This is a waltz, girls," Mrs. Anderson told us. "The band will probably play a set of three. Usually the bride and groom dance the first dance and then other people can go out on the floor and dance, too."

"How will we know when it's okay to go out on the floor," Arlene asked.

"Just watch the other people. If they go, then it'll be all right for you to go, too." That made pretty good sense, but I was getting nervous listening to the music. It was slow and mellow all right, but it sure didn't sound like *Moonlight on the Strand*. I watched the guests joining Shirley and Chet on the dance floor. They stepped, swirled, and swayed smoothly to the music. It looked so easy and graceful, I was dying to try it, but something besides shyness was holding me back—panic.

"There's quite a few people out there dancing now, if you'd like to get out in the crowd," Mrs. Anderson told us girls.

"Well, shall we try it?" Nancy asked, getting up from her seat, waiting for me to join her.

I pushed away from the table, stood, and took one step toward the dance floor, but my feet seemed frozen. "I don't know," I mumbled nervously to Nancy, but she had already turned and was walking out into the middle of the dancers.

"C'mon," she said over her shoulder, "I'll lead if you like." I forced my feet to follow her, certain we were the center of attention, with everyone in the room eyeing us curiously.

"Let's move over by the wall," I whispered to Nancy. "It's dark over there and maybe no one will notice if we're clumsy."

"Oh, all right, but no one is paying the slightest bit of attention to us," Nancy said sort of sternly. We made our way over to the wall, reached out our arms, and struck a dance pose, but we couldn't seem to get started.

"Okay," I whispered, "remember the Fox Trot—one step. Two step. Side step. Step together. Repeat."

"Right," she whispered back. "Just concentrate." In the shadows near the wall, we took one step, then another and tripped over each other's feet, nearly falling on the floor.

"Oh no," I gasped, "we're making fools of ourselves."

We tried again, but had the same problem. Then it hit me. Nancy and I probably couldn't dance to anything except *Moonlight on the Strand*. We were doomed to be wallflowers for the rest of our lives.

"Cuts," Mrs. Anderson and Arlene said, tapping Nancy and me on the shoulders.

"Mrs. Anderson," I confessed, "I just can't do this. It's no use. I might as well sit down for the rest of the night. I'll just step all over your feet."

"No, no don't worry. Just relax and listen to the music. Here I'll lead." She put her hand firmly on my waist and grabbed my hand. "Just follow along."

Concentrating, I followed along as closely as I could, but still managed to step all over her new shoes. "I'm sorry," I foolishly babbled over and over.

Then she stepped on my feet and laughed. "You'll catch on in no time. Just quit worrying," she said encouragingly. "You're already doing better than me and I've been at it for years." I glanced over at Nancy and Arlene and they seemed to be doing all right, too.

We made it through the waltz, but when the band slipped into another polka, we hit for the table and time out. "Wasn't that just grand?" Nancy bubbled. "I knew we could do it."

"Grand," I gulped, glad to have gotten through it and back to the safety of the table. We waited through the polka, through the band's intermission, and through the cutting of the wedding cake. Then, as the saxophone began to swoon with another slow tune, Nancy and I decided to brave the dance floor again. We took two steps and nearly tumbled over. We started again, tripped, and finally tried standing in one spot, rocking back and forth to the music. "I've had enough," I said finally.

"Me too, I guess. It's been really fun, but it's nearly eleven and my Dad will be here any minute," Nancy replied.

"We've got a lot of practicing to do, if we ever want to learn to dance," I said. "It looks so easy, but I don't know if we're ever going to be very good at it."

"Sure we will," Nancy said in her bright, mature way. "All we need is a little more experience. We already know how to do the Fox Trot and tonight we learned to waltz. Who knows what tomorrow will bring?"

"Guess you're right. All in all, it's been a lot of fun, hasn't it?" I was feeling pretty proud and grown up even though our dancing needed improvement.

"Just think, our first time dancing in public. Even if it was in the dark, it was an unforgettable evening," Nancy sighed, shrugging on her fleecy white jacket and sounding more grown up than ever.

"It'll probably be a long time before we get another chance to go dancing," I said.

"Maybe . . . Maybe not. Maybe next time we'll dance right out there under the lights." Nancy's dark eyes twinkled knowingly, as if they had taken a peek into the future.

Chorus Line

An intriguing white folded piece of typing paper and a stack of three by eight inch printed slips was sent from the principal's office to my seventh grade homeroom. They were placed secretively into Mrs. Pascoe's hands by a school messenger who darted silently into the room and out, with the stealth of a smuggler. Wonder and worry filled the eyes of my classmates and me as we waited for the announcement. It was always that way, with notes from the office.

It was hard to say just what the news would bring, but it was usually bad news, like the time we all had to take notes home to our parents, telling them to check our hair because it was discovered one of the kids in school had head lice. Once, they announced the death of two kids from a neighboring school who'd gone swimming in one of the local iron ore pits and drowned. Notes were sent to our parents, issuing a severe warning of danger. And then, there was the yearly immunization clinic where everyone was herded through the halls and upstairs to the school auditorium to get their shots. Like I said, it was usually bad news.

Mrs. Pascoe unfolded the note, read it silently to herself, and finally read it aloud to the concerned and curious class. "The American Legion is sponsoring a fund-raiser and the Stambaugh Legionnaires are participating. A program to be presented by the Stambaugh community will be held in the high school gymnasium on February 23, 1951. This being the month of Presidents Washington and Lincoln's birthdays, it will be a patriotic event with the proceeds going for senior high school college scholarships. Miss Carol Brown, a representative of the national organization, will be arriving in Stambaugh on Tuesday to coordinate activities for the event and plan the presentation. All girls in the seventh and eighth grades are invited to attend auditions to be held at the Legion Hall this Tuesday afternoon after school. A permission slip signed by parents is required for attendance." She refolded the note, set it on her desk, and picked up the slips. "Those of you who are interested, may come up and get your permission slips."

The boys—in their glory—snickered, snorted, and pointed at us girls as we passed their desks on our way to the front of the room. Ralph Nevempaa, "Bobbo" Maki, and Ronnie Gehloff made short grunting sounds while Bob Richard, Billy Olson, and George Brunswick tried to reach out from under their desks and grab the hems of our skirts. But who cared?

Auditions! Patriotic program! This wasn't bad news, this was great news. I couldn't wait for school to end that day so Nancy and I could talk it over. I hoped she was as enthused as I was.

"Did you get a permission slip?" I yelled to Nancy who was waiting for me, as usual, across the street from school.

"I took one, but I'm not sure I really want to be in this program," Nancy called back.

"Not sure?" I caught up with her. How could you not be sure about something as sensational as this. "Why?"

"Well, it's not very clear what we'd have to do," she said.

"Who cares? We'll probably sing. Maybe we'll read some poetry or be in a skit. C'mon, Nancy. You've just got to go. It's a chance to be on stage. I don't want to go alone," I begged.

"I suppose. What do you think your mother will say?" She had to bring that up.

"Well, I think it'll be okay. I mean the permission slips are pretty official and all." Still there was that hurdle to jump. "What about yours?"

"I don't think she'll mind," Nancy answered.

Mom was in the middle of fixing formula for my new baby brother Jim when I came in. While the baby squalled in his bassinet in the kitchen doorway, she darted between the stove where baby bottles were rattling around in boiling water, and the kitchen cabinet where she was trying to clean up the empty cans of Carnation milk, keep the Karo syrup from coagulating on the counter, and start dinner.

I started right in, blabbing a blue streak. Trying to listen to me and the blubbering baby, Mom was having a little difficulty hearing, but as usual, she was able to do both.

"I don't know about this program. We're not members of the Legion, you know," Mom said, springing to pick up the baby.

"It's a program for the community, not just members of the Legion, Mom. The announcement came right from Miss Wymore's office," I argued, rifling through a kitchen junk drawer, looking for a pencil.

"The principal's office?" Mom rocked the baby in her arms, trying to quiet him. "There, there," she sang softly.

It was the perfect moment. I shoved the permission slip on the sticky counter, handed her the pencil I'd found in the drawer, and tapped my toe as she balanced the baby in her left arm and placed her signature on the dotted line.

The following day Nancy and I hiked north on Stambaugh Main Street to the Legion Post where we found several dozen nervous girls already standing around in noisy little groups. A beautiful young woman with shimmering blonde hair met us at the door, smiling. "I'm Miss Brown. Thanks for coming. You can go ahead and find a place over there with the other girls," she said.

"How about here," I whispered to Nancy, leading the way to the center of the room.

"Okay, let's get started. How many of you know how to dance?" the young woman asked. Nancy and I looked at each other uneasily. Dance? I knew we were both thinking of Shirley's wedding reception. Could you call that dancing? We shrugged and raised our hands half-heartedly.

"Good." She gave us a brilliant smile. "Here's what I want you to do. There must be at least thirty of you, too many for one line." She silently counted the huddle of anxious girls. "I want you to form five rows of six girls each." At first, no one moved. Then everyone moved at once, creating an hysterical hubbub, but we all finally found places. Nancy and I ended up in the center of the third row.

"Group one," she said, pointing to the first row of girls, "step forward, please. Now, watch me." She stood with her back to the line and began her dance routine. "Step right, cross over, step right, cross over, kick, step left, cross over, step left, cross over, kick. Now step forward, kick right, kick left, kick right, step back. I want you all to follow along as best you can." She led the group of floundering girls through the steps, turned around, and smiled. "Okay, one group at a time, out front and center. And dance."

Nancy and I, like a couple of hungry hawks, watched the other girls try out. "We can do this," I whispered. "It's just like when we first started trying to do the Fox Trot. Remember how well we did just standing side by side? We didn't get into trouble, until we tried to dance together."

"You're right!" Nancy whispered back.

"Group three, forward and center please," Miss Brown instructed. "Once through to learn, then once through to audition." We weren't going to get a second chance to prove ourselves. We were going to have to do it right the first time. Nancy and I stepped right, crossed over, and kicked in perfect unison. Fred and Ginger! The Fox Trot had been a lot harder than this. We couldn't help smiling. Right here in the chorus line, we'd found our calling.

As soon as the last three groups had done their dances, Miss Brown held up her hand for silence and gave these simple instructions. "Please form one long line around the room. I'm going to walk past and point to the six people I've chosen to be in the program. Whether you're picked or not, please remain in your places and try not to talk until I'm through. Those of you who aren't selected will be free to leave once I'm through. The others should stay to receive a rehearsal schedule."

Nancy and I gave each other a worried glance and held our breath as we watched her walk slowly by the first several girls without pointing. My heart was thump-thumping away as I eyed the bitter disappointment on the faces of the girls passed over. Oh please, don't let that happen to me. Finally, she made her first selection. Relief and joy flooded the girl's face.

Miss Brown chose two more girls and was coming closer. She slowed, looked thoughtfully at a girl two people ahead of me, and pointed. Then she continued toward Nancy and me. There were only two spots left and a long line of girls behind us. The chances of us both being chosen were practically zero. My eyes were bugging right out of my head as I watched Miss Brown approach. She nodded at me and Nancy, but she didn't point. We looked at her questioningly. Could she possibly have meant both of us?

"You two," she said, pointing to Nancy and me. "That's it. Thank you all for coming."

We had done it. We had landed places on the program. Dancing. Who would have ever thought it possible? "We've got a lot of hard work to do," Miss Brown broke into my thoughts. "Here's a rehearsal schedule. We'll be meeting here for the next three nights after school. There will be a piano player here for you to practice with tomorrow, Thursday, and Friday, but we'll have a real live band to accompany you in the program. On Saturday night, you'll have to be at the school by seven o'clock for a dress rehearsal. I'll have your costumes ready for you in the Physical Education locker room. The show will follow at eight o'clock. Any questions?"

Nancy's mother offered to drive us to the program on Saturday night and Mom, though disappointed she couldn't attend, said it was all right with her since Dad was working and the baby was too young to be left with a baby-sitter.

Wednesday, after school, Nancy and I and the four other girls gathered at the Legion Hall ready to dance. We were as confident as could be now that we'd made it through auditions. Miss Brown greeted us with her dazzling smile, showed us where to stand, and introduced the piano player. Then she handed out mimeographed sheets with several verses of a song printed out in lavender letters. "Here's the song you'll be singing as you dance in the chorus line."

Chorus line? Nancy and I gave each other a nervous look. We had enough trouble just counting out the steps in our heads, while we tried to make our feet do what our brains were telling them to. Now we had to sing, too?

"By the time Saturday night arrives," Miss Brown said, "you'll know this whole routine by heart. In fact you'll know it so well, you'll probably never forget it. Now, the first thing I want you to do is listen to the piano and try to follow along. I'll sing with the piano so you can hear how it should sound."

The piano player gave a gutsy introduction, "Bump, bump, ta-dump, bump, bump," paused slightly, and Miss Brown began to sing, "We are Yankee Doodle Dan-dies. Yankee Doodle, Doodle Do's. Real live sisters of our Uncle Sam, wearing the red, white, and blue-ue-ue-ue . . . All right girls, let's try it all together."

We sang the Yankee Doodle Dandy song over several times. It was a catchy tune all right. "Let's try it now without looking at the words," Miss Brown said. "The sooner you let go of your song sheets, the sooner you'll learn it."

On Thursday, we learned a step right, cross over, step, kick routine that went right with the song. We struggled at first, but things were going smoothly. By Friday, we put the song and dance routine together, rehearsed it from beginning to end, worked on the rough spots, and actually felt ready for the big night.

"I can't believe we're really going to dance in a program," Nancy said as we walked home after rehearsal.

"Me either. I can't wait," I laughed confidently, tucking my coat collar and big red wool scarf tighter around my face against the gusts of icy wind pushing us along our path. "Nothing can stop us now."

Nothing could stop us, except possibly the weather. On Saturday, the Upper Peninsula of Michigan winds, gathering constant momentum, roared with a vengeance which hadn't been heard for a long time. "It's freezing cold out there," Mom said looking out the window. "I hope you girls aren't going to be disappointed if they have to cancel the show."

Disappointed? We'd just simply die, that's all. This was our night to shine. We'd come all the way from working out in the gravel at Hagerman Lake learning the Fox Trot, to tripping over each other at Shirley's wedding reception, to this day—this night—our finest hour. "But it's too cold to snow, isn't it?" I asked Mom. "They never cancel anything unless there's a blizzard, do they?"

"Honey, it's ten below zero out there and the mercury is dropping fast. It could be twenty below, or worse, by tonight," Mom said.

"Oh, who cares if it's a little cold out there." I tried to look out the kitchen window, but it was covered over in a thin icy layer of glistening star bursts. I touched my forefinger to the design and burned a print just big enough to take a peek outside. It looked like Antarctica out in the back yard.

"Well, if it was just cold, it wouldn't be so bad, but it's icy, too," Mom explained. "Even if they don't cancel the show, the roads will be bad. I really hate to have you out on a night like this."

"I can't not go! I made a promise to be there." I looked at her in despair.

"Honey, I don't want to spoil your plans, but I think you should be prepared for the possibility that you may get a call canceling the program. I just don't want you to be disappointed."

I wouldn't be disappointed, I'd be devastated. Somehow, or other, the show just had to go on. Every time the phone rang that afternoon, I jumped, worried it would be Miss Brown telling us the show had been cancelled by the weather. But the call, fortunately, never came. At six o'clock that evening, Nancy called. She and her mother would be there to pick me up in five minutes. Nothing could stop us now.

"Be careful on the ice," Mom called after me as I went out the back door. "Wear your boots!"

I didn't take time to put on my boots, and I was immediately sorry I hadn't, but there was no time to go back. Ice dangerously covered the walkway. Slipping, sliding, and freezing I made my way to the Nancy's mother's car.

"You girls think you're too grown up for boots, but you're going to break your necks one of these days trying to run around with those flimsy little shoes on," Nancy's mother said in greeting.

"Hi, Mrs. Gagne." What else could I say? I looked at Nancy, but she was silently staring straight ahead. I guessed her mother wasn't too thrilled about having to go out on a night like this.

"It must be nearly thirty below," Nancy's mother grumbled, "and icy."

"My mother thought they might even cancel the show," I offered, trying to be pleasant, clear the air.

"Well, if they'd had any sense, they would have," Nancy's mom was in a biting mood, just like the weather.

I figured I'd better not say anything else, but the sound, "Whoa!" escaped my mouth as we pulled around the corner by Judish's Gas Station onto the stretch leading to Stambaugh Hill, and did a spin right there in the middle of the road. Nancy turned in her seat and sent me a look that said, "Keep your mouth shut!"

"This is too darned dangerous," Mrs. Gagne fumed. "If it gets any worse, we're just going to have to turn around and go home. She gave the car a little more gas so we'd make it up the hill, but as soon as we started climbing, we also started sliding backwards and sideways. "Oh no you don't," Mrs. Gagne yelled at the car, the road, and the ice. "You're not getting away with this."

She gunned the motor, causing the tires to spin and grind and sound like a herd of raging wounded elephants scrambling for freedom. But the smell of burning rubber and gasoline seeping into the car seemed to give Nancy's mom all the adrenaline she needed to get that car moving forward, up the long frozen incline to the top of Stambaugh Hill.

All three of us were sweating by the time we slid into the entrance of the school yard. Nancy's mom maneuvered her big black Nash into the parking lot, stopped, and dropped us off. "I'll be back to pick you up after the show. Be out of there as soon as it's over," she commanded.

"Do you think we could go on over to Lenny's Soda Bar?" Nancy dared ask.

"Well, we'll see, Nan." Mrs. Gagne gave Nancy a little smile, her disposition much better now that she'd conquered the slippery Stambaugh Hill.

"Thanks, Mom," Nancy gushed. We both knew Nancy's Mom would be taking us out to celebrate.

The school was lit up like a Christmas tree, cars were skidding into the parking lot, and Nancy and I took small sliding steps all the way to the door where someone had thrown a couple of shovels full of sand. It was cold as the ice on Lake Superior, but, flushed with the heat of the moment, we barely noticed. We had finally arrived.

Once inside, we raced to the Physical Education locker room where we were to meet Miss Brown with the costumes. She was already there and looked up at us with her usual bright charming smile. "Get right into your costumes, girls."

Our costumes were laid out for us on the locker room benches—blue spangled skirts with silver blouses, and red and white vests covered with blue sequined stars. Black tap shoes and blue and white striped sequined top hats with red bands completed our outfits. In minutes we were transformed into first class Yankee Doodle Dandies. "The rest of the girls are on stage and the band's tuning up for a quick run-through. Let's go," Miss Brown said.

As we tap-tapped down the hall in our cleated shoes to the stage, we could feel the old wooden rafters of the school vibrating from the beat of the band's drums. The louder it got, the more excited we became. We rushed out on stage in front of the colored footlights. Miss Brown walked out in front of us, called to the band to stop, and told us to spread out just as we had practiced. "We'll do a quick run-through with the band just to get you warmed up, but don't give it all you've got until the show starts," she told us. "Wait until you have an audience, then let it rip!" We'd barely sung one stanza of the song, when she held up her hand for the band to stop. "That's enough. Save it for the show."

Back in the locker room, we waited with nearly uncontainable excitement. Whatever else, or whoever else, was on the program was a mystery to us. We heard nothing, and saw nothing, until we were escorted backstage by Miss Brown and saw, from the wings, Legion supporters had braved the weather in full force. The audience was packed.

"Bump, bump, ta-dump, bump, bump," the band boomed in introduction as Miss Brown sent us flying out onto the stage. "We are Yankee Doodle Dandies, Yankee Doodle, Doodle, Do's. Real live sisters of our Uncle Sam, wearing the red, white, and blue-ue-ue-ue . . ."

There was nothing like the thrill of looking out over the hushed crowd and experiencing their excitement at seeing us sing and dance. We stepped straighter, kicked higher than we could ever have imagined possible. We strutted, sang, and tipped our top hats like professional Chorus Girls.

"We work, we play, we dance, we sing, we do our best in everything. We are the Yankee Doodle Do's!" We'd come to the end of our song. Too soon it had ended, but as the crowd stood and applauded, I caught a glimpse of Nancy's face blooming above the beams of yellow, red, and orange footlights. Her dark eyes flashed like embers, reflecting the wonder, glow, and fulfillment of my own.

Not only had we learned to dance, we had also learned—by taking one step at a time—we could overcome obstacles, achieve success, and create memories to be long cherished. Our hands held longingly onto the red, white, and blue sequined Yankee Doodle starred and striped costumes as we went to Miss Brown to hand them in and say, "Good bye."

We didn't want the wonder, the glitter, the accomplishment of the night to pass, but then it never ever really did.

Coralie and Nancy at Lenny's, celebrating with
ice cream and a lime phosphate.

Waste Not, Want Not

Eighth grade graduation was right around the corner. It was hard to believe only three months stood between me and a whole new life as a freshman in Stambaugh High School. At long last, I would be able to break free of the confines of Couzens Grade School.

Phyllis Aho, Donna Anderson, Fran Bociek, and all the other girls in my class were buzzing about buying new dresses for the big occasion. It was just about all we could think of.

Miss Lottie Wymore, the principal, a stern, grey-haired, bespectacled woman in stark black, had other things on her mind. From kindergarten on, she had tried to convince us to pay attention, work hard, and waste not. As she stood in front of our eighth grade class at the graduation rehearsal two weeks before the big event, it was hard to concentrate on what she was saying—we'd heard it so many times before.

"Some of you are not paying attention!" she boomed from the stage of the auditorium, staring directly at me. "It would behoove you to listen and not waste your time, daydreaming—for a change." Muffled giggles of my nervous classmates rippled through the room. Bob Thomas snuck his hand behind his head and pointed back at me, sending the rest of the class into stifled hysterics. Jerry Garlick, David Wall, and Jimmy Gurchinoff sat staring straight ahead, trying hard not to burst out laughing. Ralph Nevempaa's face flushed beet red, but he didn't move, or say a word.

"Make your life worthwhile. Take advantage of every moment. Waste not, want not . . ." It was the same old story we'd heard a million times. She finally walked off stage, hoping she would one day convince us that wasting anything was the worst thing we could do.

Mom and I sat in the living room, planning what I'd wear for the commencement exercises. I already had my first pair of high-heeled black suede shoes, a new pair of nylons, and new underwear. All I needed now was the dress of my dreams.

"Here's a pretty one," Mom said, pointing to a puffy pink organdy dress in the Alden's catalog. "You'd look pretty in pink. Of course, I hate to waste the money on something you're only going to wear once."

"Well, it wouldn't be wasted. I'd wear it every Sunday. But, I really don't want pink, or yellow, or blue either for that matter. What I'd really like is green," I said, flipping the pages.

"Green?" Mom shook her head. "I didn't see a single dress advertised in green."

"Oh, nuts," I grumbled. "Why can't I ever find what I want in this catalog?"

"Because you always want to be different, that's why," Mom said, closing the catalog, leaning back on the sofa, and looking at me exasperatedly.

"I can't help it."

"No I suppose you can't," Mom said, "but maybe it wouldn't hurt for you to try to conform a little."

"Conform?" I groaned.

"Never mind." Mom knew better than to waste her time trying to get me to conform. "I have an idea. Let's go shopping. If we can find some green organdy at one of the stores in Iron River, we can buy a pattern and I'll make you a dress."

"Dreamy! I can be ready to fly in a flash!" I bounded upstairs to my bedroom, kicked off my brown and white saddle shoes, pulled out a fresh pair of white anklets from my desk drawer, carefully folded the tops down twice to form a perfect double cuff, and slipped my shoes back on. I raided my closet for my favorite white cotton ruffled blouse—the one that was murder to iron—and my blue and white striped broomstick skirt, tossed them on, and stopped in the bathroom long enough to scrub my face with Sweetheart soap, comb my hair, and smear a couple of swipes of red Everlasting VIV lipstick on my mouth.

Mom and I drove up the hill to Stambaugh, where we decided to shop Harris' Department Store for fabric, but finding nothing, we got back in the maroon Chevy and drove down the hill to Iron River to continue the search.

At the Chicago Store, we found a beautiful array of filmy organdy, but in the usual colors only—no green. Then we went to Newberry's Five and Dime, but they had only pink and blue.

"We could go to Scott's or Irene's Dress Shop, but I hate to waste the time when I know I can sew you something for a lot less," Mom said.

So, we trudged over to Kromm's Department Store, climbed the stairs to the second floor fabric section, and discovered a lone bolt of green organdy ballooning boldly out from a cloudy rainbow of pink, blue, and yellow. Mom grabbed the bolt off the shelf, turned it so a length fell open, and ran her hands over and under the material. "This will work," she said, "and if I plan right, nothing will be wasted."

"It's got a floral design on it," I said excitedly. "I love it."

"This is called flocking and it's really quite subtle, lovely, and different. Actually, it would be pretty made up into curtains," Mom said more to herself than to me.

"Curtains?" What was she thinking of anyway.

"Besides, I don't think we have any further choices," Mom pointed out. "It's either this or nothing. Let's look at patterns." She walked over to the Simplicity pattern book and started paging through. "How do you like this one?"

"The neck isn't right," I answered, looking over Mom's shoulder. "Can I just look through the book, myself?" Mom stepped aside while I leafed through the book, landed on a pattern with a scooped neckline and stopped. "Look at that neckline. It's a real dazzler."

"How many yards do we need for this dress?" Mom asked the clerk. "I don't want to get more than I need and waste fabric."

"That one? Oh, you're going to need a lot. It'll take at least six yards." She stopped, looked at the green material in Mom's hands, and gave us a concerned look. "You're not planning to use this fabric for a dress are you? This material's meant for curtains."

"Curtains?" Mom hesitated. "Well, yes I thought of that myself. But it'll make a lovely dress, too."

"Well, anyway, I don't think there's enough material on the bolt for *that* dress." The clerk seemed determined to dissuade us from buying the green fabric.

"Well, let's measure and *see*. I don't want anymore than we need," Mom said determinedly.

"We don't want to waste any. You know, waste not, want not," I said, copying what I'd heard Miss Wymore say the day before. Mom didn't seem to hear me, but the clerk gave me a odd look as she flopped the cardboard bolt over and over until the entire length of fabric lay open on her cutting table.

"You've got five and three-quarter yards here, plus— maybe—an extra six inches," she said after putting the edge of the fabric into her measuring machine, pulling it slowly through, and watching the dial spin.

"That should be enough," Mom said.

"If it were me, I wouldn't take a chance," the clerk warned, holding tightly to the bolt as if it were her own personal possession.

"I'm sure it'll be enough. Don't want any waste. We'll take the whole piece, the pattern, and two, no one, spool of sea green thread."

When we got back home, Mom pulled out the pattern's pieces, laid them over the fabric on the dining room table, and studied the situation. "I'm going to have to skimp just a bit on the skirt, but I think it'll be a cinch."

As it turned out, it wasn't a cinch. The skirt was fine, but the scooped neckline was all wrong—not that there wasn't enough fabric. No, the problem was there was too much fabric. It was too big. Worst of all, we didn't realize just how big it was, until I slipped the dress on, an hour before the graduation ceremony.

"I can't wear *this*!" I shrieked, startled at the mirror's image of me in my green flopping neckline. It was a far cry from how it looked on the demurely draped model in the pattern picture.

"You *have* to wear it," Mom sputtered. "Here, let me see that." She twirled me and my dress around like a top, took little tucks with her fingers at the arms, neck, and waist, and shook her head.

"I'll be the laughing stock of the entire school." I was close to tears.

"Oh, Coralie, you're always being so dramatic. Nothing's that bad. And, you must admit, we didn't waste one bit of this fabric—except a little around the neck." Mom suddenly burst into giggles.

"Mom," I squealed, somewhere in between giggles and tears, "I'm never going to make it to school on time."

"This whole neckline needs to be taken apart and stitched on the machine." Mom sputtered, trying to get a grip on her giddiness.

"There's no time for that!" I gasped.

"Well, I've got to get it fixed." Mom, once again sober and serious, was getting more flustered by the second.

"Why did we ever use this fabric anyway?" I agonized.

"As I recall, we both thought it was quite lovely," Mom said.

"Sure, for curtains," I grumbled. "What are we going to do?"

"Well, you're going to stand still, while I take needle and thread and hand-stitch this dress into place." Sweating, Mom pulled a long thread from the silky green spool, bit it off with her teeth, and shoved the end through the eye of a sharp silver needle. "Don't *move*," she warned, knotting the thread, grabbing a hunk of green organdy, and stitching as fast as she could, while I stood staring up at the ceiling, wishing I'd picked a ready-made pink, blue, or yellow dress from the catalog.

"I'm going to be late," I fussed. "And what if the stitching comes out during the ceremony."

"You're not going to be late. And don't worry about this stitching coming out. I'll have to cut you out of this thing once you get home." I realized she wasn't joking, but there was no time to worry about that now.

In a whirl of green frenzy, I arrived at school just on time to join Lucille Rinko, Florence Gustafson, Barbara Jacobson, Judy Sporer, and Carol Wills entering Couzens School, heading to the auditorium on the second floor where the smell of reception food—egg salad sandwiches, strawberry jello with bananas and whipped cream, iced white cake, and lemonade—greeted us.

In the double doorway of the auditorium stood Gail Pedo, Jeannie Baker, and JoAnn Nelson, waiting, looking as pretty as a summer garden. Clicking down the hall in their new high heels were Sandra Sande, Marlene Gibson, and Roselyn Holmes. Barbara Keenan and Delores Schinella, flushed with excitement, hurried up the stairwell to join the group. The girls, lovely in their gauzy new gowns, floated into the auditorium like puffy pastel clouds in a Monet painting.

Trooping along behind marched the eighth grade boys, looking astonishingly like gentlemen in white shirts, dark ties, and multi-colored sport coats and trousers. Behind the four front rows of graduates sat the chatting audience, our mothers dressed to the hilt in their best Sunday dresses, white gloves, and matching straw hats fresh from the recent Easter season. Our absent fathers, at work in their respective jobs, would get the complete low-down on who, what, when, and where from our news reporting mothers later at the dinner table.

"Hold fast to your dreams," Miss Lottie Wymore stood, once again, in front of the old oak podium on the stage of the auditorium. She and the auditorium, where we had held all of our school programs since Kindergarten, some of the more serious exams, and reading hour once a week, would soon be a part of our history. I stared at her intently, determined to listen on this most special of all days. I felt an itch under the folds at the waist of my green dress, where Mom had placed her frantic stitches, but I pushed it out of my mind and promised myself I would not squirm.

"There is nothing you cannot do, if you put your mind to it." Oh no, she was going to talk about wasting time again—I just knew it. I folded my hands in my lap and looked straight back at her. "Don't let anything sway you from your path. Never be afraid to work toward goals and ideas that are new and creative. There would be no progress in the world without the unique contributions of each individual. Use the time you have been given to its best benefit. Remember, waste not, want not!" Her gaze traveled over the group, certain she had, at last, convinced us.

I looked down at my beautiful new high-heeled black suede shoes, the trussed up neckline of my dress which only Mom and I knew was tacked in place, and my friends around me. I marveled at how I had felt transformed into an adult.

"Will the Couzens School Eighth Grade Graduating Class of 1953 please stand. As your names are called, please come forward to receive your diplomas," Miss Wymore boomed.

"Phyllis Aho, Donna Anderson, Jeanne Baker, Ralph Baker, Frances Bociek, George Brunswick . . ." I knew my name was coming up soon . . . "Coralie Cederna." I crossed the old wooden stage for the last time, received my diploma from Miss Wymore's hand, and returned to my seat, certain that success in future pursuits was just within my reach—if I wasted not.

But the celebration wasn't over until Mom and I had arrived home, taken pictures with the old box camera, and looked carefully over my diploma. The final step then was to remove the green dress from me, or me from it. Mom got out her scissors and came towards me. By this time, I was feeling so scratchy that I didn't much care. Yet, again, it was my special graduation dress and I really didn't want to part with it this soon.

"Do you think you can redesign it?" I asked.

"Well, I'm going to do something to it, that's for sure. I'm not going to have all that beautiful flocked fabric go to waste," Mom said, snipping away her handy dandy stiches and freeing me from the dress.

"That's right. Waste not, want not," I laughed, "just like Miss Wymore said."

"She did make a good point," Mom said thoughtfully.

We were barely a week into summer vacation when I started thinking about that beautiful green dress again. I bounded into the house to talk to Mom about it. Surely, she had plenty of time now to reconstruct it. I'd heard her humming away on the old Singer Sewing Machine just that morning.

At first, I didn't notice the new curtains in the kitchen. There was something familiar about them, but it didn't register, until I looked directly at the familiar flocked flowers on gauzy green.

"Oh no!" I gasped. "What's this hanging on the kitchen windows?" I yelled to Mom in the other room.

"New curtains," she said, coming into the kitchen, "and not even a smidgeon of fabric wasted.

"But, Mom, I wanted to save that dress. Now, I'll never see it again."

"Oh, don't worry about not seeing it again," Mom laughed. "You'll see it every day."

I did see the dress every day. The dress, or rather the curtains, were still flocking the kitchen windows when I graduated from high school four years later. Soon after that, they made their way out to the cottage kitchen at Hagerman Lake where they lined Dad's picture windows. Later still, when nearly all the little flocked flowers heads began to wilt, they were retired to decorate the windows on Dad's garage.

And so, Miss Lottie Wymore's dream had finally come true. She had, after years of trying, finally convinced at least one person—Mom—of the importance of conservation. Waste not, want not.

Eighth grade commencement—what a day it had been!

Bugology

Somewhere between lying on my belly in the potato field, watching grasshoppers spit, at seven, and becoming a full-fledged berry picker, at eleven, I developed a dread of bugs. It could have happened one humid summer day when I was out in the back yard and an ugly black beetle buzzed my hair, flew in my eyes, and slipped inside my blouse. I didn't stop screeching until I ran—unbuttoning—in the back door, through the house, and up the stairs to my bedroom, where I extracted the culprit and smashed it with my shoe. Talk about my skin crawling. Or it might have been the spiders doing push-ups on the walls of the outhouse at Hagerman Lake that made me nervous, or the woodticks I'd find from time to time, trying to burrow their heads under my skin. I don't know for sure. But I became very jumpy about bugs and that was making the rest of the family more than a little edgy.

"Don't let her anywhere near those berries," Mom instructed the rest of the family in the old Model A, as we prepared to leave for home after a long hot morning of berry picking on Pennola Plains, near Crystal Falls. "Remember what happened last time!"

Our pails had been piled high with blueberries for Mom's famous pies, when I'd spotted a hard-shelled, squared-headed coot, looting through one of the berry pails. I just knew any minute it would fly in my hair, buzz my eyes, and cruise inside my blouse, so I started hollering and kicking in the back seat until the floor was covered with berries and the pails empty. Then, after my grumbling brother scooped all the berries back into the pails, and the bug turned up missing, I sat the entire

way home to Dober Location tucked in the corner of the old
Model A, watching the corners of the car, ready for another
attack and bout of hysteria.

"How could a girl grow up in the U.P. and be afraid of
bugs?" Mom fumed.

"I'm not afraid of them," I insisted. "I just don't like them
crawling around on me. That's all." It was pretty embarrassing,
the way I carried on. I mean, it's not like I was enjoying acting
like a lunatic.

"You'd better get over it." Dad was pretty mad, too.

"Geez, what a drip." My brother John couldn't resist getting
into the act.

I knew what they were saying was true, but I didn't know
what to do about it. But I had to do something.

Then one day, in the summer of '53, the answer came to me
in a roundabout way. My brother John and I were sitting on the
lawn chairs out in the back yard, discussing my return to school
in the fall as a full-fledged freshman in Stambaugh High School.

"Do you know who your teachers will be?" John asked.

"I'll have Miss Colwander for English, Mr. Trebilcock for
Algebra, Mr. Wodzinski for Junior Business, and Mr. Polich
for Biology." I had my schedule all mapped out.

"'Clara' for English, 'Dike' for Algebra, and 'Silvio' for
Biology." John, who was already off to college at the
University of Michigan, rolled off the nicknames of his former,
and my soon-to-be, teachers. "They're all going to keep you
busy. No breezing by in your classes like you did in grade
school. In high school, you're really going to have to buckle
down and work. They don't fool around. You'll study English
literature, *Ivanhoe* and *Silas Marner*, in English class, equations
in Algebra, and current events and social issues in your Junior
Business class."

"What about Biology?" I was a little concerned about this class. Science was not my favorite subject and I had a hard time concentrating on it.

"Bugology?" John laughed.

"Bugology? You're such a smart aleck." I gave him the old eagle eye.

"Biology? Bugology? Same thing." There was no mistaking the mischievous look in his eyes. "You're just going to love that class." His eyes continued to glitter. "You'll get to study swamp water —"

"Quit kidding around." He sure liked to dish it out.

"Who's kidding? It's amazing how many little squirmy parameciums live in that slime. You can get Dad to take you out to the Pendleton Creek to collect some samples."

"Any other exciting experiences you want to share?" I could dish it right back.

"Sure. You'll scrape gunk from under your fingernails and create jelled bacteria cultures under glass, watch the scum grow and blossom into big green patches, then write fascinating reports. And, if you're really lucky, you'll be entertained with a bat flying exhibit in Silvio's class. That's one of his favorites."

"He let's bats fly in the classroom?" I looked him straight in the eye to see if he was telling the truth.

"I've seen him do it. Picture this: bats swooping blindly around the classroom, frantically flapping their webbed wings, and skimming the tops of your heads. You and all your girlfriends hanging on to your hair, ducking, and screaming."

"He doesn't really do things like that, does he?"

"You never know what's going to happen in Bugology, believe me. You've never lived until you've been a student of Silvio's. And the thing you're going to love best," he paused for effect, "is collecting bugs." My brother knew he had me squirming and he was thoroughly enjoying it.

"Bugs?" My skin shivered.

"Insects. One of the first assignments he'll give you in the fall is to put together an insect collection. It'll also be your first major grade—an easy A, if you put your mind to it. All you need is a jar, some common pins, and a nice big flat box."

"What about the bugs?"

"Oh, don't worry about the bugs. They'll come right to you. They always do." John, laughing at his joke, got up from his lawn chair, gave me a grin, and left me to mull over all he had said. It was a lot to think about, in view of my bugaphobia. But I wanted to do a good, no great, job in school, so I had to come up with a plan. But, the way I figured it, I needed more than a jar, pins, and a box. What I needed was courage. No, more than courage, I needed good old-fashioned *guts* and some bullheaded determination.

I thought about my insect collection night and day. The main thing, I decided, was to get started, get a good head start on the fall Biology assignment. Now was the time all the bugs were out and about. June, July, and August were by far the best and buggiest months. By September, they'd all be thinking of hibernating. There was no time to lose. I had to get to work.

So I got out there in the back yard in my bathing suit, lathered up with suntan lotion, and waited for the bugs to come. Plans for summer, filled with the promise of sunshine, swimming, and sweet mysteries of life—boys—danced dreamily in my head as I stretched out on the old Indian blanket, toasting myself in the sun. Face down, I turned one puckered cheek away from the rays to make sure the other would be evenly tanned. Sleepily, I opened one lazy lid and, lo and behold, before my very eyes sat a brilliant specimen poised for flight on a blade of grass.

I slithered to my feet so as not to disturb it, left my white sandals lying on the blanket, and ran barefooted to the back door where, just inside, I'd placed a handy mayonnaise jar. Its lid was pierced with tiny holes, just big enough to allow a bug to breathe. I grabbed it, flew back to the red beetle, and held my breath. Could I do it? It required nerves of raw steel. I thought about that A I'd get in Biology and that was all it took. I slipped the jar under the leaf, clamped the lid over the bug, and screwed the mayonnaise jar and lid back together. Even though I'd been capturing bugs for the last few days, each one seemed like the first. Elated, I ran to the house to finish the job.

"I've got another one!" I yelled to Mom as I ran through the kitchen and dining room to the front porch where I had set up my bug laboratory, complete with cotton balls, alcohol, and a display rack made from one of Mom's discarded stationery boxes. "That makes twelve different species collected in the last three days," I bragged.

"That's nice, dear," Mom murmured absentmindedly from the kitchen. She was becoming as comatose about my collecting as the bugs became once they fell into my clutches. But it didn't matter. I had enough enthusiasm for an army of bug collectors.

I retrieved a cotton ball from another jar, dabbed it with alcohol, and slipped it under the lid, in with the red beetle and his curling blade of grass. I stood back admiring my work. And my bravery.

"How's the collecting coming along?" John stepped out onto the porch, startling me out of my daydreaming. "Got any good ones?"

"Sure, all kinds! I've got twelve altogether, and I've only just begun. I'll have a hundred or more by the end of summer." I pulled out the stationery box into which I'd pinned a neat row of bugs.

"Uh huh," he said, unimpressed, "but you can do better."

"Better than this?" I didn't see how I could do any better. My collection was growing far faster than I'd hoped. "I've already got a good dozen."

"It's not just quantity that counts, it's quality. See how these insects' legs are all curled up. What you've got to do is pin them down while they're still alive. That way their legs will fan out and look natural." My brother, the science whiz had all the answers.

"While they're still alive?" I wasn't really squeamish about knocking off bugs, but I certainly didn't want to give them a chance to crawl all over me while I tried to pin them down either. While the thought of piercing little beetle bodies with a lethal weapon was a little gruesome, the big A loomed brightly. It would be worth a lot more than a few mangled bugs.

"Here, let me show you how. Hand me one of those pins." While I pulled a few pins out of Mom's pink pin cushion on my work table, John opened the jar with the quickly expiring red beetle, slid the bug out on the table, and pressed the pin slowly through the center of the red body, between its shell-like wings. Then he picked up the pinned bug and pushed the pin and pest into the thick cardboard insert in the stationery box. The beetle, shocked into action, sprawled its six legs out in all directions, trying to manage an escape. It struggled, danced, and froze. "Some take a little longer than others," John said, "but once you pin them down, you can leave and come back after they've kicked the bucket."

"Uh, thanks," I mumbled, taking out the small round magnifying glass, I'd inherited from my brother's high school days, to study the recently departed red beetle. There was no doubt about it, it was by far the best of the bunch. I'd be using the pinning technique from now on, I decided. I picked up the empty jar, replaced the air-holed lid, and closed the door to the front porch laboratory, hurrying back outside to lounge in the sun and wait for six-legged victims.

"Find any good ones today?" Dad, who had just pulled in from the mine after work, was getting a big kick out of my bug collecting. So far, no more screaming, squealing, or kicking.

Secretly, I knew he was hoping that I was getting rid of my bugaphobia and that the berry pails would be safe in the future.

"Come out on the porch and I'll show you the latest." I grabbed the Indian blanket, rolled it up on my way into the house, and dropped it inside the door as I led Dad to my laboratory. "Look at this new red one. Isn't it great? John showed me how to pin him down. Alive. See how his legs kind of fan out?" I said proudly, knowing he was impressed.

"Looks like he's gonna' take right off and fly away," Dad laughed. "By the way, I brought you something from the mine." He set his rusty dinner pail down on the table next to the box of bugs.

"Leftover lunch?" I laughed.

"Better than that." He unhooked the lid of his pail, lifted it cautiously, and then snapped it down again.

"I hope it's not alive," I giggled.

"It's alive all right." He cracked the rounded top of his pail again, peered inside, then pushed the lid all the way open. "Give me one of those pins. I've got a rip-snortin' specimen in here for you."

"Where?" I leaned over the pail, saw a thick brown mottled body wedged in the corner of his pail, and gasped at the size. "It's a monster!" One look in the pail was all I needed to forget my newfound bravery. "I'm getting out of here." I slipped behind Dad and his pail, grabbed hold of the doorknob to the dining room, and didn't look back.

"Hey, c'mon back. It's just a moth," Dad laughed, "and it's not going anywhere."

"It's as big as a bat!" I was sure I couldn't stay sane and in the same room with this creature, but then I saw Dad's eyes laughing at me, and I was determined once again to stay committed to my project. I gritted my teeth, grabbed one of Mom's common pins, and held it out at arm's length to him.

"Where's your box?" I handed him the box, trying to keep a safe distance from the moth and not let Dad see I was in a state of panic. Dad reached into the pail, carefully place his large hand around the moth, and took it out. He set it down on the box, took the pin, and stuck it through its large brown body. It was an outstanding specimen. "There you go. Nothing to it."

"Where did you find this thing?" I asked. I'd never seen anything like it before.

"In the mine," Dad said. "I was just coming up out of the shaft when I felt something tap my belt. I looked down and this thing was stuck to my shirt. I grabbed it and ran up to the men's changing area. Some of the guys were just coming out of the showers and I thought they were gonna' die when they saw it. They were running around like a bunch of goons, trying to get away."

"I can see why." The monster moth was still flapping its wings when we left the room, but I knew it couldn't last long. I felt a little bad about the poor thing squirming around, but there was that great big A in Biology to think about.

Next morning, I couldn't wait to get back into the laboratory to look at the latest addition. I could just imagine how perfect it looked with its brown mottled wings spread, black furry antennae pointing straight ahead, and long hairy legs fanned out. I went straight to the stationery box, looked at the neat rows of bugs, and gasped. The moth was gone.

It had to have wrenched free somehow and flown away. But where would it go. I gulped, an eerie feeling creeping over me. Somewhere in that room, a pair of beady eyes was watching, waiting for its moment of revenge. I jerked around to check the walls behind me, but saw nothing. I looked in every corner of the room, but saw nothing. I searched the ceiling, floor, and small book shelf, but found no sign of the little monster. I peered into the cardboard box which held an assortment of old toys and saw nothing. It gave me the creeps to know it was there, but I couldn't see it. I decided to wait until Dad got home from work. Then we could search for it together.

"It got away," I yelled to Dad as he walked up the sidewalk to the house. It had been long day, waiting for him to get home.

"What got away?" Dad gave me a weird look.

"Your monster moth. When I went out on the porch this morning to check it, it was gone. I can't find it anywhere." Dad, excited as I, slung his pail in the sink and followed me to Bug Lab.

"Keep your eyes open," he said, slowly opening the door. "It's got to be in here somewhere." He scanned the walls, ceiling, and floor. Nothing. He looked through my stuff on the book shelf, checked the corners of the room, and searched every single inch of every single window frame. Nothing. "What about that box over there in the corner? Did you look through that?"

"There's nothing in there but a couple of old toys. I already looked." Standing directly above the box, I glanced down into it, looked away, and then at Dad.

"Don't move," he whispered.

"What?" I wanted to run.

"Stay still," he ordered. Dad's eyes were big as saucers. I followed them to the hem of my brown print broomstick skirt. I didn't see anything, at first. Then Dad lunged at the moth camouflaged on my skirt, and I lost ground in my battle against the bugs, screaming like a maniac, dancing all over the room, and tipping over my bugs and bug paraphernalia. "This common pin isn't going to do it. We need something bigger," Dad yelled, clutching the adventuring moth in his fist.

"I know just the thing," I said, trying to recover my dignity. "I'll get it." I darted into the bedroom, reached up to the top shelf of Mom's closet and retrieved her new navy blue straw hat. From it, I pulled a long, pear-shaped, pearl hat pin, rushed back to the front porch, and gave it to Dad.

When it was all over, the moth spiked down with no chance of escape, my laboratory reorganized, and Dad off to his own activities, I stood looking out the window, wondering how I could redeem myself. In a few short seconds, I'd once again become the world's worst bugophobic. I had to do something to change all that, and fast.

It was then I caught sight of it—its black and yellow striped body drifting heavily through the air, looking for a place to land. I dashed into the kitchen, looked out the breakfast nook window to Mom's garden just below, and watched it hover, land, and crawl into the fluted pink bell of a tall hollyhock. I knew, at once, what I must do.

The glass jar clasped in my sweaty palms, I slipped out the back door, sneaked around the corner of the garden, and studied the hollyhocks. The bee was still there. I could hear its loud threatening buzz. Did I really want to do this? I had to it, like it or not. I took one cautious step at a time, maneuvering though the nasturtiums, the phlox, and the Shasta daisies. I stood, staring at the pink-belled hollyhock. The buzzing was even louder and told me what the outcome might be if I failed. I had to do this right. If I hesitated, I was lost.

I took a deep breath—enough air to last me until the capture was over—then lifted the lid from the jar, and closed in on the bee. The pink bell, with the bee still inside, snapped off into the jar as I twisted the lid shut. I'd done it! I had caught, captured, and collected the most important specimen of my Biology project. I'd defied the terrifying painful sting of the bumblebee. Now, no one could say I was afraid of bugs. If they did, I'd just hold up my collection and show them the mighty yellow and black body—pinned, mounted, conquered.

But I wasn't there yet. The most difficult part remained. Pinning the bee to the box. I took the jar back into my laboratory, set it on the table, and watched the bee suck the sweet nectar from the pink flower. I surveyed the scene for the better part of the afternoon, knowing I had to pin him soon or his legs wouldn't fan out in the natural pose I'd learned to accomplish. But the moment had to be right.

It seemed the bee was tiring. I placed a pin between my thumb and forefinger and unscrewed the lid with the other three fingers. Carefully, carefully, I laid the jar on its side, opened the lid and slid the pink bell toward the opening. Then, just as I was about to press the pin down on the bee, it lifted itself from the flower. I smashed the lid back down on the jar, gulped air, and decided to wait a little longer.

The next time I tried this method some two hours later, I knew I was ready. I'd come close before, but now I would finish the job. The lid unscrewed, the jar on its side, the flower slipped toward the opening, I stalked my prey like a cat. Pin primed, I moved in slow motion until I was ready to pounce. I pressed the pin through the bee, whipped it over to the box, and pressed it into the cardboard. Then I fled the room.

Afraid of a repeat performance of the mottled moth, I crept in slowly the next day to observe the results of my endeavor. Fanned out in a perfect position was the bee, its wings glistening, ready for flight—never to buzz again.

It was a red-letter day for me. Today, a bee. Tomorrow, the world. I went about my bug collecting business with new confidence, catching all manner, color, and size of six-legged creatures. My collection grew to one hundred eighty-seven. I had to add another box. And all this was leading to my big A in Biology. It was a summer of success.

Mr. Polich stood in front of the class, explaining the assignment. We were to catch six-legged insects—no spiders, they had eight legs—mount them in a display box, and bring them in the following week for our first grade. I sat smugly in my seat, knowing I would have the best collection of all. After all, I'd spent my entire summer running around with a mayonnaise jar, hadn't I?

"Do not, I repeat, do not, kill any bees! The bees are necessary to pollinate the plants, so they must be cared for. We cannot live without bees! I do not want to see a single bee in anyone's collection. I will not even grade it, if I do," Mr. Polich said.

That night after school I stood looking over my boxes of bugs pinned in perfect rows across the cardboard inserts. A fascinating conglomeration of colors, shapes, and sizes, they were beautiful, but none so lovely as the bee, the crowning glory of my insect collection.

I thought about Mr. Polich's speech. Perhaps I should remove the bee from its perch, I thought, and yet, when I placed my fingers on the pin, I could not bear to do it. It was my best specimen by far, and, anyway, it would be silly to get rid of it since it was already dead. Stubborn and still a little smug, I brought my collection, fully intact, to class. I placed it with the others—all much smaller in size—and took my seat. I would talk to Mr. Polich and explain.

"Coralie!" His voice—agitated—came from the rear of the room. I whirled around to see him staring down at my collection. "Come here!"

I slipped out from behind the lab table, hurried to the collection table, and stood next to Mr. Polich. "I can explain," I said quickly, but the look on his face stopped me from going further.

"How did this bee get here?" His eyes, dark and angry, glowered at the bee, then at me.

"I caught it last summer, and I know you said, 'No bees,' but I thought—" I stammered.

"What makes you think you don't have to follow the rules?" He stood waiting for an apology.

"But the bee is beautiful and it was already dead," I repeated, unwilling to back down.

"It doesn't matter if it was already dead, Coralie, it's the principle of the thing. You will not receive a grade for this project unless you remove that bee." He strode determinedly away from the table and took his place in front of the class.

I stood for a long while, just staring at the bee. To keep the bee, or not to keep the bee, that was the question. If I removed it, it would make the rest of the collection appear incomplete. It would be obvious something was missing. Not receiving an A from Mr. Polich would be a disappointment beyond belief, but if he had his principles, so did I. The bee was more than a beautiful bug, it was the symbol of my summer accomplishment. I'd worked hard, completed an outstanding project, and, best of all, conquered my bug hysteria.

Stubbornly sticking to my beliefs, I left the bee in place, returned to my seat, and was hardly seated when I began to worry and wonder how I would explain to Mom and Dad the lack of a Biology grade on my first high school report card.

But Silvio solved the problem. When I nervously opened my report card six weeks later, I was more than a little astonished and relieved to find a big fat B+ in Biology. I still had some explaining to do to Mom and Dad who were certain I should have earned an A, so I told them I thought the B was for Best, or Bee, or Bugology. Naturally, they did not believe a word of this.

Dad, with a twinkle in his eye, suggested the B might be for Bullheadness. Mom did not think that was funny and said I'd Better Buckle down, and fast. My brother John suggested, with a snicker, that maybe it was for Brat. Secretly, though, I still think the B+ was for Bravery—Bravery in the Battlefields with both Bugs and Biology teachers.

Classmates: (back) Bob Thomas, Bob Maki, Larry Smitham, Dick Shepich, (front) Bill Olson, and Maurice Beauchamp.

Strangers in the Cemetery

I wasn't supposed to be there and I knew it, but I was determined to follow the longings of my wild heart, even if it meant getting into big trouble. It was a risk I was willing to take. After all, I *was* a teen-ager now, a grown-up, for crying out loud. I mean, if I was still a little kid, it would be different. Maybe then, Mom and Dad would be within their rights. But to say I was too young, at fourteen, to have a boyfriend was ridiculous. These were the fifties but they were still living in the Dark Ages.

The black sky cast its velvet cloak softly over the rolling hills, its lining—a million sparkling scatter-pin stars—spread over the earth as far as the eye could see, surrounded the full-blown golden moon, and flowed in a glittering fountain to some unknown midnight rainbow's end. I studied the Northern Lights, thinking how their radiant streams seemed more a distant dream than real as they dipped and plunged to the top of Stambaugh hill, reached farther down the hill to the path in the cemetery where I stood waiting, and softly skimmed the rough cold stones, changing them into dark silhouettes with silvery shadows spreading across the dew covered grass.

Beneath the still cedars and solemn pines, the silence of the night came alive with the shrill, yet serene, chirping of crickets and from somewhere, perhaps another world, there seemed to seep the scent of old roses—sweet and sad. The summer air, moist and cool against my burning cheeks and arms, caused me to shiver. I wiped my moist palms on my new blue Levi's, avoiding the pressed creases I'd labored over just hours earlier, pulled down the elastic cuffs of my coral poplin jacket, and took a deep breath. I should have gone straight home from the library with Nancy.

I heard, then, his footsteps, the soles of thickly heeled engineer boots softly thudding toward me on the dirt driveway and my heart beat in rhythm with a thousand romantic tunes, making me forget the library, Nancy, and Mom and Dad.

The Northern Lights at his back, he was faceless, but I could make out the outline of his black leather motorcycle jacket, skin-tight Levi's, and wavy blonde hair slicked boldly back into a "duck tail." The smoke from his cigarette curled upward toward the stars, lingered in a brief fog, then faded into the night.

"Hi," I called, hooking a forefinger inside the loose knot of my new chartreuse neck scarf, twisting it nervously.

"Yah," the man of my dreams mumbled. The sound of his voice made my soul swell. In an instant, I became the heroine in the Bronte novel I'd found on the shelf of the library, for out of the night had come my brooding hero, Heathcliff. I swooned silently, imagining we were on the heathered moors of Wuthering Heights, determined to walk side by side, destined to be together forever . . .

"Did you see the Northern Lights?" It was a good opener— as good as any I'd ever heard at the movies, or read in a novel.

"They're even brighter up on the hill." He crushed his cigarette into the ground with the heel of one boot, swaggered over to a tombstone, and leaned against it. "Indian spirits," he said, gazing back at the lights.

"Indian spirits?" I'd never heard that before. I wondered what he meant.

"Studied it in history class last year." He seemed pleased with himself.

"You must have had a pretty interesting history book. All we ever learned about was the Nina, the Pinta, and the Santa

Maria—and, of course, George Washington and Abe Lincoln."
I said.

"Oh, we had all that way back in seventh grade. Last year,
we studied local history. All about the Ojibway Indians," he
said smugly.

"The ones that have their Indian Burial grounds out at
Pentoga Park at Chicaugon Lake. Right?" I was determined to
ignore his smugness.

"You're pretty smart," he teased, "for a girl."

"Oh, don't be so silly," I giggled. "Tell me about the Indian
Spirits."

"You've heard of the Happy Hunting Grounds, haven't you?"
I nodded. "Well the Indians don't really believe in death, they
believe their spirits just go on to another world. The Northern
Lights are supposed to be the gateway to the other world."

"Really?" I wondered if he was teasing me.

"See how the lights kind of move back and forth?" he asked.
"Well those are supposed to be the Indians' spirits dancing."

"That's really interesting." I studied the swaying patterns of
light, waiting for him to go on, but it appeared he had done all
the talking he was going to do for the moment. One minute,
we'd been talking like old friends, the next minute, we were
awkwardly aware that we barely knew each other. We stood
shy and uncomfortable, shifting from one foot to another, wondering what to do, or say, next.

"C'mon over here and sit down," he drawled finally, zipping
open one of the dozen gold zippered pockets on his black
leather jacket, slipping in his hand, and withdrawing a fresh
pack of Camels.

"Sit? On a tombstone?" It didn't seem like a very reverent
thing to do. "I don't think we should do that."

"Why not? Afraid the graveyard spooks are gonna' get
you?" He gave a disdainful laugh as he heaved himself up, sat

on the edge of the coarse stone, and pulled out a book of matches.

"No, it's not that." I didn't want him to think I was a silly little kid. "It's just that I don't think it's right—you know, sitting on someone's tombstone."

"Oh c'mon." He lit another Camel, blew a stream of smoke into the air, and tossed the lit match on the ground where it glowed for a second, then burned out. "You can't hurt anything by sitting down."

"Oh, all right." I tiptoed over to the gravestone—cutting a path far and wide around the grave—and sat down next to him.

"Wanna' see a match burn twice?" he asked suddenly, breaking another long bout of silence.

"Huh?" He was trying to trick me.

"Wanna' see a match burn twice?" he asked again.

"I guess." I didn't know what he was up to.

"Keep your eye on the match. Watch carefully. Okay. Here goes." He thrust the Camel in his mouth, ignited another match on the matchbook cover, and blew it out. He waved the match in the air for a few seconds, then grabbed my hand, and touched the still hot match tip to my skin, all the while laughing like an idiot.

"Cut that out!" I shrieked, furious with myself for being so gullible.

"Never heard that old joke before? Boy, you must really be from the sticks." He was having a great time at my expense.

"I suppose, you're not?" Heathcliff or not, he sure was making me mad. "Don't pull anything like that on me again or—"

"Or, what?" he challenged.

"Or—oh never mind." We weren't exactly getting off on the right foot with this romance.

"Oh never mind," he mimicked.

"And don't tease me!" Now I was getting even madder.

"Did you ask if you can go to the show?" He'd wisely decided to change the subject.

"I can't. I'm not allowed to date." There it was out—he'd probably never want to see me again, but I couldn't let him think I didn't want to go.

"Geez, it's just a movie. Everybody goes to the show." He was sounding smug again.

"Not me—not with you, anyhow—I mean not with any guy." There was an edge to my voice. I'd pleaded with Mom and Dad, but it was no use. There was no way they were going to let me go out with a boy. Maybe in a couple of years, they'd said. It seemed like forever.

"So how did you get out of the house tonight?" There was the question I didn't want to think about.

"I told them I was going to the library with Nancy."

"Don't tell me you lied." The word, "lied," sort of slithered off his tongue.

"No, of course not. Well, not exactly. I did go to the library with Nancy. Then she went home and I came here." My stomach started to churn.

"So what did you do today?" he asked after an uncomfortable pause, drawing deeply on the glowing Camel.

"Went out to Hagerman Lake with my dad," I said, noticing how the aroma of leather and tobacco mingled sweetly with the fresh night air.

"Your old man let you drive?" He jumped down from the tombstone, crossed to another stone, and leaned against it.

"He always lets me drive," I said, annoyed. I didn't like hearing Dad referred to as, 'your old man.'

"That must have been a real trip." Even in the dark I could see the smirk on his face.

"Uh huh." Change the subject—talk about him, not me—that was what this conversation needed. "What did you do today?"

"Rode out to Ice Lake on my bike," he answered.

"Did you go swimming?"

"Why would I go out to Ice Lake and not go swimming?" He sounded like he thought I was a real drip.

"I don't know, maybe you wanted to just look at the lake. Or maybe you wanted to go fishing. Or maybe you just felt like riding your bike." If he could be sarcastic, so could I.

"You've got quite a temper, don't you?" he said, sounding much more mellow than he had before.

"I guess you could say that." Heathcliff or not, he wasn't going to make fun of me.

"Well, good for you. Gotta' be able to take care of yourself, you know. Don't let anybody get the best of you." He flipped the burning cigarette onto the air, ground it out when it landed, and folded his arms across his zippered, leathered chest.

"I guess." He seemed so mature, it was hard to believe he was only fifteen years old.

"What's that you've got around your neck? Is that some kind of dog collar, or something?"

"No, it's not a dog collar. It's a neck scarf. Chartreuse. It's new." He sure had a knack for getting my dander up.

"Temper, temper," he said sweetly. "Just come on over here and let me see your chartreuse neck scarf." Maybe there was some hope for this romance after all. I got up off the tombstone, walked slowly over to him, and stood just out of his reach—knees knocking. How embarrassing. I hoped he couldn't hear them or my heart thump-thumping away at break-neck speed.

He took one step toward me, reached out, and flipped my scarf so the fluted edges popped up into my face, tickled my nose, and made me giggle. Then before I could stop him, he took the two ends of the silky pleated scarf in his hands, slipped the knot, and slid it off my neck.

"Give that back to me," I laughed.

"Say, please," he teased.

"Give it back." I yelled.

"Shh!" He wiggled the scarf at me. "You'll wake the dead."

"Give me my scarf," I whispered.

"Say please, or you'll have to come and get it." This last he threw over his shoulder as he shot swiftly back up the path toward the Northern Lights.

"All right, I will." I took off after him, but he'd broken into a quick sprint and I couldn't keep up. I saw him slip off the path, duck between two large tombstones, and disappear into the soft black darkness but, when I followed, I couldn't see him anywhere.

"Come on. Give it back!" I couldn't see any movement, just rows of cold dark stones.

"Say please." Suddenly, from out of nowhere, I felt his arms go around my shoulders, tackling me and taking me to the ground. He pinned me down with one arm, fluffed the scarf in my face, and tickled me until I thought I'd die laughing . . . but it didn't seem so funny when I realized we were rolling around right on the ground above a grave.

"Stop it! Give me my scarf." I grabbed at it.

"Say it!" I couldn't get away.

"Let go. You're crazier than a loon." I couldn't stop giggling.

"Say it!" He was going to win.

"Please!" Struggling, I reached again for the scarf, but grasped only handfuls of air. "I said, 'Plea—'" It happened so quickly, at first I wondered if it had happened at all. But it had. Heathcliff, oh Heathcliff, had kissed me. Dazed, I watched him spring to his feet, brush himself off, and pull out yet another Camel as if nothing at all had happened.

I took the scarf, flicked off the wet blades of grass, and tied it around my neck. I patted my hair which I knew must be tangled, vigorously rubbed my face where I figured my Ever Loving VIV lipstick must be smeared, and brushed the knees of my new blue Levi's, hoping they weren't spotted with grass stains.

"I've got to go." I had thrown caution to the wind, now I had to hurry home and hope no one had figured out where I'd been.

"Already? You just got here." Heathcliff stepped toward me, took hold of my neck scarf, and was just about to give me another quick nervous kiss when it happened. We suddenly, frighteningly, found ourselves bathed in a flood of brazen light—unable to escape.

Pitch black and rattling, it seemed to have appeared from nowhere, sputtering down the cemetery path. There was no mistaking the sound, the car, or the driver as they rolled relentlessly down the hill toward us. It was Dad in the old Model A.

"Geez, it's your old man." Heathcliff dropped his hold on my scarf, stepped back, nearly tripping over the base of a tombstone, and stood there like a statue, staring at me as if I'd suddenly become a leper.

I stood—frozen—at the side of the path, watching in dread and wonder as the old Model A approached, its cockeyed headlights casting eerie flashes of light over slick fronts of cemetery stones. This couldn't be happening to me, I thought. I'll wake up any minute now and find out I've been dreaming— a nightmare of the worst kind.

The old Model A stopped dead on the path, its black boxy body and windows glinting in the star-swept night. Dad's face, framed in the rolled down window opening, eyes flashing like flames of fire, left no doubt about his feelings on finding me with my forbidden friend.

"Get in this car," he growled at me. "And you," he said to Heathcliff, "Get lost!"

With great speed, and not a single backward glance, Heathcliff strode purposefully away into the night, while I cranked the flat metal door of the car open, climbed into the passenger seat, and clanked the door shut—frightened and furious at the same time.

"Haven't you got any sense at all." It wasn't a question, it was a statement of fact. Dad jammed the stick shift into first and pulled on down the hill.

"I wasn't doing anything wrong." He was right. I didn't have any sense at all. Anyone in their right mind could have figured out Dad was on the brink of bursting a gasket.

"Don't say another word," he cautioned through gritted teeth.

"Oh for crying out loud." The words just sort of slipped out of my mouth.

"Not *another* word." The message was painfully clear. Even I, Dad's golden girl with the glib tongue, knew the situation had been pressed to its limits.

Silence, fierce and foreign, filled the old car, as we rumbled down the path to the white metal gingerbread gates. Irresistibly drawn to the scene left behind, I turned and looked back. Heathcliff's footsteps had taken him quickly away from the tombstones, on into the velvet night, and out of my life. Nothing was left but the glow of my storybook sky.

I gave Dad a sideways glance, noting the rigid way he held his head, as if his neck had been set in cement, and suddenly a haunting feeling crept over me. It seemed I was sitting next to a stranger.

I wanted to talk to him but I didn't dare. I thought of all the things I might say to him—if I had the courage—like, "Can't you just let me grow up?" or, "I finally find a boy who likes me and you have to come along and wreck everything," or, "If you ever read the Bronte sisters' books, you'd understand about love."

Then again, I didn't want to be mad at Dad. I wanted to laugh and say, "Silence reigned and we all got wet," and then hear him laugh, too. Confused, we sat side by side, divided by a deep gorge of disappointment. I gulped back angry, frustrated tears.

"Play with fire and you're gonna' get burned," Dad said, still staring straight ahead. There was something besides anger in his voice. Was it pain?

I turned my head away from him toward the window and watched as the Northern Lights, undulating in rays of waving gossamer gold, spun down from the heavens, swept over the rows of cemetery stones, and spread shimmering stardust over the magical place where the sweet memory of my short-lived romance would long linger.

"I'm sorry," I said softly, knowing he would forgive me one day soon, but also painfully aware that things would never ever again be exactly the way they had once been between Dad and me. It was called growing. Growing up. Growing apart.

Coralie at one of her favorite haunts.

Ah, Romance!

Following the scene in the cemetery, it took a week or so before Dad stopped scowling every time he saw me. But it soon became apparent he held no grudges and had returned to his old cheerful self. I breathed a big sigh of relief, but barely had time to exhale when I realized what was happening.

The FBI couldn't have engineered a better plot against me. I had been assigned a spy—undercover, of course. My nine-year-old sister had been put on the case. She seemed to turn up everywhere. I went to the library; she was there looking for books. I sunned on a blanket out in the back yard; she got a blanket and set it next to mine. I visited my girlfriends; she rode by on the old blue Zenith bike—which had now practically become a family heirloom—pretended she wasn't really looking, then went home to report to the "Agency." I had no secrets from my sister, likewise from Mom and Dad. I was getting cabin fever. I had to have some privacy—a life of my own.

"I just want to go to the movies. I don't see why I have to take *her* along," I griped. I was standing at the kitchen sink washing the supper dishes.

"Connie likes to go to the movies, too," Mom said, scrubbing off the stove and piling more and more pots and pans on the counter for me to wash.

"Well, can't someone else take her?" I grumbled, rinsing a stack of dishes and slinging them in the dish rack.

"No." Mom dipped her dishrag in my dishwater, wrung it out, and went back to scrub some more.

"I don't see why she has to go with me. Nobody takes their little sister with them to the movies. I'll be the laughing stock of Stambaugh." This was one slick snow-job she and Dad were pulling on me.

"I'm sure you can handle it." An unmistakable note of sarcasm slipped into Mom's statement. "If you want to go to the movies, your sister will go with you."

"You're lucky we're letting you out of this house at all." Dad grabbed a toothpick from the kitchen cabinet, gave me a sour look, and headed out the back door.

"Yes, you'd better be glad we're letting you go to the movies at all," Mom said quietly.

"Oh for crying out loud," I said, "I don't see why—"

"You *know why*." I stepped to one side of the sink, my hands still in the dish water, to let Mom rinse her dishrag, ring it out, and set it on the edge of the dish rack to dry.

"You know why," I mouthed in sassy silence. She was in my way and I didn't like it.

"Dad will drive you there," Mom said, "and if you need a ride home, you can call. Dad will come and pick you up."

There was no point in pushing the issue any further. At least we could walk home—that's when most of the excitement happened, anyway. All the popular boys, in their souped-up coupes and convertibles, cruised the Stambaugh streets right after the movies, while the girls made every effort to act like they hardly noticed. As we swung busily along in our white bucks and broomsticks skirts, they'd drive past, whistle, and wave. Sometimes they'd slow to a crawl, make some cute remark to get our attention and then carry on a conversation as they followed alongside, pumping their brakes and making the fuzzy stuffed dice that dangled over their mirrors bob back and forth.

"Wolves," Dad called them, but it was the way a small town teen's social life started. It was the only way we got to meet anyone outside of the boys in our home room at school—and since we'd known them since kindergarten, they were practically like our own brothers.

And so it began . . . me and my shadow . . . driven by Dad to the movies, given money for tickets and popcorn, and dropped off at the brass handled doors of the Perfect Theatre in Stambaugh on Sunday night.

The first couple of weeks weren't too bad. Connie and I gobbled popcorn, saw our favorites stars, Rock Hudson, Doris Day, Marlon Brando, and Marilyn Monroe in their latest movies, and afterward strolled slowly home down the mile long hill from Stambaugh to Dober Location. The convertibles cruised by, curved back around the blocks, and caught up with us. Who cared if my little sister was with me—even if I did have to make her promise not to tell each time I talked to a boy. Romance still bloomed and I was in seventh heaven.

Heaven, however, didn't last long. It lasted approximately three trips to the movies. Then, on our fourth trip, after we'd stuffed ourselves with popcorn, watched the movie, and stepped out into the evening still bright with sunlight, my little sister looked at me and said, "I'm not walking home anymore." She wouldn't budge from the spot.

"Oh come on," I coaxed. She couldn't really mean it. I'd talk her into walking somehow.

"No! I'm not walking home!" Her hands were set determinedly on her hips, her head was cocked to one side.

"Why not?" I asked, demonstrating patience while denying an irresistible urge to scream, holler, and stamp my feet.

"It's too far and it takes to long." Her mouth formed a full lower-lipped pout.

"It won't take that long," I said sweetly. "I promise we'll stop and take a rest whenever you get tired."

"No! I want to call Dad to come and get us!" Her blue-green eyes narrowed, her pout became more pronounced. "I want to go and call him right now!"

"All right, we'll walk down to Lenny's Soda Bar," I said slowly, trying to calm her down. Maybe, I could get her to change her mind by the time we got there. We set off down the two blocks to the soda bar. When we arrived out in front of Lenny's, I stopped, looked at her, and gave her my best manipulative smile. "Well, see that didn't take much effort, did it? How about we just take it slow and easy and start walking home?"

"No! I'm not walking." She was a tough case, no doubt about that.

"Look . . ." I said, playing for time, trying to come up with some scheme to keep her walking. "I'll . . . I'll tell you what . . . I'll give you a nickel if you walk home instead of calling Dad."

She thought about it a minute. I could see almost hear the wheels in her head clicking away, considering all the treats a nine-year-old could buy with a whole nickel at Vic Shepich's grocery store in Dober Location.

"Okay," she finally said, holding out her palm.

Who cared about the money. I could do without milk for one lunch period. I forked over the dough and we made our way past the Stambaugh General Hospital, past Mrs. Mahlberg's mossy lavender rock garden, and finally down the Stambaugh Hill. While I happily waved at cruising convertibles, Connie clutched her nickel.

The weeks went by, one nickel turned into two, then two nickels into two dimes. My piggy bank was going on empty. Connie's was beginning to bulge. I quit buying myself popcorn at the movies so I could pay her off. I was hungry, but I was happy.

I should have seen it coming, but I didn't. My little niece Cheryl Detterbeck had come to visit from Chicago. With Connie and Cheryl barely a year apart in age, they were nearly like twins and ended up being double the trouble for me. I had to take them both with me to the movies.

Having just watched Shirley Jones and Pat Boone in *April Love*, I left the theatre absolutely smitten with romance. I forgot all about my sister and her sidekick. It was a perfect evening for a long dreamy walk home.

"We're not walking home," Connie and Cheryl announced in unison, dissolving my daydreams.

"Oh come on," I said.

"No!" I could tell, instantly, that they really meant it. I felt in my pocket and came up with a shiny silver quarter.

"Here," I said, holding it out to Connie. "You two can have this whole thing if you'll just walk with me."

"No, we're going to Lenny's to call Dad and you'd better not try to stop us, or I'm *telling* on you," Connie pouted.

"Telling what?" She had plenty to tell, but she had been paid to keep quiet. Surely, she wouldn't turn me in now.

"Tell how you're always talking to boys!" She tipped her head, twirled around, and tripped on down the sidewalk toward the soda bar—Cheryl following fast in her footsteps.

"You two are a couple of little brats!" I yelled.

"I'm *telling*!" Connie yelled back.

"But you promised not to." I caught up with them, tried to shove the money into Connie's hand, but it was no use.

"So how was the show?" Dad asked as the three of us climbed into the car.

"It was okay, but . . ." My sister hesitated when she saw the warning look in my eyes. "But we didn't feel like walking home." She gave me a threatening look.

"It was a great movie," I said to Dad, changing the subject. As we drove the rest of the way in silence, I figured

I was home free. But as spies do, even bribed spies, Connie went right into the house and *told* Mom and Dad everything.

Grounded from the movies, and warned to get my act together, I took the warning literally, turning my attention to other endeavors. Along with Jeannie Baker and Gail Pedo, I joined the Thespian organization at school. I tried out for a play, and was cast as Julie in *Liliom*, the play version of *Carousel*. The sad sweet story turned the audience of parents and friends to tears and me to further dreams of romance, remembering, long after the play ended, the acacia blossoms drifting down from the decorous paper mache' treetop to the park bench where I sat on stage, speaking my feverish lines of love to Liliom.

Ah, romance, I seemed to find it wherever I went. I joined the Latin Club and read the required books from the suggested reading list. The Romans, I learned, were, to put it mildly, a passionate bunch. Completely enthralled with the stories of wars, conquerors, and maidens, I spent all my study hall hours oblivious to my surroundings, devouring one tale after another. I wondered if Mrs. Anderson, our Latin teacher, had really read all those books or if she just didn't remember how racy they were.

In English class, we were assigned the task of reading a chapter a day in Dickens' *A Tale of Two Cities*, but for me it was no task at all. I was hooked from the first page and couldn't stop until I'd finished the stunning conclusion and words of Sidney Carton, '. . .'. it is a far, far better thing that you do, than I have ever done; it is a far, far better rest that you go to than I have ever known.' Even La Guillotine became a romantic symbol in my dreamy teen world.

From all outward appearances, a book always flopped open in my lap as I lounged in the living room next to the radio, I had become the epitome of every parent's dream, a studious, serious student. Mom and Dad didn't guess I was reading the hot new bestseller, *Magnificent Obsession*, while at the same time listening to the Lux Radio Theatre on low volume and mooning over Tallulah Bankhead in her latest love story, *Lifeboat*. So it was only natural that they let down their guard and finally agreed to allow me to go to a school dance with a boy. The only hitch was that it had to be a double-date with another couple.

My girlfriend, Phyllis Aho, and I got our heads together and figured out that with a little encouragement our classmates, Bob Richard and Dick Shepich, would ask us to the Mid-winter Freshman dance. Mom said Phyl could sleep over and we could stay out until 11:30 P.M., an unheard of late night hour for us. Dick was still too young to drive, but Bob had just gotten his permit. He assured the three of us he'd have wheels.

When he drove up in his dad's old black pick-up truck and the two fellows in suits and ties lumbered out of the vehicle, down our sidewalk, and to our backdoor, Phyl and I, watching through the window, caught a serious case of the giggles which was to last throughout the evening. Four bodies forced into the front seat of an old pick-up truck may sound like it had romantic possibilities, but, with two of those bodies giggling idiotically, I could honestly assure Mom and Dad there hadn't been even the remotest chance of that.

Following this first big date, the Mid-winter dance ordeal, the entire high school plunged into plans for the spring prom. We girls sauntered to and from our classes, loitering in the halls as much as possible, hoping a junior or senior boy would realize that, even though we were only sophomores, we were prime candidates for the prom.

Getting asked and actually going to the prom were practically of equal importance. Who you went with was of much less importance. As long as they were at least a B-student, didn't drink or get into fights, and brushed their teeth more than once a week, they were acceptable.

When my friend John, a senior, who more than met the minimal requirements, invited me to the prom, I couldn't wait to tell the other girls, Mom, and Dad, in that order. I know Dad would liked to have said no, but Mom, wrapped up in the pastel pageantry of the event, made the decision for them both. I could go.

John called for me dutifully at 6:30 P.M. with a beautiful band of pink roses, which Mom promptly pinned on my wrist. In a mist of blue lace and taffeta, pink roses, and a hefty douse of Eau de Toilette Water, we waltzed out the back door, John promising to have me home no later than it took to drive to Eagle River with our double-dates, have dinner at the Czechko Club, and drive back home again.

Along white picket fences bordering the dance floor in the high school basket ball court, we wove our way in, under, and around white trellises decked with rainbows of tissue rosettes and trailing with fake ivy, getting our dance cards filled. Then, we swished the night away in our waltz-length gowns inflated with hoops and copious layered crinoline underskirts, while mothers listening to the romantic strains of *Blue Moon, Sentimental Journey,* and *Let Me Call You Sweetheart* from the balcony above, singled out their sons and daughters, followed their every move, and sighed with passionate pride.

Swirling in a sea of rainbow dresses stroked by strobe lights softly stealing over the crowd, I turned heavenward, caught Mom's eye and waved, then dreamily invited the blue moon in the song to engulf me with its pale blue light and promise of romance. Once again, I was lost, smitten with romantic notions, infatuated with spring.

As a finale to the evening, Mom had invited John to stop in for a piece of freshly baked chocolate cake. When we arrived home, her best Moss Rose dishes were set neatly in the breakfast nook. She poured coffee into demitasse cups, set out a tiny set of tongs and sugar cubes in a neat little stack on a rosebud dish, and cut us each a piece of cake.

"Go ahead," she said to John, "have a seat."

"Thank you Mrs. Cederna," John said politely, sliding into the narrow little nook.

"I'll just set this all out for you," she smiled, "and then you can help yourselves to seconds."

Dad was working the night shift. My brothers and sister had been sound asleep for hours. The moment couldn't have been more special. Romance was in the air.

"Do you have everything you need?" Mom asked.

"It's wonderful, Mom." With that, I plowed into the breakfast nook, remembering at the last second to compress my hoop with both hands so I could fit between the bench and the table. "Thanks!" I said dismissing her, hoping she would take the hint and discreetly retire to the living room, leaving us to a few private moments.

"Oh, the cream, I almost forgot." Mom stepped toward the refrigerator, instead of stepping toward the living room. This romance was never going to get off the ground with my mother in the room.

"I'll get it!" I shot up from the bench, forgetting about the hoop, and everything from then on seemed to happen in slow motion—only I couldn't stop the sequence. My hoop actually lifted the table. The filled coffee cups rattled a warning, then toppled over onto their saucers, sending the spilled brew running along the table, over its edge, and down the entire front of my misty blue prom dress. Trying to stop the disaster, I tried to upright the coffee cups but missed and plunged my fingers instead into the middle of my chocolate cake. John had jumped out of the nook, found a place by the outside door, and was standing there, like petrified wood, alarm darting about in his eyes.

"Get over to the sink," Mom yelled, turning the water faucet on fullblast. She grabbed the bottom of my skirt, lifted it above the hoop, and held it under the cold water. "Oh no, I can't remember if it's hot or cold that takes out coffee stains . . . Here," she hollered to John, throwing a dishrag at him. "See if you can get that mess cleaned up!"

Dutifully, John nabbed the dishrag in mid-air, dropped to his knees on the kitchen floor, and started sopping up the streams of coffee stretching out across the kitchen floor.

When offered a fresh piece of chocolate cake, John managed to say, "Uh, no thanks," as he gave Mom, me, and my dripping dress one last startled look, before darting out the door to freedom.

Stumbling stubbornly along on my rocky road to romance, I somehow managed to find romantic interests no matter where I went—even in church.

On a overcast spring evening in 1954, Mom and I drove to Iron Mountain, Michigan to attend a Diocesan Choir meeting of which we had become charter members. The group of organists and directors from all over the U.P. sat in wooden folding chairs, in a circle, listening intently to Fr. Sartorelli explain the changes that would be coming in the near future.

"It is inevitable," he said, "that in the very near future, most of the music we are using now will be prohibited. These Masses we are using are just too flowery. How can the congregation pray when we are performing a concert?"

A heated discussion ensued in which the members openly argued against the changes, but Fr. Sartorelli was quick to caution that we must heed the word of the bishop and that sharp tongues do not a place find in heaven. The evening had turned into an upheaval of disappointment.

But that all changed when *he* walked in the door.

"Oh, let me introduce you all to Luigi Valentini, who comes all the way from Italy," announced Fr. Sartorelli. "He's here this evening to give you a real concert performance. If you'll all just come up to the choir loft, Luigi will play for you."

We all trooped upstairs, Luigi pulled out all the stops on the organ, and Mom and the older members of the group nearly cheered when they realized he was going to play "flowery" music. However, Carole Frighetto and Loretta DeMilio from Caspian; a few other teen-age girls from Iron Mountain and Marquette; and I weren't concentrating on the music. We were too busy swooning over the suave, silk-suited Italian with slick dark hair and eyes.

Then, to my astonishment, as we filed down the stairway following the concert, Luigi eased up silently beside me, took my hand briefly in his, and said, in broken English, "How do you like my concert?"

"Oh, it was wonderful," I gasped, speedily removing my hand so Mom wouldn't lecture me all the way home.

"You are leaving already?" he asked.

"Yes." Mom came walking over to us. "We have a long way to drive yet tonight. We have to be on our way."

"Well, I have to be on my way, too . . . You don't suppose you could give a poor-r-r boy a lift home, could you?" Luigi said, rolling his R's in a fascinating way.

"Uh . . ." Mom was at a loss for words. I knew she was thinking that giving the poor guy a lift home was the Christian thing to do, but the weather was becoming more overcast by the minute. "I suppose we could—"

"Oh, per-r-rfecto!" Luigi walked right over to our new 1953 blue and white Chevy, opened the front doors for Mom and me, and, before Mom or I could say another word, eased himself into the back seat.

"Where to?" Mom was now looking worriedly out the window at the blackness of the night and the fog collecting under the streetlights.

"Oh, just to my dear-r-r fr-r-riends home. You know, the Pissacar-r-r-o's, where I'm staying? I hope it is no tr-r-rouble . . ." He was looking a little pathetic.

"No, I guess not." Mom started the car. "Which way?"

"Oh thank you, thank you. You are so kind to a poor-r-r boy! Take this street to the end. It is not far. You will see." For as quiet as he'd been in church while playing the organ, he sure was talking a lot now.

"You've been in this country long?" Mom asked, trying to make the best of a bad situation while studying him apprehensively in her rear-view mirror.

"Oh no, how kind you are to ask. No. No. No. I have been here only three months now and I am all alone. Only the Pissacaro's. They are wonder-r-rful people. Do you know them?" he asked. I loved hearing him roll those R's.

"No, I don't think so." Mom shot me a worried look and I shot her a glowing smile. I wasn't a bit concerned. I was, as usual, having the time of my life. The handsome Italian was practically a captive in our car.

"They know my family in Italy. Friends many years. 'Come to American,' they said to me. Many, many times, they say this. And so, I come." He waved his hands in the air as he spoke.

"Uh, huh," Mom remarked, staring at the houses as we reached the end of the street, hoping the Pissacaro's place was coming up soon.

"Oh there it is. Stop. Right there. They are so kind. The Pissacaro's. Yes. Yes. So kind to poor-r-r boy."

Mom pulled to a quick halt, flicked the light on in the car, and turned around to peer at Luigi, giving him a not so subtle look that he should leave. But he wasn't willing to notice. He had our full attention and wasn't about to give it up so easily.

"Yes, yes, I come to this country. Alone. Poor-r-r boy is all alone here in United States. United States can be very lonely, yes?" He wasn't even making a move toward the door.

"Yes?" Mom repeated, completely unnerved now by our situation.

"Yes, I see how you understand. I come from fine family in Italy. Am only son of good family. No brother. No sister. Just my me—poor-r-r boy." The poor boy routine was getting a little old. Even I was getting worried about our trip home in the fog now.

"It's been very nice meeting you," Mom said pleasantly, "but we've got to get on the road home now—with all this fog and all—"

"Yes, yes. I play organ in cathedral ever since I was small boy. Many years I go to church every day and play for six, sometimes eight hours. Sometimes more. There I study how to play with these fingers." He showed us his fingers. They were long, slender, and perfectly manicured.

"I see," Mom sighed. "Well, you do play beautifully."

"I give concerts in my country. But still I am a lonely boy. Just a poor lonely boy." I was beginning to think I understood why he was so lonely—he never quit talking. How could anyone put up with that night and day? Still he had that certain irresistible charm.

"Concerts, huh?" Mom was still trying to be polite, but it was becoming more difficult by the second.

"Oh, many concerts. I play in Rome, even for the Pope." Suddenly, the porch light on the Pissacaro's house flashed on, and we all turned in time to see the figure of a man standing just inside the door, looking out at us. "My friends put porch light on for poor-r-r boy. I should go in now."

"Yes, they're probably worried about you," Mom said anxiously, not much caring now if he realized she wanted to get rid of him. I was squirming in my seat, wondering if we were going to have to push him out of the car in order to get him to leave.

"Oh yes, they want poor-r-r boy to be happy. They worry I won't find right woman to wed." He laughed a silly little rippling laugh. "I tell them I am only young boy of thirty-two."

Thirty-two! The goofy guy was ancient. Not only was he a foreigner with a mouth that never shut up, but he was also old as the hills.

"We have to go *home* now," I said, speaking up for the first time since we'd all gotten into the car. "You'd better *leave.*"

"Oh certainly, I take up too much of your time." He opened the door, slipped out, and around to Mom's window in one lithe movement. Then he leaned down and looked across Mom to me. "Arivederrrci!" He called. Then, at long last, he turned, and finally left.

"Geez, what a snail," I snickered to Mom.

"He seemed real nice at first," Mom said, "but he sure got on my nerves after a while."

"You mean when he said, 'Poor-r-r boy, poor-r-r boy'?" We both burst out laughing.

"Coralie, you stop that this minute," Mom giggled. "Look at this fog. This is serious business."

"It's been a whole evening of serious business," I giggled. "Let's get out of here. I hope I never see that nut or this town again as long as I live!"

"Well I think you can rest assured that Mr. Luigi is nothing but a bad memory. I think it's safe to say we'll never see him again," Mom said with relief. "Poor-r-r boy will have to find someone else's ear to bend."

"Well, I hope he finds someone else quick before he keels over from old age," I giggled harder.

The fog, dense in Iron Mountain, seemed to get even thicker as we hit the highway for the dangerous forty-five mile trip home. Mom edged the car along, not daring to drive over twenty miles an hour.

"Get out the rosary," Mom gasped, nodding at the glove compartment where she kept a spare set of beads. "We should have left for home a lot earlier than we did."

"Well, how could we, with poor-r-r boy in the car?" I grasped the beads firmly, still giddy from our adventure. "Okay, let's pray . . . Hail Mail full of gr-r-r-ace . . ." I said with an Italian accent.

"Stop that! Your-r-r making me ner-r-r-vous," Mom giggled, struggling to stop herself.

"Not as nervous as that idiot from Italy," I sputtered.

"Well, we'll never see him again, thank goodness," Mom said.

"I hope you're right."

"Of course, I'm right. He doesn't have the faintest idea of where we live. And even if he did, I'm sure he's forgotten all about us by now."

Unfortunately, Mom was wrong . . . It was a beautiful spring Saturday evening when disaster struck. The big regional forensic meet had been held in Marquette, Michigan at Northern Michigan College that day and I'd attended along with my classmates and our advisor, Miss Helen Dunham. Our group had done especially well in our Dramatic Monologue, Dramatic Dialogue, and Humorous presentations, so we girls were ready to celebrate when we returned to Stambaugh. The boys decided to go on home, and Miss Dunham had other plans for the evening.

We all agreed we'd go to the Riverside Pizzeria, but we wanted to change from our performance clothes to blue jeans. One of the girls had her Dad's car so she was elected to drive each of us home to change before we went out.

"I'm home," I hollered as I tripped in the back door in my three-inch heels. I could hear voices in the living room, but no one answered me. I guessed they were making too much noise to hear me. "I'm home," I yelled again as I walked through the kitchen into the dining room.

At first I didn't realize what was going on. I saw strangers chatting with Mom and Dad and drinking coffee out of Mom's, now infamous, Moss Rose cups. They seemed to all be talking at once. Then they stopped and looked up at me. That's when I saw him. Poor-r-r Boy sitting in my living room, talking to Mom. And Dad! It was a nightmare.

"Look who's here, Coralie," Mom said. "The Pissacaro's have brought Luigi Vallentini to visit."

No! I looked from one face to another until they came into complete focus. This nightmare couldn't be happening. I couldn't even bring myself to say, "Hello." I was too embarrassed, horrified, and shocked. And Dad was looking at me as if I was responsible for the whole thing. I bit my lip and glared at Luigi.

"I told the Pissacaro's I must find my new friends and they tell me they will call their friends from Caspian who must know the organist and choir director of the Stambaugh church. So here we are." His smile was as big as the Cheshire Cat's. The Pissacaro's beamed with delight. Dad was concealing a scowl I'd come to know too well.

It was too much for me. I practically ran into Mom's and Dad's downstairs bedroom. Mom followed me in and closed the door. "They've come a long way to see you. You'd better come out and sit with us a while," she whispered.

"I don't care if they've come all the way around the world. I'm not going out there with that *nut*. I wouldn't sit in the same room with him for all the tea in China."

"This is no way to act in front of guests," Mom sputtered.

"Who asked them to be guests, anyway? Not me. They've got no business coming here. Mom, please . . ." I wailed.

"Shh . . . they'll hear you," Mom warned.

"My friends and I are planning to go to the Riverside for pizza. Now I can't even go up to my room to change as I'd have to walk past that lunatic."

"Calm down." Mom hesitated. "What do you need from your room?"

"Just my Levi's, white shirt, and white bucks." I looked at her with pleading eyes.

"I'll be back in a minute." Mom was gone less than two minutes, returning with an armload of clothes and shoes. "Here's your stuff. Have a good time." Then she left me to return to her Moss Rose teacups and our uninvited guests.

I threw my high heels in Mom's closet, hung up my new navy suit, and pulled on the Levi's, blouse, and bucks. Ready to leave, I gripped the knob on the bedroom door. I started to sweat, trying to think of some polite way to get out of my predicament. But when I heard a car horn tooting outside the house, I threw caution to the wind. I pulled the bedroom door open, plowed through the living room, and shot out the front door, never giving a backward glance. I'd had enough of romance. I was going out with the girls.

An hour later, seated at the Riverside, fingers happily dripping with tangy tomato sauce, mozzarella cheese, and spicy sausage grease, I decided it was time to put romance on the shelf for a while. It was nothing but trouble. What I needed was a change, a new way to spend my leisure time. I needed some fresh air, a new challenge, some peace and quiet. But what would that be? Then it hit me. Deer season was right around the corner. I decided to take up hunting.

I needed some peace and quiet!

A Killing Age

Alone in my upstairs bedroom, I perched on the edge of my unmade bed and toyed with the folds of my pink woven spread, tracing the tulips that trailed their way from top to bottom and side to side in a pulsing pattern. With the door closed I could easily ogle my collage of Kirk Douglas clippings pinned along with pennants and prom programs to the homemade heart-shaped bulletin board left behind by my sister Corinne when she got married and moved to Chicago. I'd inherited her room, her bulletin board, and her kidney-shaped vanity with pink ruffled skirt and a secret drawer. The secret drawer held my diary, but I had no time for writing tonight.

I stared at the empty wall above the vanity, fighting a painful memory. At thirteen, in a fit of rage, I'd fearlessly flung Mom's gift, a long coveted mirror, down the stairway—only to find another would not be forthcoming and the scattered sharp splinters were mine to retrieve. It killed me to think I had once been so immature. But I was just a kid then. Now I was fifteen—almost sixteen.

Anyway, I knew what I looked like. Attractive and willowy like my dad with light brown hair and eyes; slim and so-phisticated like the models in Seventeen magazine; and with teeth like a Pepsodent advertisement, I carried myself with an air of self-confidence that concealed loneliness, uncertainty, and confusion.

Life was not easy in this household. No one seemed to understand I was mature and responsible. No one seemed to understand I couldn't always follow their rigid rules. No one seemed to understand I was an adult. Tomorrow would be my sixteenth birthday!

I reached under my pillow and grabbed the rabbit's foot Dad cut from a carcass and gave to me a long time ago. I stroked it for luck. He just had to let me go with him tomorrow. I'd just die if he didn't.

Savory kitchen smells—roast beef, mashed potatoes, and gravy—were rising up through the heating ducts, pouring through my register, and invading my room. I was hungry, but not quite ready to go down to dinner. I had work to do.

I reviewed my strategy, efficiently organizing my argument, planning my position, and mentally ticking off each point of persuasion. First of all, my brother John, Dad's usual hunting partner, was in his first year of dental school at the University of Michigan and wouldn't be traveling home for the Thanksgiving holiday. Second, school was closed for four and one-half wonderful days. Third, I'd been badgering Dad for years to let me go along on one of his yearly deer hunting expeditions and he'd told me one day, when I was old enough, I could go. So finally—and here was the clincher—my sixteenth birthday was about to dawn. I would get my driver license. I would be an adult. I was old enough to hunt with the guys. It was time.

Finally armed and ready, I went downstairs to make my attack.

There, as usual, Dad was seated and eating in the breakfast nook while Mom darted about her blazing blue and canary yellow kitchen, finding ways to serve him. She, a pretty dark-haired fun-loving Finn of medium height with flighty ways and fetching hazel eyes, was a good wife. I couldn't see myself in that kind of a role—subservient—but I guessed for Mom it was okay. She seemed to like it.

Dad was absorbed in his private thoughts—his great sense of humor masked by his naturally intent and serious expression. A tall handsome, fair-haired Italian, Dad wore his aristocratic arrogance, as always, like a second skin which suited him well. He did not acknowledge my presence.

"Food's on the stove, dear. Help yourself," Mom sang out like a sweet songbird as she swooped into the living room to answer a cry from one of the younger kids.

"Looks good," I called back, measuring out my meat and potatoes. I didn't want anyone serving me. I would be sixteen tomorrow. A grown woman.

I slid into the nook, sat down across from Dad, and started eating—keeping a sly eye on his progress. I knew as soon as he was done, he'd be off on some creative carpentry project. I also knew my younger sister Connie, who was reading, and younger brothers Jim and Jerry, who were wrestling in the living room, would be vying for his attention any minute. Like thieves they seemed to lie in wait for Dad, ready to rob me of his attention and affection at the most inopportune times.

Dad was almost done with dinner. I had to ask now or I'd miss my chance. I felt myself losing courage . . . it was now or never.

"So, can I go with you tomorrow?" I plunged right in, forgetting my carefully planned presentation.

Dad took a sip of the coffee which appeared in front of him like magic from my mother's hand.

"Well, I don't know, Dodie Ann . . ." Dad hesitated only a second, then shot a well-aimed look past his coffee cup, across the table, and directly into my eyes—like a bullet right on target. "You think you can handle a gun?"

"Sure. Sure I can. You know I can. Remember how you took me target practicing last fall?"

Dad kept his eyes on mine—a frown festering on his face. I could lose out any minute and my dream would go down in history as something that had never happened. I needed to build a little confidence—quickly.

"Remember, how you said I was such a good shot?" I gave him my most sincere and serious expression.

Dad polished off his coffee, got up from the table, and toted his dishes to the sink. He was leaving! No, I couldn't let him get away.

"You said I could go! You promised me!" I was getting nowhere fast—from diplomat to daredevil in one ruthless second. I had to get my emotions under control. "I mean, I've been thinking about going deer hunting with you since I was ten, and since John can't go this year, I thought maybe I could go in his place. Please, Daddy, please can I go with you tomorrow? I get out of school at eleven-thirty tomorrow morning. I'll get to the police station by twelve to take my driving test and be home and ready to go by one o'clock. It will be the best birthday present I could ever get from anyone ever. Please!"

Well, there it was. My soul laid bare. I'd resorted to begging, but maybe it was just as well. There could be no doubt about what I wanted.

"Remember, the Ladies' Club Thanksgiving Tea is to-morrow at two!" The magical songbird had flitted back into the kitchen from the living room. "Eva Williams and her daughter Bev will be there and Bernadette LaViolette and her daughter Diane. It'll be fun and a chance to wear that gorgeous new dress!"

Not now, Mother!

"She has the prettiest new dress, Daddy," Mom chirped away as she expertly stacked the dishes, scraped the pans, and wax papered the leftovers all in what seemed like a single movement. "It's iridescent—satiny grey—and when it swishes, it shines like a rainbow—baby blue and pearly pink. It's just darling on her!"

Oh, Mother, please!

The situation was getting out of hand. I had to think fast . . .

"I'll bet it is." Dad sort of smiled at Mom but turned his attention to me. "You'd better wear your long johns. It gets pretty cold out there, you know."

"What?" I thought I was dreaming.

"And you'd better be ready to go at one o'clock sharp, or we leave without you." Dad was already out the door. "You can use John's old twenty-two. You remember how to use the safety, don't you?"

"You bet I do!" I couldn't believe I was getting my long awaited wish, but here it was.

"Mom, I'm going with Dad tomorrow, okay?" I knew the subject was settled. If Dad said I could go, I could go. I figured Mom would be a little disappointed, but she and I did all kinds of wonderful (cultural) things together. We were always dressing up and performing for some church or civic group (she sang—I played the piano), or going to style shows (she watched—I modeled), or going to concerts (we actually both listened).

"Okay, honey, but you be careful," Mom warbled as she flew into the living room where my brothers' wrestling bout had turned into a full-fledged fist fight.

I could hardly wait for my sixteenth birthday to dawn. It would be a red letter day—a birthday to remember long into the future. Someday, I would look back and know that my sixteenth birthday had been the best one ever . . .

Alone, I sat on a snowy stump in the middle of nowhere— the Upper Peninsula of Michigan, west Iron County, about one-quarter mile from the banks of the Pendleton Creek and somewhere near the old gravel pit—wondering what I was doing there. I shivered, looked around at the wondrous expanse of wilderness surrounding me, and watched for signs of the other hunters. Nothing moved.

Towering timbers, enormous evergreens, and stubborn saplings rose from shadowy thickets of underbrush, casting black silhouettes as they stretched toward the sky, competing for light. Clumps of matted moss and clusters of frozen ferns formed icy tufts on the snow-covered ground. The scene, crystal clear, cold, and crisp was soundless.

With each breath I could smell the sweet scents of cedar, spruce, and pine. I watched my breath make smoke signals in the air and, trying to entertain myself, blew slow tedious breaths to see how long I could make them last before they disappeared forever.

I kicked my boots in the snow to keep my feet warm, careful not to break the silence. Any minute now, a deer would meander into the small clearing in front of my stump. I would take careful aim, shoot, and prove to my dad that girls were just as resourceful as guys.

The minutes dragged. Hours passed. There was a lot of time for thinking—too much time . . .

It had been ages since Dad and I had shared time together. When I was nine, he taught me to drive. When I was ten, eleven, and twelve, he took me with him almost every day to Hagerman Lake where he was building the family a summer cottage. Here we spent hour upon hour working together, eating crackers and peanut butter for lunch, and trying to outdo each other spotting wildlife. We were sole witness to a family of squirrels playing on a solitary stump, loons languidly skimming the lake, beckoning us with their lonely calls, and magnificent eagles soaring and plunging for perch. He taught me to shoot a rifle, take the boat out by myself, and use a compass in the woods.

But when I turned thirteen, Dad and I no longer found time for each other. Could I help it if I discovered lipstick, high heels, and boys?

I missed being with Dad. But here I was finally back in the swing of things . . .

When would the action start? Dad, brother John, and all their hunting buddies had been talking about this exciting experience for years, telling story after story about their accomplishments. I'd have killed to be with them.

For the twentieth time, I peered down the path the other hunters had taken when leaving me behind. When would they come back? I was getting colder by the minute. I checked the safety on my gun. Yes, it was off. I thought about smoking one of my two smuggled cigarettes, but decided a Lucky Strike wouldn't taste much good out here in the cold. I shook the ice from my gloves, took them off, and blew warm air on my freezing fingers. I sure was having a great time. What a way to spend a birthday.

Suddenly, I was startled by an astonishing noise—the pounding of hooves, then loud snorting sounds! My eyes widened in terror and disbelief as three large deer came charging out of the woods, running directly at me. I was dead meat! I felt my body flush with heat and was shocked to feel sweat on my palms and forehead. I thought deer were soft and gentle—and wise enough to stay away from people. Heaven help me, I thought frantically. I was boiling hot! I didn't move a muscle, but the threesome must have caught my scent for they stopped dead in their tracks not sixty feet away.

Frozen in place, we regarded each other cautiously. But curiosity overpowered caution and the leader doe moved a few steps closer.

As if in slow motion, I stood up, raised my gun, and placed the bead of my site on the big doe. Our eyes locked. My feet, face, and fingers were on fire! There were no antlers, but violating was not considered a crime by this bunch of hunters. I released the safety. I felt sweat trickle down my underarms. Why had I dressed so warmly? I aimed for the chest cavity— Dad had told me to go for the heart as he didn't want to track a wounded deer.

I flexed my index finger just a little to make sure it was still working. But I didn't pull the trigger. Those eyes—beautiful brown—soft and sensitive, stunned me with their wild trust and innocence. I flexed my index finger again. But just then the leader doe raised her head high in the air, gave a flick of her white tail, and began leading the tawny group toward me. My instinct was to back away, but I held my ground and held my breath in utter amazement. I could almost feel their smoky breath as they passed on either side of me, gliding gracefully through the bushes and trees, and gently disappearing into the thick underbrush.

I shook my head as if to wake myself from a dream. But, it was real—the beauty of nature at its best. I wanted to savor those moments as long as I could.

But the hunters would be back soon. Too soon. They would probably think I was a big baby. Dad would probably be embarrassed by my inability to kill a doe. I found myself feeling cold and chilled again. I hoped they wouldn't come back for a long time. I didn't want to see them.

Their merry voices ricocheted off the trees, glanced off the ground, and echoed through the woods, announcing their return. I wished they hadn't come back so soon. They'd think I was just another silly girl for not shooting.

I held my breath as the colorful crew appeared—first Bill Lepisto and his son Emil, then Bill Barna and his son Kerry—decked in a rousing variety of reds—red wool pants and hats, red plaid jackets and shirts, and red socks and mittens covered to the ankles and wrists by leather boots and choppers (leather mittens). And then came John Cederna, my dad. He, too, was decked in red but with that self-reliant swagger of his, he looked like he was sporting a three-piece suit. I was proud to have him for my dad. He was my hero. I didn't want to let him down.

"So, did ya' see anything?" Bill Lepisto called.

"Uh, no . . . uh, yes . . . uh, just a couple of doe—nothing to shoot at." I tried to sound nonchalant. "They stood right there in front of me. I could have shot, I guess, but I figured . . ."

"Well, Johnny," Bill Barna laughed, "at least one member of your family ain't a violator. Where'd she ever learn that from?"

With that, the group roared with laughter. I groaned inwardly, trying to convince myself I'd been absolved.

With Bill Lepisto in the lead, we started the long trek back to the car. Single file, I fell in behind the men and their sons, and Dad followed in the rear behind me.

I turned my head back toward him as we trudged down the trail. "I could have got one," I said adamantly.

Dad just kind of smiled. I knew he didn't believe me.

I was feeling like a real washout as a hunter. The trail was getting slick, so I concentrated carefully on not making a fool of myself by falling. We crossed over, around, and under low tree branches, dodging patches of ice, rocks, and fern clusters. My gun felt a lot heavier now than it did when we walked in.

"Gun getting heavy?" Dad chuckled.

"No. Are you kidding?" I'd die before I'd admit I was freezing and exhausted with a gun that felt like a canon.

Suddenly, Bill Lepisto stopped dead in his tracks. I caught myself just before losing my balance and saw him raise a finger to his lips. Shh—his lips formed the sound. He nodded to a fir tree just ahead and to the left.

All eyes followed his nod to the snowy mound at the base the tree. There sat a little ruffed grouse roosting—his smart little crown perked in alarm.

Kerry, Bill Barna's son, raised his gun, but Bill put his hand on the side of the barrel and gave it a nudge. "Let the girl have a chance," he ordered.

I understood immediately what was happening. I was being given a second chance—a chance to prove myself. I could feel the exhilaration and excitement of the group. They were like a huddle of fanatical football fans just before the final play in sudden death. I knew what they were thinking. I hoped I could prove them wrong.

There was no more time to think. I glanced at Dad and his expression was obvious. He was firing me a stare that was hard as steel. He hoped I could, by some miracle, shoot the bird but he didn't think I had a chance in hell—still he himself had taught me to shoot. "Go ahead," he ordered with an urgency I knew meant, "now!"

In one single determined second, I raised the gun, released the safety, and sited the bird. A shot rang out. The bird slipped to its side—dead.

"Good shot!" I was being congratulated from all sides.

"Johnny, ya' could take a lesson from that girl," Bill Lepisto teased. "At least she don't miss when she shoots."

"Yah hey, Johnny," Kerry and Emil chimed in.

Dad strode over to the bird, grasped it by its talons, and held it high for all to see. He beamed with pride.

My father had never looked at me like that before. Admiration showed plainly in his eyes. I wasn't just a giddy girl with romantic notions who went to fancy teas and wore fancy dresses anymore. I was someone special—one of the guys.

Drenched in his excitement, I let the feeling flood me—like a desert in a downpour. I had won my dad's full and undivided attention—and his respect.

But, I had had to kill to do it. If anyone had told me I could feel so much pain in my joy, I would not have believed them. It didn't seem possible to be so happy and so miserable at the same precise moment. I gulped back the threatening tears, gritted my teeth, and grinned.

I could be just as strong and proud as my dad. I refused to acknowledge the intense pain and guilt I felt upon viewing the lifeless body of that poor innocent bird. It was a matter of survival—the bird or me.

The November sky, brilliant blue a few hours earlier, had turned grizzly grey. I don't remember the rest of the walk back to civilization, or the ride home, or dinner that evening.

But later that night, alone in my upstairs bedroom, I do remember going to my sister's vanity, opening the secret drawer, and taking out my diary.

I wrote, "November 23, 1955: Today I celebrated my sixteenth birthday. I got my driver license and finally got to go hunting with Dad. I shot a partridge right through the head. Dad couldn't believe his eyes. I think he was actually proud of me. It was so exciting! It was the best birthday ever! I'll never forget it as long as I live."

Then I turned off the light, crept under the traveling tulips, and closed my eyes. I lay there like a corpse, thinking, agonizing, pining—imagining I had wings and was flying free.

Coralie Cederna Johnson on a visit to the Ojibway Burial
Grounds in Pentoga Park on Chicaugon Lake.

About the Author

Coralie has had articles and poetry published in *Above the Bridge Magazine. The Porcupine Press*, and *Peninsula People Magazine* for which she was a contributing editor in 1991-1992. Her story, *A Killing Age,* won an award in the Jackson Community College 1992 Literature Department's Essay Contest.

Her original craft designs, stories, and instructional materials have appeared in *McCall's, Woman's Day, Family Circle, Decorating and Crafts, American Legion Auxiliary, Love and Money Needlecrafters' Magazine,* and *Workbasket.*

Coralie lives in Ypsilanti, Michigan with her husband Jim and is employed at the University of Michigan Dental School as a Clinic Coordinator.

She is the mother of four and grandmother of three. Her son Paul is a dentist in Escanaba, Michigan. He and his wife Paula have two children, Bryan and Allison. Son Peter, also a dentist, lives in Manistique, Michigan, with his wife Therese and their daughter, Jaclyn. Daughter Tamara Sorelli is a free-lance writer in Yuma, Arizona. Daughter Carrie Noesen, a social worker, and her husband Brook live in Ann Arbor, Michigan.

Her favorite hours are spent with family members, friends, and her dogs, Angel and Hesper. Besides journalism, her hobbies include collecting antique children's books, nature and animal photography, and researching family history.

A recent family gathering at Hagerman Lake.
Front: Coralie, Connie, Shep, Mom, Corinne.
Back: Jerry, Jim, John.

The Cederna Family

Corinne has retired from her career as an interior designer in the Chicago area. Her children Cheryl, Lester, Wendi, Bruce, and John have families of their own and visit often with Corinne and her husband Bob.

John has recently retired from a thirty year career in dentistry and built his own "cottage" in South Carolina. He and his wife Pat enjoy visits from their seven children, John, Marie, Tom, Ann, Joe, Paul, and Joan, and their families.

Connie teaches Social Studies and general elementary education to fifth graders at Anderson School in Trenton, Michigan. She resides in Dearborn, Michigan with her dog, Cody, and cats, Loki and Lawrence.

Jim, is president of an international carbon black company. He and his wife Carol live in Atlanta, Georgia and have two college age children, Channon and Jeff.

Jerry, formerly a high school teacher, and his wife Joyce reside in Escanaba, Michigan in the U.P. and work for the U.S. Postal Service. They have three sons, Kurt, Joshua, and Jeno.

Coralie's mother, Carrie Cederna, still resides in the Upper Peninsula of Michigan and, though her father, the late John Anthony Cederna, passed on in 1980, the extended family gathers often at the Hagerman Lake cottage to reminisce, paddle on down to the little islands in the bay, and look for the return of the loons.